The Religious Origins of Democratic Pluralism

The Religious Origins of Democratic Pluralism

Paul Peter Waldenström and the Politics
of the Swedish Awakening 1868–1917

Mark Safstrom

☙PICKWICK *Publications* · Eugene, Oregon

THE RELIGIOUS ORIGINS OF DEMOCRATIC PLURALISM
Paul Peter Waldenström and the Politics of the Swedish Awakening 1868–1917

Copyright © 2016 Mark Safstrom. All rights reserved. Except for brief quotations in critical publications or reviews, no part of this book may be reproduced in any manner without prior written permission from the publisher. Write: Permissions. Wipf and Stock Publishers, 199 W. 8th Ave., Suite 3, Eugene, OR 97401.

Pickwick Publications
An Imprint of Wipf and Stock Publishers
199 W. 8th Ave., Suite 3
Eugene, OR 97401

www.wipfandstock.com

ISBN 13: 978-1-4982-2509-0

Cataloguing-in-Publication Data

Safstrom, Mark

    The religious origins of democratic pluralism : Paul Peter Waldenström and the politics of the Swedish awakening 1868–1917 / Mark Safstrom

    xii + 292 p. ; 23 cm. Includes bibliographical references.

    ISBN 13: 978-1-4982-2509-0

    1. Waldenström, Paul Peter, 1838–1917. 2. Pietists. 3. Religious pluralism. I. Title.

BX8080 S15 2016

Manufactured in the U.S.A.   01/05/2016

Cover Illustration: "Hercules at the Crossroads." Edvard Forsström. Reproduction: Kungliga biblioteket.

Excerpts from chapter 2 appeared in the Introduction to *Squire Adamsson: Or, Where Do You Live?* (Pietisten, 2013). Excerpts from chapter 8 appeared in *The Pietist Impulse in Christianity* (Pickwick, 2011).

*To the circle around
Pietisten,
its readers, writers, and staff
past, present, and future.*

Contents

List of Figures and Tables | ix
Acknowledgments | xi

Introduction | 1

Part I: Crafting a Strategy of Pluralism

Chapter 1: Locating "The Middle Way" in Waldenström's Discourse | 15
Chapter 2: Modeling Pluralism through Allegory—*Squire Adamsson* | 31

Part II: Separating Church and State

Chapter 3: Pietism as the Re-Emergence of Religious Pluralism in Sweden | 47
Chapter 4: Print Media and the Mobilization of Reform | 60
Chapter 5: Religion in Public: "Private Matter" or "Matter of Conscience"? | 76
Chapter 6: On Conscience and the Rights of Dissenters | 87
Chapter 7: The Limits of Democracy in the Kingdom of Christ | 101

Part III: Brokering Confrontation and Exchange: Pietism and Socialism

Chapter 8: Pluralism as Productive Tension | 111
Chapter 9: Branting v. Waldenström: The Debate to Define Absolutism and Moralism | 124
Chapter 10: The Impact of the Free-Church Vote | 135
Chapter 11: Majoritarianism v. Proportionalism: Making Space for Dissent | 151
Chapter 12: An Exchange of Words: A Re-Socialized Christian Vocabulary and a Democratized Socialist One | 174

Part IV: Tempering the Politics of Temperance

    Chapter 13: Defining Moderate v. Absolutist Abstinence Politics | 189

    Chapter 14: Pragmatism and Experimentation with Best Practices | 201

    Chapter 15: A Preference for Education over Legislation | 216

Conclusion | 223

Endnotes | 237

Bibliography | 281

Figures and Tables

Figures

    Waldenström in academic robe at Yale | 6
    "The New Jonah" | 8
    Squire Adamsson receives wisdom from Mother Simple | 26
    Title page from *Brukspatron Adamsson* | 33
    George Scott | 50
    Amy Moberg | 53
    Carl Olof Rosenius | 56
    Covers of *Pietisten* | 62
    Waldenström in park at Lidingö | 64
    "Through North America's United States" | 69
    The Common Seminary in China | 70
    Gävle Högreläroverk | 88
    Erik Jakob Ekman | 97
    Rosenius in the pulpit at Bethlehem Church | 103
    "Saint George and the Dragon" | 106
    "Hjalmar Branting tries to scrub clean Hinke Bergegren" | 122
    Lina Sandell-Berg and C.O. Berg | 125
    "In the free-religious voting school" | 134
    "Dance around the Midsommar pole" | 137
    "The summer promenade of politics" | 141
    "Hercules at the crossroads" | 142
    "Before the masterpiece" | 145
    Oscar Ahnfelt | 146

"The Quick-Change Artist P.P.W. on tour in America" | 154

Waldenström and a corps of volunteers | 172

"Look where all this terrible drunkenness will lead!" | 195

"Thus far hath the Lord helped" | 221

Tables

1. Comparison of the outcome of four elections | 138
2. Outcome of the 1899 elections in Gävle | 155

Acknowledgments

A GREAT NUMBER OF people have supported this project in many ways, such that written thanks are hardly sufficient. Nevertheless, I wish to thank my doctoral committee members Terje Leiren, Steve Pfaff, Lotta Gavel Adams, and Marianne Stecher for their advice in envisioning and revising this project from start to finish. It was Terje who initially introduced me to Waldenström's travel literature, which has turned out to be a wise suggestion. Special thanks to Lotta for her generosity in making available her apartment in Stockholm on two extended occasions, without which research at *Riksarkivet* and *Kungliga biblioteket* would have been considerably more expensive, if not impossible. Thanks are in order to Steve Pfaff, who despite the fact that I was not in his field, got me up to speed on enough sociological vocabulary to be able to think of religion and social movements in the terms of a social scientist, as well as a historian. I am eternally grateful for the generous financial support of the American-Scandinavian Foundation, the Swedish Women's Educational Association (SWEA San Francisco), and the Foreign Languages and Area Studies fellowships (Jackson School of International Studies), as well as the support of the Department of Scandinavian Studies at the University of Washington. This aid made it possible for me to live in Uppsala and Stockholm over the course of several summers between 2005 and 2010, in order to complete my research, as well as continue to develop my language skills.

I owe a great debt of gratitude to my wonderful relatives in Täby, Leif and Agneta Eriksson and Jesper Eriksson and Elin Björneheim, who have opened their homes and schedules on several occasions, as well as shown me a great time in Stockholm, Gävle, and Gotland. Thanks to Agneta, for making inquiries about Waldenström at her and Leif's former school, *Vasaskolan* (*Gävle Högreläroverk*). Thanks are also in order to my SVF College Line friends, Karin (Larsson) Hedin (who showed me around Stockholm and the inner workings of *Svenska Missionskyrkan* on several occasions), as well as Erik and Elin Gert, Henrik and Amanda Kihlström, and Charlotta (Birgersson) Korslind for their hospitality and company.

I am also indebted to a large circle of people over the years who have demonstrated their interest in my research, by enduring my lectures, providing good conversation, asking thoughtful questions and offering sage advice. This interest has on countless occasions allowed me to feel that the research that I had stumbled into was meaningful and relevant, and without your interest I would, quite frankly, probably have chosen to do something else. This includes the great circle of *Pietisten's* readers and friends; the congregation of First Covenant Church in Seattle (notably Bryce Nelson, who once convinced me to teach a lecture series on Pietism, about which I knew nothing; I have been benefitting ever since); the congregation of Wiley Heights Covenant Church in Yakima, Washington; the congregation of Immanuel Church in Stockholm; the Waldenström family, who graciously received me as a guest at their extended family reunion, and to Bertil Oppenheimer in particular for initiating this relationship; many wonderful members of the Swedish-American Historical Society, the Society for the Advancement of Scandinavian Studies, and the Society of Historians of Scandinavia; and the archivists and directors of the Archives at North Park University, Chicago (Steve Elde and Anne Jenner) and the Swenson Swedish Immigration Research Center at Augustana College, Rock Island, Illinois (Dag Blanck and Jill Seaholm).

Several friends and relatives have provided support and encouragement throughout this six-year journey and deserve deepest thanks; my cousin, Johanna (Knudsen) Staman, who has an endearing knack for putting things in perspective when they have ceased to be so; Mark Swanson, a good friend with an inexhaustible appetite for theological and church-historical discussion, which I have appreciated enormously throughout this period of research; to my parents and sisters, who, in addition to their unwavering love and support, have also been good sports in allowing me to drag them through endless old churches during their visits to Scandinavia—thanks for taking an interest in things that matter to me. *Tusen tack!*

Mark Safstrom

Seattle, Washington
Thanksgiving, 2010

Introduction

THIS STUDY WILL FOCUS on explaining one of the riddles that puzzled political scientists and historians through much of the twentieth century, namely the origin and development of Swedish Social Democracy. While other countries in Europe experienced dramatic swings between radical and conservative political parties, which resulted in tragic experiments with totalitarian regimes, Sweden by contrast managed miraculously to avoid these extremes. What made this "middle way" appear miraculous was the fact that between the 1860s and the 1910s, Swedish society had rapidly been transformed from a patriarchal, agrarian society in which parliamentary representation still reflected the medieval "four estates," to a bicameral legislature with universal suffrage and true parliamentarianism. The conclusions that will be drawn from this study indicate that this rapid, yet successful, transformation was facilitated by political actors who crafted the discourse of these societal debates in such a way that pluralism came to be valued as an ethical good and then vigorously defended. This ideological preference for pluralism allowed the very emergence and maintenance of civil society, despite the fact that the political climate was far from tranquil, as various parties with contrary interests vied for control in this fledgling democracy.

At the center of this study is one Swedish politician, Paul Peter Waldenström (1838–1917). In addition to a career in politics, Waldenström was a clergyman, revival preacher, educator, author, and newspaper editor, who has typically been identified as one of the foremost figures in the spiritual awakening of the nineteenth century.[1] His contributions to spiritual life and his theology have received a great deal of attention, particularly by those religious groups directly impacted by his ideas. The two chief custodians of his theological legacy have been the church institutions directly founded by his followers: the Mission Covenant Church of Sweden (*Svenska Missionsförbundet,* now part of *Equmeniakyrkan*) and the Evangelical Covenant

Church, located in North America. By contrast, his very long and active political career has received little attention, perhaps eclipsed by the interest in his theology, perhaps indicative of the secular orientation of much of contemporary Swedish society. Waldenström's political career began in 1868, with his participation in the Church Assembly of the Church of Sweden (*Svenska kyrkans kyrkomöte*), a consultative body to the Swedish parliament (*Riksdag*), and expanded during his years of service in the *Riksdag* from 1884–1905. Furthermore, he remained a frequent commentator on politics and societal developments throughout his career and until his death. The years 1868–1917 thus serve as the framework for this discussion.

That Waldenström was merely a religious figure and not a consequential political actor is an assumption that will be challenged in this study. Historians of Swedish history have long been aware of the active participation of religious figures in politics during the so-called "folk movements" of the nineteenth century and the subsequent breakthrough of democracy after the turn of the century. However, this participation has at times been evaluated as having been non-conclusive in the nature of its impact, as historian Sven Lundkvist suggested as late as the 1970s. Lundkvist, furthermore, encouraged more research into the connection between these religious revivals and overall political developments.[2] Even today, the ambiguity that remains in evaluating the role that religious movements and their ideologies played in Swedish politics risks overlooking a dynamic aspect of nineteenth century popular culture. Waldenström serves as an ideal subject for better understanding the view of democratic values among the religious revival groups for three reasons: he was a prominent leader within this population, he was vocal on democratic values and praxis, and he was directly connected to the debates on these matters within the *Riksdag*. He thus serves as a direct point of contact between a large popular movement and the apparatus of government. His political speeches and newspaper articles frequently contain commentary on the development and maintenance of pluralistic values and debate, as well as prescriptions for how these ideals could be implemented and safeguarded.

This study brings a new perspective to the discussion of this period, in that many of Waldenström's writings have never before been analyzed within the context of democratic pluralism. Some of these writings have rarely, if ever, been analyzed at all. Among the primary sources used during the research for this study is a collection of Waldenström's carbon copy books from 1906–1915, which include imprints of numerous letters to the editors of Swedish newspapers and private persons. This collection was rediscovered in 1988, when it was catalogued and transferred to the Swedish National Archives (*Riksarkivet*) in Stockholm. Analysis of these writings alone brings new material to the discussion of Waldenström's career, and a fresh perspective on his evaluation of the Swedish political and social developments after his career in politics formally ended in 1905. Also included in this study are contemporary critiques of Waldenström as they appeared in several Swedish newspapers preserved at the Royal Library (*Kungliga biblioteket*) also in Stockholm. Finally, the development of Waldenström's political philosophy has been traced as it appears in the great body of his theological books and writings. These writings have seldom been analyzed with political questions in mind, and so this study has intentionally re-read these theological works with an eye to understanding how his theology informed his engagement in political questions.

If Waldenström has been a neglected figure among Swedish scholars, he remains virtually unknown outside of Sweden. Born in Luleå in northern Sweden in 1838, Paul Peter Waldenström was the son of a country doctor and, as such, was privileged to attend Uppsala University, beginning in 1857.[3] By 1863 he had earned a doctor of philosophy degree, and the following year, he completed an examination for ordination as a priest in the Lutheran Church of Sweden (which until the year 2000 functioned as the Swedish state church). Although ordained, Waldenström chose not to serve in a congregation, but instead in an educational position. His primary occupation was as a teacher at several upper secondary schools (*högreläroverk*) where he taught theology and classical Greek, Hebrew, and Latin. The first of these positions began in 1862 in the town of Växjö, followed by schools in Umeå and Gävle, the longest of these being his tenure in Gävle from 1872–1905. In 1868, he took over as editor of the religious devotional journal *Pietisten* ("The Pietist"), a central organ of the revival movement within the Church of Sweden, which enjoyed a subscription base conservatively estimated at around 10,000 subscribers in 1860 (roughly one out of 385 Swedes was a subscriber).[4] *Pietisten* retained its significant influence for the remainder of his life. Even as late as 1914, *Pietisten* had grown to 17,000 subscribers,[5] thus remaining slightly ahead of population growth (one in 340 Swedes subscribed). As the name of the paper suggests, the community of readers that it served drew heavily from the religious heritage of Lutheran Pietism. Waldenström's own gravitation toward the revival movement had begun following a conversion experience at the age of nineteen, at which point he had become familiar with the writings of classical Lutheran Pietism, including the German theologian Johann Arndt (1555–1621) and the preachers within the contemporary Swedish branch of that movement, known as "new evangelicalism" (*nyevangelismen*), such as Peter Fjellstedt (1802–1881) and Carl Olof Rosenius (1816–1868).[6] His avocation as a revival preacher also began shortly after his conversion, and it was his preaching and authorship which launched him to national prominence.

Waldenström became branded as a radical in 1872, when he came into conflict with the authorities of the Church of Sweden regarding its doctrine of the atonement. The orthodox Lutheran view on the atonement held that the sacrifice of Jesus Christ on the cross had functioned to reconcile God to human beings, who, according to Christian theology, had been estranged from God as a result of original sin. Swedish Lutheranism, as well as the early revival movements, had traditionally emphasized the interpretation of the atonement as informed by Anselm of Canterbury, which implied that God had allowed himself to be reconciled to fallen humanity as a result of Christ's sacrifice.[7] Waldenström's 1872 sermon in *Pietisten* defended an alternate (though not entirely new) critique of this view, asserting that it was not God who was reconciled to human beings by the crucifixion, but instead human beings who were reconciled to God, since the nature of God cannot be expected to change.[8] The climate of strict orthodoxy among the clergy at the time opposed this, as it denied the teaching on the issue as articulated in one of the Church of Sweden's founding documents, the Augsburg Confession, which had been binding since 1593. Following a prolonged and heated public debate on this matter, as well as on the nature of the congregation and communion, a large group of his sympathizers, dubbed "Waldenströmians," broke away from the Church of Sweden and in 1878 founded a free association of congregations called the Swedish Mission Covenant (*Svenska Missionsförbundet*). This was not the first such group to break away from the religious monopoly of the Church of Sweden, but it quickly became the largest, which by the time of Waldenström's death had surpassed 100,000 members (roughly 2 percent of the population). The editors of the encyclopedia *Nordisk Familjebok* in 1921 estimated that the church had 270,000 adherants (thus 4–5 percent of the population), and further postulated that as many as one million Swedes had at one time in their lives looked up to Waldenström as their "spiritual father" (about 16–17 percent).[9] Although a central inspiration to the creation of this church, Waldenström maintained a distance, and it was not until 1904 that he assumed the principle leadership role as president (*föreståndare*). This position increased his already active travel schedule as an itinerant preacher.

In the course of his career Waldenström made several extensive tours through North America, made frequent trips to Germany and Europe, a trip to Palestine and Asia Minor, and a visit to China to inspect the Swedish missionary stations there. His trips to North America were prompted by requests from the large community of Swedish immigrants who had settled there, and who had founded a church denomination inspired by the

Swedish Mission Covenant in 1885, *Svenska Missionsförbundet i Amerika* (now the Evangelical Covenant Church). Waldenström enjoyed a long publishing career, writing no fewer than 34 books on devotional topics, including six travelogues and one novel, numerous pamphlets, monthly articles for *Pietisten* and several other newspapers, both religious and secular. A handful of his books were translated into English, including *The Blood of Jesus. What is the Significance?*, 1888 [*Jesu blod: Betraktelser* 1880]; *The Reconciliation*, 1888 [*Om försoningens betydelse* 1873]; *The Lord is Right*, 1889 [*Herren är from* 1875]; and the novel *Squire Adamson; Or Where Do You Live?*, 1928 [*Brukspatron Adamsson; Eller hvar bor du?* 1863]. The English translations reflected the fact that his audience of Swedish immigrants had begun transitioning into their English-speaking context. It also was an indication of a certain amount of recognition that he had gained within the English-speaking academic world. The foremost example of this was the distinction of being awarded an honorary doctorate from Yale University in 1889. The school of theology maintained an interest in Waldenström in subsequent years, and included him as a guest of honor at the university's 200th anniversary celebrations in 1901. With this distinction, he shared prestigious company, as the celebrated and controversial Mark Twain had also been awarded such a degree that same year. Another indication of the attention he had garnered was the fact that Waldenström had been one of the international figures invited to participate in the world parliament of religions in 1893 in Chicago (though he was not able to attend).

Waldenström's political career began in 1868, when he was elected as a delegate to the Church Assembly of the Church of Sweden. This body had been a compensatory measure to the church following the parliamentary reforms in 1866, which abolished the four-estate structure of the *Riksdag* (nobility, clergy, burgers, and farmers), and thereby deprived the clergy of the house they previously held. Under the new model, all questions that arose in the *Riksdag* regarding religion and the state church would be referred to the Church Assembly, thereby preserving some indirect representation for the Church of Sweden. In his participation in the Church Assemblies of 1868, 1908, 1909, and 1910, Waldenström was most known for his attempts to pass measures that would separate the church from the state, as well as democratize its structure (critical aspects of this are addressed in detail in Part II). In 1884, Waldenström was elected to represent the city of Gävle in the *Riksdag*. In his seven terms as a representative, Waldenström emerged as one of the leading supporters of temperance legislation, as well as an opponent of protectionism during the so-called "tariff debates" of the 1880s, an advocate for educational reform and the reform of the state-church relationship, and a prominent critic of socialism (his stances on socialism and temperance are treated in detail in Parts III and IV respectively).

Waldenström in academic robe at Yale University in 1901, one of many guests of honor at the anniversary celebrations. *Nya Färder i Amerikas Förenta Stater*. 48.

There have been several waves of interest in Waldenström as a historical subject, including at least sixteen biographies. The first major period of interest in Waldenström came during his lifetime. In 1872, the controversial sermon that he published in *Pietisten* started a flurry of responses, and in the next few years, several hundred books and pamphlets were published both supporting and refuting his theory of the atonement. He was not the first in history to present such an idea, but his very public challenge of this doctrine made a sensation throughout the Lutheran world, and even in other denominations and abroad. Even as late as 1889, when he arrived in the United States on his first American preaching tour, both English and Swedish language newspapers heralded him as the "Martin Luther of Sweden" . . .

or as an "Anti-Christ" among those seeking to defend Lutheran doctrine. The *Chicago Sunday Times-Herald* referred to him as one of Sweden's "four greatest living men."[10]

While Waldenström's theory was significant on theological levels, the implications for religious practice among Swedes were far-reaching. Through his close reading of scripture and his plain-speech explanations to the Swedish layman, Waldenström had turned theology into a spectator sport. Like other religious reformers before him, he had made the case that anyone who could read should be able to understand Christian truths and challenge whatever incorrect assumptions might exist in the dominant paradigm. For lower- and middle class Swedes, this became an opportunity to challenge the rigid hierarchy of the Lutheran state church. Many embraced Waldenström's slogan "Where is it written?" (*Var står det skrivet?*) and took this as an opportunity to discontinue their participation in the state church and formalize their own private Bible studies into congregations and denominations in their own right, the so-called "free churches" (*frikyrkorna*, adj. *frikyrklig*). The movement marked a general trend away from a unified, centralized, and hierarchical form of faith toward a very diverse, decentralized form that exalted the layman participant. The implications that this religious paradigm shift had on Waldenström's understanding of the relationship of church and state will be treated in Part II. What should be pointed out now is what this early period (the 1870s) did for his legacy. Waldenström's bold challenge of church doctrine created an opening for others who were dissatisfied with the Church of Sweden to make their own protests, both likeminded Pietists, as well as people with other motivations. He was seen as a threat by the religious establishment. The commentary on him during this period was therefore sharply polarized and primarily concerned theological issues. His reputation as a radical reformer emerged at this time.

The second era of high public interest in Waldenström occurred during his two-decade-long career in the *Riksdag* from 1884–1905. The interest this time was centered on social issues, namely those issues surrounding the labor movement, temperance legislation, and the separation of church institutions from the state. For those people engaged in the temperance movement, Waldenström was generally the object of high praise, with the exception that he was sometimes seen as too moderate on the issue of prohibition (see Part IV). However much of the attention he received from the press was that which appeared in the newspapers covering the labor movement (see Part III). Waldenström's criticism of socialism gained him plenty of enemies in the Social Democratic and left parties. The sources used in this study come from the Swedish newspapers of the period, but particularly from the city of Gävle, which Waldenström represented in the *Riksdag*. The coverage by the Socialist-leaning newspapers in this period was often starkly negative, as these papers worked to support Waldenström's political opponents. In his campaign against socialism, Waldenström even estranged some of the temperance people and free-church members, who were rather centralized within the Liberal party.[11] The net result of these political debates was that Waldenström increasingly came to be regarded as a conservative, an evaluation that will be problematized in this study.

"The New Jonah." Waldenström is pictured being ousted from politics in Gävle, only to be attacked by the whale of the Swedish Mission Covenant. Reproduction: Riksarkivet Marieberg, Stockholm. Waldenströmska släktarkivet, P.P. Waldenströms samling I, volym 20.

The posthumous interest in Waldenström has also come in waves. The majority of this attention has been from within the Swedish Mission Covenant. After his death, several commemorative biographical works helped to enshrine him as the founder of that church. These served the purpose of defining his role as a church builder, and focused mostly on the positive contributions of his theology. Around the 100th anniversary of his birth in 1938 came another wave, which lasted through the 1940s. It was during this time that the most critical and comprehensive biographies were written. It was started by a short, but critical book by Jakob Grundström, *Waldenström och Samhällsfrågorna* ("Waldenström and Social Questions"). This book represented a turning point between earlier generations which had had a laudatory view of Waldenström as church father and visionary. Instead Grundström presented Waldenström as having been firmly planted in the classical liberal tradition of political thinking, and despite some radical tendencies, was in fact no radical at all when it came to politics and social questions. What is clear in this analysis was that Grundström was representing a younger generation of free-church leaders who thought it time to take Waldenström down from the pedestal on which previous generations had placed him. A divided image emerges at this point, in which Waldenström retains his legacy as a radical in terms of his reforms of church institutions, but in politics he began to be seen as solidly conservative.

Grundström's critique seems to have inspired one of Waldenström's former assistants, Ragnar Tomson to respond to Grundström's assessment that Waldenström was not a radical. Thus Tomson took on the momentous task of tracing Waldenström's activity in politics, writing not one but three biographical works in the 1940s, each taking up a different aspect of Waldenström's career. *En hövding* ("A Chieftain") is a general summary of his career, and *En politisk vilde* ("A Political Maverick") outlined Waldenström's political career in twenty years of the *Riksdag*. The third and most important book came in 1945, *Den Radikale Waldenström* ("The Radical Waldenström"). Here Tomson laid out a detailed account of Waldenström's engagement on a series of social issues, including the tariff debates of the 1880s, the "muzzle law" of 1889 concerning freedom of speech, and the rights and protections of workers. Tomson presents Waldenström as an essentially radical politician, who only grew conservative after the turn of the century toward the end of his career. In it he sketches a portrait of Waldenström as having two phases, an early radical phase pitted against a later one, in which he became a reactionary conservative.

One of the critiques of Tomson's portrayal of Waldenström is that while a progression of ideologies is assumed to have taken place in Waldenström's development, the reasons for this change are not sufficiently accounted for or traced. This weakness was pointed out by William Bredberg, who wrote one of the definitive Waldenström biographies in his 1948 dissertation *P. P. Waldenströms verksamhet till 1878* ("P. P. Waldenström's Work up to 1878"). Although this work focused on Waldenström's earlier career, Bredberg also commented that Tomson failed to account for the evolution of Waldenström's philosophy, particularly why Waldenström became so conservative in his later years, if indeed there was a change. Bredberg does not go into depth on this, but does point out that the contemporary Swedish view of the era when Waldenström was active was dominated by a Social Democratic bias.

> *For those who believe that Christianity in and of itself is the most radical of all and comes with the farthest reaching claims, then it is not necessary to hesitate in using the attribute "radical" on the*

young Waldenström. On the other hand, it will seem odd for the person who judges his position from the modern social democratic viewpoint. Such a person will find a great resemblance between him and "the bishops."[12]

The 1978 centennial of the Swedish Mission Covenant was another opportunity for re-evaluation of Waldenström. Bror Walans *Året 1878* ("The Year 1878") and Erland Sundström's *Arvet från Waldenström* ("The Inheritance from Waldenström") served the purpose of reasserting some of Waldenström's lost place as patriarch, albeit with more critical distance than Tomson. These works also reflected modern tendencies to de-emphasize "great men" and place leaders against the background of broad popular movements, particularly asserting the influence of other church leaders such as Erik Jakob Ekman (1842–1915), who occupied almost as central a place in the Mission Covenant as Waldenström.

The most recent and perhaps also one of the most interesting of these works is Harry Lindström's 1997 dissertation on Waldenström's novel, *Squire Adamsson*. This religious allegory was a bestseller in Sweden, being reprinted nearly a dozen times since its initial publication in 1862, as well as in English, Norwegian, and Danish. The valuable addition that Lindström's dissertation gives to the study of the religious revivals is that it identifies Waldenström's novel as having had widespread influence in Swedish popular culture and engaging broader social issues than simply theology. Furthermore, Lindström pointed out that religious authors have typically been ignored in modern Swedish history, and made the case that those authors who have the most influence in their own time are not necessarily those who end up being enshrined in the national canon. As evidence of this, he notes the fact that Waldenström's book sales rivaled even the most popular secular authors of the day.[13] Furthermore, Lindström identified that there still remained unresolved questions regarding the influence of the religious awakening on general developments in Swedish society.

This study will attempt to fill out the previously under-researched political side of Waldenström's career and shed light on the influence that he had in the era of the Swedish popular movements. Since pluralism, both religious and political, was a central idea in his career, it is only fitting that pluralism serves as the common thread of this study. This book has been organized according to the three main social questions that Waldenström addressed in his political career—questions of religious freedom, democratic practice, and the role of the state in enforcing standards of public health. These three subjects correspond to the three traditionally recognized "folk movements" (*folkrörelser*), which included the religious awakening (*väckelserörelsen*), the labor movement (*arbetarrörelsen*), and the temperance movement (*nykterhetsrörelsen*). The point of analyzing them together is to help answer the question of how these movements were interrelated. Part I will offer a definition of pluralism as it appeared in Waldenström's discourse and as it pertained to the unique political situation at the turn of the century. Part II will focus on Waldenström's attempt to implement ideas of religious pluralism within the complicated context of Sweden as a Lutheran kingdom. How to disentangle the institutions of church and state was the first question, but was followed up by the equally important question of what role religion should take on once Sweden evolved into a more pluralistic society. Part III will focus on the reasons for Waldenström's opposition to socialism and his concerns over the nature of its revolutionary discourse. This chapter will also suggest ways in which Waldenström's critique influenced the evolutionary development of the Social Democratic party ideology, as well as the overall shape that Swedish democracy took in the decades that followed his career. Part IV will analyze the insights and contradictions that the temperance movement posed to notions of pluralism, focusing on Waldenström's leadership in this debate.

PART I

Crafting a Strategy of Pluralism

> ... On the left side, just as on the right side of the road, there is a ditch. Just as it is dangerous to drive into the ditch on the left, it is equally dangerous to drive into the ditch on the right, and as one has to react against the one situation, so must he react against the other.
>
> There is an old story, which the majority of us have heard, about a landowner who was hiring a coachman. There were many who applied for the position. "How close to the ditch can you drive?" he asked the first of them. The first one answered: "So close, that there is only the breadth of a hair between the wheel and the ditch." The second one boasted just as much. The third one answered: "I never drive near the ditch, I keep myself right in the middle of the road, for that is the safest." The landowner was of the same opinion. But in our political parties it is the case, that the one who is considered the best and most trustworthy, is the one who can drive so close to the ditch, that at least half of the wheel is hanging over the edge.[14]
>
> —P. P. Waldenström, political speech in Karlstad 1908

CHAPTER 1

Locating the "Middle Way" in Waldenström's Discourse

THIS BOOK WILL FOCUS on the career of Paul Peter Waldenström, with the ultimate goal of shedding light on how the popular spiritual movement that he led could have influenced the democratic values of the country as a whole. While he was thrust into the media spotlight for asking spiritual questions regarding the accomplishments of Jesus Christ on the cross, when Waldenström entered politics he turned to very tangible questions regarding the constructive value of pluralism and the nature of the emerging Swedish democracy. In order to explain the connection between these two seemingly different sets of questions, it is important to define pluralism, and offer an introductory perspective on how Waldenström understood pluralism.

One starting point is that pluralism should be differentiated from "plurality," or the simultaneous existence of multiple points of view. Pluralism, as it is being referred to here, is a deliberately orchestrated strategy for dealing with the conflicts that result from a plurality of opinions and competing interests. In both religious and political questions, plurality presents the opportunity for conflict whenever a single dominant regime is lacking or is challenged and thereby unable to establish uniformity by force. In the case of Sweden in the second half of the 1800s, the national unity that had been inherited from generations of absolutist monarchy, a hierarchical society, and a unified state church gave way under the pressures for democratic governance and a growing diversity of worldviews. This unprecedented level of ideological conflict between opposing groups was so strong after the turn of the century that historian Berndt Schiller has identified the years 1906–1914 as "years of crisis."[15] Despite such a situation of volatility, it is a remarkable achievement that Swedish politicians were able to establish a democratic praxis that favored pluralism when some of its neighboring countries were not. To the extent that plurality can be transformed into a strategy of pluralism, in which conflict is mitigated and even funneled into constructive dialogue, then pluralism should be seen as an important historical accomplishment. It is with this in mind that Catholic Church historian George Weigel makes a careful distinction between what can be understood as a passive acceptance of plurality and an active strategy of promoting pluralism:

> *Plurality is sheer difference: a sociological fact, a staple of the human condition. Pluralism is a civilizational achievement: the achievement of what [John Courtney] Murray called an 'orderly conversation'—a conversation about personal goods and the common good, about the relationship between freedom and moral truth, about the virtues necessary to form the kind of citizens who can live their freedom in such a way as to make the machinery of democracy serve genuinely humanistic ends. [. . .] It must begin, as Jefferson began the American democratic experiment, with the assertion and defense of truths.*[16]

To the degree that plurality often becomes a social "problem," then pluralism, as described by Weigel, becomes the response and solution to that problem. The problem occurs whenever there is a conflict of ideologies or interests. These conflicts could be the result of any of the diverse concerns of the human condition; in the case of this study, these disagreements were sparked by conflicts between religious worldviews (prompting the religious awakening), class and economic status (prompting the labor movement), and public health (prompting the temperance movement). The consequences that came from the erosion of uniformity in Swedish society were twofold. First, the members of these groups were forced to come to terms with the new reality that conflicts of ideologies and interests would no longer be adjudicated solely by elites (by the government or by the church), but instead needed to be debated in public arenas, such as in the media, voluntary societies and congregations, and in the new bicameral *Riksdag*. New ideologies challenged old ones and competed with other new ideologies for dominance. Understanding pluralism is thus first a matter of orientating oneself amid the diverse landscape of competing ideologies and interests that were vying for top position after the parliamentary reforms of the 1860s. Second, they had to develop strategies for dealing with that situation. In crafting these strategies, the members could take different approaches. A natural impulse would be to attempt to establish dominance for one's own group by trying to prevent pluralism. However, if pluralism could be identified as being to the advantage of a group, then such groups could be expected to defend and promote a situation of pluralism. For members of minority groups or for groups who saw themselves as threatened, pluralism could be seen as advantageous to the extent that it allowed their own survival. While there is a certain amount of idealism associated with pluralism, it is also important to acknowledge the pragmatic dimensions. Group survival for minorities is often dependent on allowances for pluralism. Pluralism is first necessary for groups trying to carve out a place for themselves. Once this place is relatively secure, pluralism can take on a more idealistic character, as more of a luxury than a necessity.

As it will be referred to here, pluralism will be understood as a strategy for dealing with conflict, and furthermore, that this strategy is made with both idealistic and pragmatic motivations. In its most basic political usage, pluralism implies an agenda that values and defends the presence and participation of more than one interest group in the collective decision-making process. Beyond this basic meaning, however, pluralism can take on quite sophisticated ideological meanings. When pluralism becomes a political strategy, it tends to involve questions regarding the nature of power-sharing between different groups. One political scientist who has focused on the question of power-sharing is Arend Lijphart. Lijphart's interest in exploring this question was motivated by the national and tribal conflicts of African nations in the second half of the twentieth century. In many places on the continent, the end of colonial governments had been followed by experiments with European-style democratic systems. When many of these experiments collapsed into internal conflicts, it became apparent that political ideologies were superseded by other identities, namely "primordial" tribal ones.[17] While some political scientists continued to assert that it was necessary for national identities to trump tribal ones in order to establish unity, Lijphart remained skeptical. His solution to such situations was a form of governance he termed "consociational," often simply referred to as "power-sharing." Although the replacement of segmental loyalties by a common national allegiance appears to be a logical answer to the problems posed by a plural society, it is extremely dangerous to attempt it. Because of the tenacity of primordial loyalties, any effort to eradicate them not only is quite unlikely to succeed, especially in the short run, but may well be counterproductive and may stimulate segmental cohesion and intersegmental violence rather than national cohesion. The consociational alternative avoids this danger and offers a more promising method for achieving both democracy and a considerable degree of political unity.[18]

The consociational form of government as presented by Lijphart is a form in which all major groups in a region are intentionally represented.

This diversity is made mandatory by policies that stipulate that all significant groups receive a seat at the decision-making table. While this pluralism might be enforced by laws requiring the inclusion of minorities, it is also aimed at generating a culture that values pluralism in the society as a whole. The intention is that if minority groups who are vying for position, as well as majority groups who are trying to defend their dominance, can both understand that pluralism is in their own interests, they will be more likely to tolerate and work with other competing groups. Lijphart's observations reflect the difficulty of achieving unity of purpose in a heterogeneous social environment, as well as touch on the central questions regarding pluralism that have been discussed since the Enlightenment. He also focuses his critique on the weaknesses of democracy by "majority rule," namely its shortcomings in protecting minorities and dissenters. The consociational/power-sharing approach to dealing with ideological conflict thus places value on strategies of pluralism as a way to overcome the weaknesses of democracy by sheer majority rule. When ideological actors intentionally approach conflict with a mind to preserve the rights of dissenters and protesters, these weaknesses are minimized, and then conflicts have the opportunity to become transformed into productive exchanges between opponents.

This productive type of pluralism—where opposing sides of an argument inform one another in a dynamic tension—is a type of pluralism that closely resembles Waldenström's own views on democracy. Though not a political scientist, he was a politician with an experiential understanding of how the Swedish political system worked, as well as how it could fail. Drawing on this experience, he offered an endless stream of anecdotes, warnings and proverbs regarding the political system. An example of this imagery is included as an introductory quote at the beginning of Part I. Simple speech and folksy imagery like this quote in Karlstad in 1908 was typical of his writing and preaching style. Such imagery was both an asset and a liability to Waldenström, and for it he was both admired and ridiculed. With it he was able to captivate audiences of thousands, as well as generate fodder for columnists and tabloid cartoonists. An expert teacher and translator of Latin, Greek and Hebrew, Waldenström understood well that words and images can be interpreted differently and that one text is not always read by two people in the same way. He built a career and a church denomination on the notion that unity could be achieved in the midst of diversity, that pluralism does not destroy truth, but instead enhances the human understanding of it. His famous motto for biblical study, "where is it written?," became a slogan picked up by Swedish Pietists looking to reform an archaic state church monopoly. Picking apart the established religious paradigm word by word, Waldenström became the figurehead of a movement of democratization within a previously hierarchical and doctrinally-rigid Lutheran church. Simple speech can indeed have profound effects.

The simple language that Waldenström used in his speeches is also problematic for the study of his political philosophy precisely in that it is folksy and often prefers parable-like explanations instead of a standardized political vocabulary. It is also masked in theological imagery, which has the potential to make it unattractive to secular ears. Despite these challenges, the pluralism that Waldenström advocated in his speeches and sermons bears similarities to the explanations of the concepts articulated by Weigel and Lijphart. The introductory quote was selected as a starting point in explaining Waldenström's particular understanding of pluralism. This image of the cart on the road appeared in one of the political speeches that he gave after his career in the Swedish parliament formally ended, in this case in Karlstad in 1908, in which he passionately urged his listeners to vote against the Social Democratic party (*Socialdemokratiska arbetarepartiet*) in the upcoming elections. It had been the result of the work of members of this same party which had helped to end Waldenström's political career in the election of 1905 through an ambitious and successful media campaign directed at unseating him.

As a result, the simple reading of this speech and the rest of Waldenström's political commentary has been to explain him as a defeated, conservative reactionary, bitterly attacking the ascendant political ideology that had beaten him and which would come to dominate Swedish politics throughout the following century. This was the interpretation given by the newspapers in Gävle during the elections of 1902 and 1905, as well as the enduring interpretation demonstrated by the debate over Waldenström's legacy among the historians Grundström, Tomson, and Bredberg. Even Tomson, who most advocated the interpretation of Waldenström as a radical, conceded that he had become reactionary in his later years. However, there are several limitations to a perspective that divides the political arena into "conservatives" versus "radicals." The first is that this dichotomy does little to explain the interaction between opposing political ideologies, particularly how they influenced one another, and instead initiates a cyclical process of weighing the radical qualities of a person against his or her conservative qualities. Oftentimes, whenever one political party or ideology has emerged as the victor following a debate, those groups who had protested the now dominant group find themselves in the situation of having to defend their contribution. This often results in attempts to either justify their conservatism or herald the radical aspects of their program. This kind of process of justification is evident in Tomson's analysis, as his work is framed as a defense of Waldenström "the radical." While there is value in being able to identify someone as being a conservative or radical, this presents a bias, where radicalism is favored, irrespective of whether or not this radicalism promoted progress. It also creates the risk of overstating the contributions of radicals or incorrectly identifying people as radical for the sake of validating their careers. It can suffice to say that Waldenström had his moments of both radicalism and conservatism.

The second limitation of this perspective is that once these labels of conservative and radical are affixed to a group or ideology it can obscure their contribution to the debate. This seems to have been the case with the groups involved in the religious awakening in Sweden. These groups are often named as being part of the overall emergence of democracy, but only indirectly credited with this development. That is, the democratic ideologies of these communities, which gave greater freedom to the individual participant and democratized the hierarchy of religious life, are credited as serving as a catalyst to create a general culture of democracy and a precursor to more radical reforms. But there has been a paradox in Swedish historiography in that at the same time as this general assessment has been made, there has also been a tendency to assert that when religious personalities were directly engaged in politics through official channels, they were seen as defending conservative values and being resistant to democratic reforms. This assumption perpetuates a traditional bias that has been present since the Enlightenment, in which religion is viewed as the opponent to reason and progress. Operating within this assumption, social scientists have sometimes treated the positive outcomes of religious ideology as unanticipated byproducts of fanaticism, as though the religious participants were acting irrationally and not aware of what they were doing.[19] This assumption can even be seen among sympathetic observers. For instance, at a centennial event for the Swedish Mission Covenant in 1978, former prime minister and Social Democrat Tage Erlander (1901–1985) made the observation that Waldenström's life's work had been decisive in the overall breakthrough of democracy in Sweden.

> *Waldenström's teaching on the atonement took on a decisive significance for the breakthrough of democracy in Sweden. He tossed out a difficult dogmatic question of doctrine to the people and let anyone and everyone take a position for themselves on how one should understand the atonement. Now it no longer mattered what was stated by the parish priest and the confessional documents. Read about it in the Bible, and see for yourself! [. . .] If people could now decide for themselves on heavenly things, they were naturally competent to make decisions regarding communal*

*affairs about the schools and church building and even regarding national political questions.*²⁰

At the same time that Erlander credits Waldenström as starting a process of democratization, his language also preserves the assumption that these religious developments were still disconnected from the political arena. It is as if Waldenström as a religious actor instigated something that he later did not participate in; his activity in the spiritual world simply allowed people to make the application to politics themselves, without him making the connection directly.

Other historians have sometimes made the claim that these religious movements served as "lessons" in democracy for lower- and middle class Swedes who were in the process of abandoning their agricultural and patriarchal society.²¹ The official website for the Swedish parliament identifies the emergence of Swedish democracy as having been due to the influence of the folk movements:

> *It is often said that the temperance movement together with the free-church and trade union movements in the late 1800s had a positive bearing on the development of democracy in Sweden. They helped people to learn the procedures for meetings, to write minutes, to argue in favour of their cause and to handle contacts with public authorities. The political parties as we know them today also began to emerge just over 100 years ago, and together with the various popular movements they helped to bring about universal franchise.*²²

These religious movements appear not only to have set the stage for the development of democracy, but also as having had a long-term impact on the direction that society took. This exploration of Waldenström's view of pluralism and his participation in Swedish politics aims to identify some of the missing links between the religious awakening and the emergence of democracy in Sweden. Specifically, this involves an assertion that Waldenström directly applied the democratic aspects of his theology to his political philosophy.

The simple imagery in Waldenström's analogy of the coachman steering a wagon on a road speaks volumes about his philosophy and introduces his positive view of ideological tension. In this image, the tension between conservative and radical forces in politics is identified as bearing the potential for productive dialogue if it can be brought into balance. And conversely, if this debate is not balanced, societal breakdown is immanent. Balance is achieved by allowing open debate between opposing groups. This debate is necessary for the steady development of society as a safeguard against extremism and the totalitarian elimination of minority groups. Innovation is being encouraged here, but at the same time there is the caution that innovation does not automatically lead to progress. In this analogy, Waldenström reflects an understanding of the history of ideas that resembles the philosophy of Georg Wilhelm Friedrich Hegel (1770–1831), most notably the dialectical progression between thesis, antithesis, and synthesis. Determining the degree of influence of Hegel on Waldenström is elusive, but it is unlikely that he could have remained ignorant of Hegel's works during his studies in philosophy and theology at Uppsala University. Among Waldenström's influences at Uppsala were the idealist philosopher Christopher Jacob Boström (1797–1866) and one of his disciples, Sigurd Ribbing (1816–1899).[23] Although Waldenström cannot exactly be cast as a disciple of Boström's, William Bredberg suggests a significant level of Boström's influence, particularly in the rationalized vocabulary that Waldenström himself employed as well as his own Christian idealism, which reflected that of Boström.[24] Hegel's Christian idealism and worldview is certainly amenable to the rational characteristics in Waldenström's own spirituality. At any rate, Waldenström's political philosophy demonstrates an application of various strains of rational idealism to the theological and cultural context of Pietism. Waldenström's articulation of his political view was minimalistic at best, and is primarily visible in his explanations of specific items of debate in the *Riksdag*. In and of itself, his understanding of pluralism in the political arena was not highly theoretical, and was left largely undeveloped. However, the novelty of Waldenström's political philosophy is that it represents a fusion of this Hegelian-style dialectic, a rational idealism, and the missional focus and democratic commitments of Swedish Pietism as expressed by the "new evangelicals." Here is a tangible point of convergence between Enlightenment philosophy and Pietist spirituality, which Waldenström not only inherited, but also developed and promoted. At its best, this fusion of diverse ideologies bore with it the potential for harmony, something which seems to have been a goal of Waldenström's political activism.

In addition to the Hegelian and Boströmian impulses in Waldenström's worldview, there are also a few connections to the cultural phenomenon known as Romanticism. In terms of his future vision for a democratic Sweden, there are points of resonance with the ideas of poet and historian Erik Gustaf Geijer (1783–1847) in particular. Historian Henrik Berggren has explained that Geijer had a conservative vision for a Sweden that would remain composed of small, independent farmers (known as "Little Sweden"), which would be able to withstand the threats of industrialization and urbanization, and which could avoid the extremes of chauvinistic nationalism ("Greater Sweden") on the one hand, as well as the version of socialism that advocated an international, industrial utopia on the other.[25] For the proponents of Little Sweden, democracy was heralded as an age-old national characteristic, which dated back to the free farmers of the Middle Ages, and which was threatened by modernity and needed to be recovered and defended. Waldenström himself made comments to this effect, in which he championed the Romantic ideal of the free farmer and saw democracy as a Swedish value, which was in stark contrast to the alleged totalitarian characteristics of socialism. For example, it may have been out of a preference for an idyllic, pastoral vision of Sweden that Waldenström came to support the "own-your-own-home" movement (*egnahemrörelsen*), which was a more palatable alternative to socialism that was more in line with traditional Lutheran social welfare strategies. The options for poor relief that Waldenström preferred reflected his desire to answer the critiques of socialist agitators, without forfeiting a classical liberal basis for the Swedish economy and political system. His socialist opponents would consider this kind of solution to social inequality as an example of the "old charity" model, however. Waldenström was the leader of a folk movement that depended upon local, grassroots associations, and which presupposed that its members were voluntarily engaged in idealistic charitable, missionary enterprises. His version of the new "Little Sweden" (though he did not call it that) would have been to complement the parish council / municipal council (*sockenstämma / kommunalstämma*) with free-standing mission societies, whether in rural or urban settings, which would be engaged in rebuilding society from the bottom-up with popular involvement.

Historian Bo Stråth has made a generalization about the folk movements, which could rightfully also be applied to Waldenström: "They wanted to reform society, not make revolution. They did not seek to do away with the targets of their criticism, but to transform them and take them over."[26] As a reformer Waldenström drew from an eclectic mix of ideologies of the time, among them the Romantic tradition. He was not a Romantic in the full artistic and cultural sense of that term, but did think in terms of a renewal of the nation-state that fits with larger currents within Romanticism, sometimes progressive and sometimes conservative. On the eve of World War I, he did express support for the "Farmers' March," which called for an increase of the national defense force, and he did support the monarch's constitutional privileges when these were attacked. However, these two concerns were pragmatic, rather than Romantic; in regard to the former, for the ability of Little Sweden to defend itself, and in regard to the latter, to maintain consistency in constitutional interpretation (these two topics will be treated in Part III). Despite making his share of patriotic statements,

Waldenström ultimately made a poor nationalist, as his citizenship in the Swedish kingdom (whether "Little" or "Great") would always be trumped by his citizenship in Christ's kingdom. On a foundational level, conflating these two kingdoms would have amounted to blasphemy for him, even if he found himself tempted by it at various points. Better to leave Sweden in the hands of small, voluntary societies, which could grapple with the challenges of modernity in a pluralistic, democratic public discourse. Patriotism may have been part of a healthy expression of civic duty, but national citizenship was no more than a coincidence of birth. By contrast, Christ's kingdom was of a transnational variety. Its international character was inescapable to the participant of the mission societies and free churches, which had a clear, two-fold division of their enterprises: "inner mission" (work in Sweden) and "outer mission" (in foreign locations such as Congo, China, and Alaska).

This preference for Little Sweden is also evidenced in Waldenström's statements in his account of America, in which he compared the United States and Sweden.

> *America seems to me to be like a young, rich, nervous lady with plumes, rings, brooches, dressed in silk and velvet, bustle and high heeled shoes, which make her taller than she really is. Old Sweden resembles more a shy and unpretentious mother with kerchief and cotton apron. There is more gold adorning the exterior of the young woman, but the old woman has more gold dwelling in her heart.*[27]

Elsewhere in his accounts, he presents America as an innovative, fascinating place with high ambitions, but also demonstrating a culture that has perfected the art of exaggeration and fraud in advertising itself. Whereas old Sweden might be this poor little woman in cotton rags, her superiority rests in being confident in her authentic identity and drawing her wisdom from time-honored traditions. These Swedish traditions he imagined were liberal, democratic ones, derived from a general romanticized view of the free farmers (*bönder*), whose common sense was more to be trusted than the nobility or the captains of industry. It is telling also that in his novel, *Squire Adamsson*, the hero is not the *brukspatron* (factory owner) but rather a *torpare* (cotter or crofter), from the lowest rung of the social hierarchy. It is "Mother Simple," who lacks formal education and all pretentions, and is engaged in sewing circles and community revival, who ends up saving the Squire and implicitly advocating societal transformation from the bottom up. The paradox of Waldenström's exaltation of agrarian values was that in the early twentieth century, this way of life was quickly disappearing. Nevertheless, there remains to this day a widespread Scandinavian mentality which hearkens back to the values of this bygone society, in which moderation and mediocrity were seen as positive traits, even if satirized. One of these is the "Law of Jante," a comical list of "ten commandments" adhered to by the village of Jante depicted in a work of fiction from the 1930s.[28] These laws effectively prevent anyone from being exceptional, and frown on attempts at innovation and self-promotion. It is best for the individual to "fit in" and join the consensus of the community. The Swedish word "*lagom*," almost always used positively, similarly refers to a cultural preference for doing things "just right," not too much, not too little.[29] With humorous self-criticism, Scandinavians often deride themselves for being conformists to this oppressive cult of mediocrity. But it is also used as a way to distinguish "how things are done in Sweden" from "how things are done out in the rest of Europe and abroad," in which political haste, excess, fervor, and self-promotion can lead to bankruptcy, revolution, entanglement in war, and social and economic inequalities. *Jante* and *lagom* represent "the golden mean." These terms have been popularized after Waldenström's lifetime, but he in many ways demonstrated this kind of mentality of moderation as he formulated his political philosophy.[30] This is particularly evident in how he imagined international socialism as being a foreign, extremist threat to homegrown, common-sense traditions of democratic pluralism. For Waldenström, the more organic variety of liberalism represented by the humble farmers had cultivated a domestic democratic praxis. One qualification of this is that while he may have advocated moderation, he himself was a man of high ambitions. Mediocrity was not compatible with his role as the leader of hundreds of thousands of free-church participants, the editor of an internationally read journal, a prolific author, and a politician. The revival was a growth industry, in which he expected to see results in concrete terms: numbers of saved souls, increased memberships of societies, changed laws, and a transformed society. There is a tension here with what Waldenström says about "little mother Sweden." On the one hand, she should be prudent, frugal, moderate and wise, but on the other hand ... she should get busy and reform the world.

Central to Waldenström's understanding of democratic praxis, was the safeguarding of a pluralistic public sphere, in which dissent was possible and opposing political groups were able to critique one another and shape each others' ideological development. Waldenström made several assumptions in crafting this political worldview. One assumption was that societal progress is best achieved through steady evolution. Abrupt revolution and rejection of foundational principles would spell disaster. Another assumption was that these classical liberal values just mentioned (values of free speech, democracy, and equality) permeated the essence of what Swedish society was in the late 1800s, despite many blatant contradictions and inequalities.

Achieving the social and economic equality desired by large portions of the lower classes would be best served by reforming society in such a way that took its liberal heritage into account, rather than abandoning the liberal perspective for a wholesale endorsement of socialism. His third assumption was that socialism left unchecked would all too naturally devolve into revolution, revolution into anarchy, and anarchy into tyranny. The liberal traditions of democracy and pluralism, as they had slowly emerged through the reforms of the 1800s could easily be lost. With these assumptions in mind, it is easy to understand the urgency with which Waldenström warned against this in his political speeches. For him, the potential dominance of the Social Democratic party likely meant the end of free speech and parliamentary process. In short, the budding pluralistic discourse that Sweden was experiencing in the late 1800s could easily be replaced with a unipolar political landscape, governed by a rigid Marxist ideology.

The wealthy factory owner, Squire Adamsson, receives the common sense wisdom of the old cotter woman, Mother Simple. *Brukspatron Adamsson, Eller Hvar Bor Du?*, 181. Illustration by the celebrated National Romantic artist, Jenny Nyström. Used by permission. © 2015 Jenny Nyström / Kalmar Läns museum / Artists Rights Society (ARS), New York.

His opponents in the Social Democratic and Communist fold disagreed strongly with him. Waldenström was in their eyes a reactionary, and in being reactionary defended the status quo, the monarchy, the bourgeoisie. However, in surveying the records of the internal quarrels that occurred within the Social Democratic party, it seems that some of the party leadership had many of the same concerns that Waldenström did, particularly during the pivotal years of 1908 and 1917.[31] The specifics of these confrontations will be explored in more depth in Part III, but what can be said briefly here is that these internal conflicts demonstrate that as members of the party worked to dismantle Waldenström's political career and dismiss his concerns, there were many who also seemed to take his criticisms seriously, namely Hjalmar Branting (1860–1925) and Kata Dahlström (1858–1923). The party, as it emerged in the 1920s, was not the same party that it had been in the 1880s. The more radical and anarchistic elements had been marginalized or even banned in some cases, and the party members in the *Riksdag* had more often than not opted for cooperation with the Liberal party, rather than open confrontation. The hindsight of a century gives the modern observer the ability to see that by the 1920s, important precedents had been set by the party which allowed the survival of pluralistic political discussion and the maintenance of democratic practices. The party would go on to dominate Swedish politics for the majority of the twentieth century. However, at the time that Waldenström died in 1917, Europe was horribly shaken by the Great War, revolution was in the air, and the anti-establishment rhetoric of Socialist agitators continued to pick away at the older Liberal political paradigm. Waldenström could not confidently assert that Sweden was yet out of the woods, nor could he admit that the Social Democratic party was in many ways a different party than the one which had almost driven him out of office in the 1902 election and then finally succeeded in 1905. Right up until his death in 1917, his media presence continued in the newspapers, and so did his warnings to the Swedish people about the dangers that radical socialism posed to free speech, to parliamentary process, to Swedish constitutional law, and to the overall health of pluralistic social discourse.

The goals of individual liberty and social security have been persistent dreams throughout human history, but the attainment of one has often come at the expense of the other. The ideological battles that were fought during the twentieth century between American-style capitalisms and Soviet-style socialisms created a unique opportunity for Swedish society to be identified as a "middle way" between these two extremes. To mid-century political analysts, such as journalist Marquis Childs, Sweden appeared to have fused socialism's concerns for social justice with the freedoms and democratic structures of classical liberalism in a unique balance.[32] Although these assertions would later be critiqued and modified, the "middle way" still remains current in the popular imagination as a convenient way to locate Sweden on an ideological spectrum. The assumptions that are generally made from right and left, respectively, are that liberalism "tamed" socialism or that socialism "humanized" liberalism. Alternately, recent analysis by political scientist Sheri Berman has demonstrated that it was neither liberalism nor socialism that triumphed in the struggles of the twentieth century; instead it was Social Democracy, which was a new product produced by the confluence of both.[33]

Regardless of how much one ideology is credited over and against the other for having contributed the most to this exchange, one assertion that can be made is that the successful development of this new Social Democracy was dependent on the maintenance of a pluralistic public sphere. That is, unlike the dramatic ideological revolutions that took place in some European governments, such as Germany, in which one party eliminated its opposition, the practice of parliamentary democracy was maintained and managed to flourish in Sweden. Pluralistic discourse and exchange can be seen as having been essential to fostering this environment, and as such constitutes the basis of any kind of political middle way that might have developed. If Swedish society can indeed be seen as a middle way, it would be to the degree that political actors were able to maintain this atmosphere of pluralism in a public sphere where diametrically opposed ideologies were able to coexist and continue to influence one another in an ongoing political dialogue.

Furthermore, the understanding of pluralism that is being advanced here is one that contends pluralism to be a positive and even a deliberately orchestrated situation. This would be opposed to an understanding in which pluralism is seen as a *modus vivendi*, or undesirable situation, along the lines of a cold war or passive-aggressive conflict. In this positively defined pluralism, the actions of those who hold power and of those who seek power become delicate balancing acts. Affirming the agency of dominant groups as well as underdogs not only makes for more nuanced history, but also frees historical inquiry from the assumptions that only those in power determine outcomes. A positively defined pluralism also depends on generous provisions for free speech that allow dominant political paradigms to be criticized and challenged. In moments when power changes hands, freedom of speech allows ascendant political regimes to be criticized. This type of transfer of power between groups creates a situation in which the ascendant regime is confronted with criticism, and in addressing this criticism, can shift its developmental trajectory. Such can be seen to have been the case in the ascendancy of the Social Democratic party from the 1880s through the 1920s. As will be argued in Part III, Waldenström took on this role as a critic of socialism during this period, and interacted with key figures within the party who were in turn forced to respond to his criticisms.

The perspective that political exchange is a balancing act can be seen as a simple-minded generalization of a complex situation. However, it can also be seen as an intentional rhetorical strategy, employed in order to maintain a pluralistic public sphere. Common in Waldenström's sermons as well as his political speeches was the presentation of societal progress as a journey along a road, as already seen in the Karlstad speech. Hazards existed to the right and to the left, he claimed, and the proper course was that navigated somewhere in the middle. The subsequent direction society would take was determined by a struggle between opposing viewpoints. Each pulled the wagon to one side or the other. The net result of this struggle was, in Waldenström's view, a positive outcome. This was reinforced in part by the fact that he remained an independent in the *Riksdag*, never formally aligning with any political party. His political philosophy was to throw his weight to whichever point of view he saw as being underrepresented and at risk. That said, he most often took up the cause of the Liberal party and later with the Moderates (conservatives), after the Social Democratic press cranked up its media campaign in 1902. However, he tended to play the devil's advocate and found himself at times defending causes normally advocated by Socialists. Such political ambiguity often makes classifying Waldenström on a political spectrum difficult. However, when read from his own perspective—that the maintenance of pluralism was of the utmost importance in facilitating any reform at all—one is able to better understand the way in which Waldenström hoped his political strategy would serve to promote pluralism. Waldenström's dire predictions of a tyrannical new world order ruled by Marxist ideology have never been actualized in Sweden. Swedish Social Democracy evolved in a hybrid form, having co-opted existing structures rather than supplanting them. As is being argued here, the Social Democratic party seems to have responded to criticism from opposing parties and modified their priorities, charting a course of dialogue and reform, rather than open confrontation and revolution.

If Swedish society managed to develop in a pluralistic direction, despite the ominous warnings of opponents a century ago, then why is the study of Waldenström's political philosophy and activism of interest today? For one, if the outcome of Swedish politics is to be seen as the product of a pluralistic dialogue rather than a one-party triumph, then any insights into the discussions that took place during this seminal period in Swedish political development are valuable. The common narrative in Swedish history during this period, however, has frequently opted for the one-party-triumph motif. Due to the dominance of the Social Democratic party through most of the last century, there has been a tendency for the predominant historical narrative to be written from that party's perspective.[34] This narrative developed naturally due to the fact that during the twentieth century, the party enjoyed long periods of political dominance—in fact, the longest unbroken rule of any political party in a European democracy was that held by the Social

Democratic party from 1932–1976.[35] This perspective is rather teleological in the sense that the historical conflicts that the party had with oppositional groups were seen as triumphs of the Social Democratic agenda, rather than as moments of contingency, in which ideas were exchanged across party lines and the ultimate outcomes were altered by the presence of a plurality of voices.

CHAPTER 2

Modeling Pluralism through Allegory—*Squire Adamsson*

WALDENSTRÖM'S CAREER AS A politician was informed heavily by his religious worldview, and in order to understand his various viewpoints in both religious and political questions, it is essential to begin with an exploration of his theology. The religious and the political were interconnected for Waldenström, who saw activity in both of these divergent spheres as being part of a holistic living out of faith. As a politician, he spent little time explaining his political philosophy, instead focusing his life's work on his theological writings. It is first here, in the process of crafting his devotionals and sermons, that he worked out his understanding of pluralism, and then applied these ideas in the political sphere. Historians looking for a Waldenströmian political treatise written in secular terms will come up empty-handed, as no such document has surfaced. Waldenström was no stranger to controversy, and it is likely that it was from his own first-hand experiences with theological controversy that he developed a strong interest in ideas of pluralism. This effort to reconcile conflicting sides of theological arguments had begun as early as his childhood. According to historian William Bredberg, the conservative orthodoxy ("Old Pietism," *gammalläseriet*) that had been present in his home province in Northern Sweden in his childhood would come to drive him into the circle around Carl Olof Rosenius, whose "new evangelicalism" (*nyläseriet*) featured a strong ecumenical message and a commitment to keeping the Pietists united within the Church of Sweden and avoiding separatism.[36] Despite this aversion to dogmatic conflicts, Waldenström himself became responsible for generating one of the most famous episodes of public debate after the 1872 atonement controversy, which culminated in the exodus of the Waldenströmians from the Church of Sweden in 1878. For the rest of his career, he appears to have been seeking to fix this separation by promoting an ecumenical cooperation between all Christian groups, high and low.

Understanding pluralism was a major theme in his work even a decade before the atonement sermon was published. Waldenström's debut as an author was due to the success of his novel, *Squire Adamsson*, first published in 1862 as a series in the newspaper, *Stadsmissionären* (the "Stockholm City Missionary") and then expanded into a novel the following year. At the time of this writing, there have been eleven editions of the novel in Swedish, with translations having also appeared in English, Norwegian and Danish. Despite the wide readership of the novel in the nineteenth century as well as the residual interest, the book has been all but forgotten within general Swedish literary history. As has been maintained by Harry Lindström and by Lars Furuland, literature of this popular variety has been ignored and left out of the national canon, not because of a lack of popularity or influence, but quite simply because it was not accepted by the dominant class of the time, nor the ideological groups that would later come to dominate the twentieth century.[37] On the contrary, Lindström maintained that Waldenström's novel ranks among the most widely read Swedish novels of the nineteenth and early twentieth centuries, building on the observations of literary historian Henrik Schück. In his inventories of Swedish literature in the 1890s, Schück concluded that Waldenström enjoyed a wider readership than either Oscar Levertin (1862–1906) or Verner von Heidenstam (1859–1940), two of Sweden's most popular authors at the time.[38] The omission of Waldenström's most popular novel from Swedish literary history, as well as its neglect by historians has much to do with the fact that it was embraced by the wrong public, i.e., lower- and middle-class church-goers, rather than the bourgeois class that was dominant at the turn of the century or the Social Democratic elite of the twentieth century.

Contributing to the marginalization of the book in the consciousness of posterity are certainly its dominant religious themes. If it is seen as being merely a religious work, then one might assume that it was a product of a subgroup within Swedish society, and thus lacks universal appeal. Admittedly, the novel was indeed first and foremost addressed to members of the religious awakening, or at least people who were engaged in the discussions surrounding the awakening. However, two qualifications are warranted. First, it would be incorrect to assume that the impact of the book was limited to this public. From Harry Lindström's research (1997), a strong case has been made that the novel reached a broad enough public to have made a significant impact in general societal discussions. Second, the religious aspect of the book alone should not be used to disqualify it from having borne universal significance in contemporary society. While modern Sweden is a famously secular society, Sweden of a century ago was in contrast quite religious, steeped in the traditions of both a state-sponsored Lutheran education, as well as revival activities sponsored by the various free churches.

Title page from *Brukspatron Adamsson*, fifth edition. Artwork throughout by Jenny Nyström. Used by permission. © 2015 Jenny Nyström / Kalmar Läns museum / Artists Rights Society (ARS), New York.

With good reason, *Squire Adamsson* has been compared to another religious allegory, John Bunyan's *Pilgrim's Progress* (1678) (available in Swedish as early as 1727). Rather than having simply been an imitation of Bunyan's classic book, Lindström asserted that *Squire Adamsson* was also a provocative departure from this earlier allegory. Waldenström had, he argued, taken the literary and religious ingredients of the allegorical genre and thrust them into the contemporary Swedish cultural context. This was evident in the comparison of the main characters of both books, Christian and Adamsson.

> *Christian is an anxious refugee from the world, Squire [Adamsson] is in certain respects a modern human being, conflicted, constantly searching for a spiritual identity, a participant in the new age of self analysis, reflection and restlessness. Waldenström's allegory is to a high degree a Swedish allegory, characterized by the complex problems concerning faith in Swedish society.*[39]

Furthermore, Lindström pointed out that the allegory presented by Waldenström lacked the closure of *Pilgrim's Progress*. The readers who follow Adamsson on his pursuit of truth find themselves on a much less predictable and more troubling journey than that undertaken by Christian. Waldenström presents enticing alternatives to the worldview that Adamsson attempts to follow, thus creating a far more elusive journey for the truth, but therein a more realistic depiction of what the search for truth entails. Lindström identifies *Squire Adamsson* as having been fully engaged in the existential questions of Swedish culture of the period, and not at all isolated from the dominant culture.

> *The book's presentation bears witness to a well thought out awareness of culture, an attempt to discern the alternative worldviews of pluralism and take a position on them. Not least interesting is the fact that the author provides the reader with so many objections to the culture of Evangelium and so many attractive arguments for alternative cultures.*[40]

Despite their differences, it is accurate to ground *Squire Adamsson* in the tradition of religious allegories represented by Bunyan's *Pilgrim's Progress*, as well as John Milton's *Paradise Lost* (1667). Common to such allegories is an important experiential element. As the reader follows the main characters on their spiritual and existential journeys, he or she vicariously experiences the discoveries that the main characters make, and thus is able to come to similar conclusions about morality and truth. Because authors in this genre often lead their readers to predictable ideological conclusions, some critics have problematized the way in which such works lead readers in search of the truth. Stanley Fish is one scholar who has identified a weakness in this genre, in part due to its linear construction. In other words, the plot is linear in that the main characters move on a one-directional journey from ignorance to understanding, from being "lost" to being "found," and other binary opposites. In his explanations of *Paradise Lost*, Fish linked this linear construction to the inherently linear nature of the pursuit of the truth in the Judeo-Christian historical worldview and the scientific method of the Enlightenment. The goal of this construction, according to Fish, is to force the reader to take part in a centuries' old argument between rhetoric and philosophy. Experiential readings, like allegories, are designed to pull the reader on a journey of discovery, with the final destination being truth. However, there are pitfalls along the way, which have the potential to distract and mislead the main character away from his or her final goal. Fish claims that rhetoric has often been situated in the role of "distraction," while reason and rationally defended theology have been given priority of place. In Western intellectual history, the subordination of rhetoric to reason was solidified by the rise of Christian scholasticism, but also had strong roots in classical philosophy.[41] Fish writes:

> *Although the transition from classical to Christian thought is marked by many changes, one thing that does not change is the status of rhetoric in relation to a foundational vision of truth and meaning. Whether the center of that vision is a personalized deity or an abstract geometric reason, rhetoric is the force that pulls us away from that center and into its own world of ever-shifting shapes and shimmering surfaces.*[42]

Perhaps due to this bias toward rhetoric as devil's advocacy or sophistry, rhetoric has gotten a bad name, whereas other traditions of argumentation, such as theological ones, have not been called into question in the same way, Fish explains. The reader of an allegory, assuming that he or she is being brought along on an objective explanation of the truth, may be less prepared to identify that this too is a rhetorical strategy and that the narrator is making choices in how the pursuit of truth is being framed.

In *Paradise Lost*, for instance, the story of the expulsion of Adam and Eve from paradise is used as an allegorical way of mirroring the average believer's transition from sinfulness to redemption. As the protagonists make their way on their journey to redemption, rhetoric is employed to pull them off course. These rhetorical arguments are identified by Fish in the characters of fallen angels like Belial, which Fish identifies as Milton's reinforcement of traditional arguments against rhetoric.[43] This is a common quality in Christian thought, which Fish traces back to Saint Augustine, who was important as a pioneer in facilitating the transfer of Western philosophy from classical to Christian paradigms. Augustine continued the tradition of Aristotle in subordinating "eloquence" to "wisdom," but diverged on the source of that wisdom.[44] Whereas the classical mind had looked for truth by analyzing perceivable phenomena in the natural world and through mathematical analysis, the medieval Christian mind depended on divine revelation to reach truth. The human soul was on a journey, being separated from original union with God and seeking reunion with him.

> *Although [God] is our native country, He made Himself also the Way to that country [. . .] Thus He is said to have come to us, not from place to place through space, but by appearing to mortals in mortal flesh . . . But since men were made comfortable to this world by a desire to enjoy creatures instead of their creator, whence they are most aptly called "the world," they did not know Him, so that the Evangelist says, "The world knew Him not." Thus in the Wisdom of God the world could not know God through wisdom.*[45]

In the view of Augustine, not only is rhetoric held in suspicion, but even human wisdom on its own is not sufficient to reach the ultimate truth of God's salvation. What is needed is an encounter with divine revelation, found in the historical person of Jesus Christ. To be more specific, this encounter needs to be experienced in order for truth to be understood. The experience of revelation completes human knowledge and allows it to penetrate into its ultimate field of inquiry, the truth of God. As the coming of the Gospel had "completed" the previously incomplete wisdom of classical civilization, so too Augustine believed that the proper study and teaching of the Gospel could correct and guide all of humanity in the solution of their social ills.[46]

This essential belief that complete truth was discoverable and absolute was a concept that continued to shape Western epistemology through the age of the Enlightenment. With the Enlightenment came an emphasis on the scientific method as a means of approaching the truths of the natural world. What Fish points out is that this system has frequently become a constricting force on progress. The belief that truth is ultimately knowable has created a blindness to the limits of the paradigms created by scientific, rational discourse. This anti-rhetorical pursuit of knowledge has emphasized a notion that the perils of rhetoric and the deficiencies of language can be solved by linguistic reform, bringing humanity to a point where words could directly express the objects and concepts they signify.[47] Such a development of direct signification is not possible, according to Fish. While Enlightenment philosophy has perceived itself as moving vertically toward absolute truth, what it was actually doing was simply moving horizontally from one paradigm to the next. The scientific method was not a means of moving people closer to truth, but of convincing them to exchange one "monadic totality" for another.[48]

Fish's stated intention in his discussion of religious allegory is part of an effort to free rhetoric from its negative stigma in order to allow its imaginative capabilities to be used to creatively restructure law, politics and society. This assertion finds some support in the writings of Richard Rorty, who also suggests that rhetoric can aid in the never ending process of deconstructing paradigms. Rorty explains that questions of absolute truth are irrelevant to this process, and concludes instead that a pragmatic approach should be used to solve specific problems of society.

> *There is no activity called "knowing" which has a nature to be discovered, and at which natural scientists are particularly skilled. There is simply the process of justifying beliefs to audiences.*[49]
>
> *[The anti-rhetoricians] are the ones who are confused, because they think of truth as something towards which we are moving, something we get closer to the more justification we have. By contrast, pragmatists think that there [. . . is] nothing to be said about justification in general. [. . .] There is nothing to be said on the latter subject not because truth is atemporal and justification temporal, but because the only point in contrasting the true with the merely justified is to contrast a possible future with the actual present.*[50]

These critiques of the biblical-historical interpretive framework are somewhat accurate in terms of the often linear nature of some of Christian historiography, as well as the sometimes negative view of rhetoric.[51] The allegories in question, *Pilgrim's Progress* and *Paradise Lost*, at least on a superficial level, also do tend to have a linear characteristic to the degree that they present humanity's progression on a spectrum from being lost to being redeemed.[52] Since the perception of truth rests on the individual's subjective experience of revelation and his or her interpretation of that revelation, this is a point of vulnerability in the genre of religious allegories. While the narrator assumes a posture of objectivity, there are certain points of "revealed" truth which remain unquestioned. This creates an inherently static conception of those truths. It is this vulnerability which Fish and Rorty find inherent to presentations of truth that are linearly defined.

The point of exploring this debate about religious allegory and the linear nature of the traditional Christian view of history is to determine how such a critique would apply to a theologian like Waldenström. Certainly there are ways in which *Squire Adamsson* demonstrates some of the linear characteristics discussed. However, it would be incorrect to identify Waldenström's allegory as simply an imitation of these previous allegories, in that it also demonstrates a significant departure. Rather than containing a completely linear pursuit of truth, the path of discovery for Waldenström's protagonist is also decidedly circular and lacks the resolution found in the other allegories. While the traditional salvation narrative is at work in this novel, the plot is not primarily concerned with salvation (i.e., a progression from being "lost" to being "found"). Instead the main focus is on exploring the nuances and limits of God's unconditional grace. The point is to problematize simplistic understandings of grace, and the net effect of all of these speculations is that by the end of the novel, the reader is left unsettled because the matter is not neatly resolved. The novel's circular construction is underscored by the inclusion of the same scripture verse as both a foreword and epilogue.

> *Now to him who relies on works, the wages are not counted as grace but as debt. But to him who does not rely on works but believes on him who justifies the ungodly, his faith is accounted as righteousness.*[53]

By invoking this passage from the book of Romans, Waldenström engages his readers in experiencing the complexities of Saint Paul's discussion of the nature of grace. The main character, a wealthy landowner named Adamsson, must repeatedly grapple with the meaning of the free gift of divine grace rather than trusting his own good deeds and his intellectual powers to understand divine truth. Adamsson's journey is not easily classified as a linear progression from ignorance to enlightenment. The "truth" concerning grace is presented to Adamsson within the first several pages of the novel, and is thus seemingly anti-climactic. In the end, Adamsson is redeemed, but not due to his arriving at a perfect understanding of the truth, but simply because his life has run its course and at the time of his death he is found trusting completely on God's grace. He arrives at this trust numerous times throughout the course of the novel, but each time quickly strays, being led away by his own doubts, his strong inclination to "works righteousness," and the pull of rhetoric (not only by rhetoricians who are secular, but also by "theologians"). This cyclical movement persists right up to the end, leaving the reader in question as to whether or not Adamsson has learned anything more about grace than what was presented to him in the first few chapters.

One thing that can be certain about Adamsson's journey is that by the end of the novel he has accumulated various experiences with grace, and that these diverse, subjective experiences have conditioned how he perceives the truth. His experiences have marked him, represented in the names of the cities he has lived in, as well as in his name, which changes from Adamsson, to Abrahamsson, to Agarsson, and finally back to Abrahamsson.[54] This emphasis on experience is not only an inheritance from the allegorical tradition already discussed, but is also a hallmark trait of

Lutheran Pietism.[55] Experience is symbolized by education, and two teachers take on the role of teaching Adamsson about grace. The most important teacher is "Mother Simple" (*Mor Enfaldig*), who accompanies Adamsson on his journey through life, correcting him when he goes astray. Adamsson begins the story as the wealthy owner of a large factory called "Industriousness" (*Arbetsamhet*), in the city "The World" (*Världen*), which produces good works, driven in part by the power of a river called "Self-Centered-Piety" (*Självfromhet*). His good deeds, while a product of his good intentions, are done out of vanity, a vice that prompts correction from Mother Simple.

> "Things are not as well as the Squire might believe. The Squire is false-hearted. All his good deeds and his practice of godliness is simply an attempt to escape the sorrowful realization that things are not as they should be with him."[56]

Her advice to Adamsson is that he should stop relying on his good works, and instead trust grace, leave his factory to move to the city "Evangelium." This he does, but not until after the ruler of the land, "Justus All-Powerful" (*Justus Allsvåldig*), calls in all of Adamsson's debts and throws him into prison. Once Adamsson realizes that works do not bring justification, he allows himself to be moved by "Immanuel" to Evangelium, where Mother Simple takes responsibility for his development. Mother Simple is "simple" in that her wisdom comes from her experiences, not through university or seminary education. What she knows she learned from "Father Experience" (*Fader Erfarenhet*), who also becomes Adamsson's other teacher in Evangelium. Father Experience teaches in "the class of the wretched" (*Ömklighetsklassen*). Mother Simple warns Adamsson that this class will soon bring an end to his honeymoon phase with grace. It is only through trusting grace through the various trials of life that people can be justified before Justus All-Powerful and have their debts cancelled. Grace is administered by Immanuel, who according to the law of the city of Evangelium, is the only one who can accomplish justification.

Waldenström not only uses the format of this allegory to comment on the truth, but especially to comment on the pursuit of truth. Here it is significant that he denies full insight to any of his characters. Not only do the residents of The World have incomplete and even false understandings of truth, but the residents of Evangelium too have arguments among themselves as to the truth. The main point of disagreement between the various characters is over the nature of their relationship to Justus All-Powerful.

> *In a city called Holiness, there ruled at that time a mighty king by the name of Justus All-Powerful. There were many peculiar*

> *rumors circulating about him among the citizens of The World. Many considered him to be an inhumanely strict man, which is why they feared him tremendously. Others were of the persuasion that he was a good-natured master, of whom there was nothing to fear. Some even wondered if he really existed, or if he wasn't just some kind of saga hero. In short, everyone had their own ideas about him, but no one truly knew him.*[57]

Ultimately, there is no one who has arrived at complete knowledge, including those who have presumably completed their journeys. Even the constant Mother Simple is at one point shaken in her trust in grace.[58] The allegorical environment that Waldenström creates allows him to comment on various ways of pursuing truth, including the dispute between rhetoric and logic, as well as the ideal method for Pietists to discern truth by relying on a collective evaluation of their subjective experiences. The various perspectives on the nature of Justus All-Powerful and his relationship to his subjects are symbolized in the names of the cities, such as The World and Evangelium, as well as "Loose Living" and "Theology." Adamsson and the other inhabitants of this universe run the risk of being misled by the rhetoric of Beelzebul (the devil), who manages to distort the truth in all of these places. However, the reader also becomes aware that rhetoric is not only being used by secularized academics, but also by theologians. Thus, one of the skills being imparted by the narrator to the reader is an awareness of the difficulty in arriving at the truth, as well as training in critically evaluating the rhetoric of even those characters with the best intentions.

Even though there is a relatively equal critique of all parties in this allegory, there is a tendency to stack the deck against "the learned" and the traditions of the Enlightenment. In these cases, the pietistic emphases on subjective experience, homespun common sense, and mistrust of scholarly and scientific approaches to the pursuit of truth come through loud and clear. It would be easy to argue that Waldenström is demonstrating anti-intellectualism, which was a strong current in the Pietist movement in Sweden and America.[59] However, Waldenström was an academic himself, holding an advanced degree in classical languages and was a formally trained Lutheran minister. His presentation of rational approaches to questions of faith is more of a commentary on the elusive nature of the truth, rather than a dismissal of a role for higher education in Christian communities. The fact that he aims his critique at both Christian and secular scholars results in a common warning against false confidence regarding all assertions of truth. This can be seen in one episode in particular, in which three men succeed in pulling Adamsson away from Evangelium: these characters are named "Confident," "Straight-Forward," and "Enlightened," yet are alternately called "Bold," "Dead-Sure," and "Self-Wise."[60] These men come from the community of Theology, and with their convincing arguments manage to bring Adamsson to doubt his trust in unconditional grace that he has learned from Mother Simple and Father Experience. Mother Simple cautions Adamsson that he has been given a dangerous poison by these men; in other words, he has become overconfident in their mathematical understanding of grace. Her assessment of these men and their scholarly approaches to the truth is that the qualifications they make in trying to objectively define the nature of grace actually serve to dismantle its potential to transform the subjective individual.

> "Even Mr. Self-Wise tries to find assurance for his heart by speaking about Immanuel's grace. But since he does not understand that it is exactly in this assurance that its power lies, so he thinks that he can guard against sin with the addition of 'however,' which he has derived from Logic, I expect. By doing this, what happens is that with all of his 'howevers' he destroys all assurance and thus diminishes its power. In this way, he opens the windows and the doors to sin."[61]

Only an understanding of grace that allows it to retain its dynamic vitality can effectively allow a person to be saved. Qualifications of grace lead to self-confidence and a validation of one's own abilities, when it is rightfully Immanuel alone who should be credited with accomplishments of grace. Since the truth of grace is presented to Adamsson at the beginning of the novel, there is an intentionally anti-climactic nature to Waldenström's presentation of grace. By beginning and ending with the same biblical text, Waldenström is able to demonstrate how different contexts will affect the interpretation of any given text. Indeed, Adamsson has modeled how this verse has taken on a rich nuance of meanings in each of these phases of his life. Waldenström does retain a place for revealed truth, namely the concept of the freeness of grace for all who believe. However, this revealed truth is extremely minimalistic. Adamsson is able to form a composite understanding of grace by weaving together these episodic conclusions he has made. Adamsson is able to see in part, but he is never able to know fully, and therefore has to take a leap of faith.

Another important non-linear aspect of the Waldenstromian pursuit of truth is the fact that there is so much repetition in the plot of *Squire Adamsson*. Adamsson repeatedly becomes frustrated in this process and strays from the truth he is struggling to believe. In contrast to what Fish has asserted about the pattern of falling away from the true path that one can find in religious allegories, in the case of Waldenström's novel, this process of falling away is not simply a consequence of rhetoricians acting to mislead and bring the destruction of the protagonist. Rather, this repetitive struggle of grasping the truth and losing it actually proves to be a constructive process for the protagonist. Furthermore, it is also an essential aspect of the experiential model of pietistic faith. Simply giving intellectual assent to the objective truth about grace will not cause one to be justified. Grace has to be trusted and put into subjective practice through repeated experiences. Mother Simple is the catalyst for this repetitive motion for Adamsson. As she repeats the same advice to trust grace each time, this repetition forces Adamsson to reflect on his situation in a new light. Although the message is the same, it is received by Adamsson in a new way in each instance because the circumstances of his life have changed. While Mother Simple appears "simple" in the beginning, by the end she emerges as the only truly wise character due to the fact that it is only she who has correctly anticipated that the perception of truth is affected by subjectivity. Though an academic, Waldenström chooses not to present the reader here with a scholastic system explaining the nature of grace, but instead offers a strategy for dealing with a pluralistic world in which the truth about grace will continue to be debated and remain unresolved.

Reading Waldenström's allegory as a circular—as opposed to a linear—presentation of the pursuit of truth may be used to re-evaluate how religious allegories can function. The critics mentioned above have pointed out how allegories can represent a sort of self-fulfilling prophecy, by seeing truth as something knowable and the attainment of truth as the goal of history. Waldenström's circular allegory complicates this assertion, and offers an alternative view of the pursuit of truth as reflecting a dynamic tension that is enhanced by instances when truth claims remain unresolved. In this perspective, the protagonists can model for the reader the possibility that the truth will become nuanced, rather than threatened, by a diversity of subjective experiences. Conversely, whenever the characters attempt to construct certainty, they fail. Waldenström breaks down his characters' self-confidence in order to differentiate between which principles can be regarded as "essential" (the basic concepts necessary to hold a community together and navigate the pitfalls of life) and those that are "non-essential" (the particulars of those concepts).

Squire Adamsson is a vivid representation of the way in which some Swedish Pietists attempted to pursue truth. Essential in this process is the freedom for discussion and disagreement. In order to enter this discussion, certain assumptions about the truth had to be accepted, such as the existence of God, the authority of scripture, and the divinity of Christ. However, when lesser doctrinal issues came into question (such as the specifics of how and when to baptize a believer), the practice of certain Pietists was to discuss these questions, but to avoid making totalizing statements about them. Despite the accusations that Waldenström had broken with the spirit of Rosenius, and thus with classical Pietism, there was more of the spirit of Rosenian piety in Waldenström than perhaps any other single influence.[62] On the whole, he remained concerned more with the activity and experience of faith, rather than nailing down doctrines for the Swedish Mission Covenant (SMF). Although his career as a religious leader had been launched by a theological controversy, doctrine was an area where he preferred to be a minimalist. On the issue of baptism, for instance, Waldenström and the SMF chose to observe both infant and adult baptism, a practice that is unthinkable in many Christian denominations.

The theological battles that Waldenström became embroiled in during the 1870s served the purpose of confirming his earlier understandings about the dynamic tension of truth. This acceptance of the necessity of pluralism, without conceding to relativism, shaped his career as a religious leader, as well as profoundly influenced the way he participated in politics. Waldenström retained an idealist's loyalty to the core principles of Christian theology: the existence of God, the constancy of God's grace, the peril of sin, and the promise of salvation. These essentials of the faith he did not call into question, and he eschewed relativism. However, at the same time, in non-essential questions, such as the minute definitions of these concepts of faith, he encouraged his audience not to defend rigid doctrines. Complete understanding of these matters was elusive to human minds, and as such, it was better to be flexible in these non-essential matters. Waldenström was generous in his own orthodoxy, and as such warned his readers against constrictive orthodoxies, both in the theological and political spheres. Discussion and debate on contentious matters allowed for a nuanced view of truth.

It is unlikely that Waldenström wrote *Squire Adamsson* with political questions in mind, especially as it was first written two decades before he entered the *Riksdag*. It did, however, remain in print for the remainder of his life, and his continual revisions to the manuscript demonstrate an on-going engagement with this text. *Squire Adamsson* offers insights into the mind of Waldenström, particularly how he viewed the debate about truth as a constructive process. When read in light of political discussions of the day, it emerges as a general defense of pluralism. As discovered by the characters of the novel, truth needs to be understood in terms of historical circumstances and developments. The Hegelian dialectical understanding of progress, which seeks a synthesis between conflicting perspectives about the truth, is perceptible in Waldenström's allegory, and his systematic exploration of truth represents both the influence of Enlightenment rationalism of the type presented by C. J. Boström, as well as the earnest defense of essential truths typical for Lutheran Pietists.

In the remaining parts of this book, the impact of Waldenström's understanding of pluralism will be explored as it manifested itself in three of the social movements of the period, the religious awakening and reform of the church-state model, the labor movement and the development of Social Democracy, and the temperance movement and the challenges that this movement posed to pluralism. Pluralism was an ethical good that Waldenström desired to promote as a political virtue, and as such, it was the prism through which he viewed each of the three folk movements and evaluated their claims to reform Swedish society.

PART II
Separating Church and State

In necessariis unitas, in dubiis libertas, in omnibus caritas.

Im Notwendigen herrsche Einmütigkeit, im Zweifelhaften Freiheit, in allem aber Nächstenliebe.

I det nödvändiga, enhet, i det flertydiga, frihet, i allt, kärlek.

In essentials, unity. In non-essentials, liberty. In all things, charity.

—Moravian Pietist motto[63]

CHAPTER 3

Pietism as the Re-Emergence of Religious Pluralism in Sweden

As THE NAME SUGGESTS, the religious revival referred to as the *den svenska folkväckelsen* ("the Swedish national awakening" or "popular awakening"), involved a large scale, nation-wide transformation in the way Swedes participated in religion. Whereas the religious model of the preceding centuries was hierarchical, with an elite group of clergy presiding over one unified national congregation, the popular revivals were radically democratic. In contrast with the formal structures of the national church, where decisions were reached in exclusive meetings of bishops, the decisions of revival groups were made in congregational meetings driven by lay people. This shift had begun even as far back as the 1700s, whenever Pietists met in their secret and illegal conventicles, but reached greater significance between the 1820s and 1850s with the emergence of dissenting mission and communion societies, as well as religious periodicals. Matters of doctrine and practice became the prerogative of the mission society or congregation instead of the clergy. The expectation of a "unity of truth" that had been undermined by the Reformation was further undermined by this decentralization of the interpretation of truth. As the clergy lost authority in dictating doctrine and religious life, this brought changes in the perception of their authority in both the private sphere and politics. The state church had traditionally been represented in the *Riksdag* as one of the four "estates," but the governmental reforms in 1866 minimized this role when the four estates system was abolished. Clergymen had to re-evaluate their role in an increasingly democratized spiritual landscape and compete with new types of spiritual leaders, many of whom were laymen and lacked formal education. Success as a politician and religious leader became less dependent on wealth and birth, and instead was facilitated by such things as talent in public speaking or celebrity status in the media. The success of politicians and religious leaders alike became more dependent on the sentiments and opinions of average people. In many cases, despite the abolition of the estate of the clergy, seats in the parliament could continue to be held by religious figures if they managed to evolve to function within these new expectations and practices.

This section will focus on how church and state were separated during this period, and how actors like Paul Peter Waldenström articulated how this increased pluralism should be defined and understood. It will discuss some of the implications that this new order had for individual religious life, as well as the relationship of religion to the Swedish state. Waldenström's career can be viewed as having been concerned with addressing two main questions. The first was how Sweden could transition from a society in which national solidarity was based on identification with one unified Lutheran state church to a societal model that would increasingly allow space for a plurality of religions and freedom for dissent. The second question was how religious freedom could be accomplished in such a way that this would develop into an atmosphere in which partisan conflicts could be overcome and productive exchange could be fostered. Answering this second question would be essential in navigating between extremisms and guaranteeing that the project of establishing pluralism would be successful. For Waldenström this hinged on the necessity of avoiding two perils; on the one hand preventing religious pluralism from devolving into the extremes of either apathy or polarized conflict, and on the other hand preventing religion from being completely privatized, and therefore excluded from the public sphere. Both of these extremes were to be avoided for the reason that they risked replacing one monoculture with another. The ideals of pluralism could be compromised or lost if any ideologies, religious or secular, were restricted from public life.

Beginning in earnest with the revolutions of 1848 and continuing through the first decades of the twentieth century, the countries of Europe were engaged as never before in a dramatic discussion of the role of religion in society that eventually resulted in the diminished influence in politics and public life, the process referred to as secularization. From the seventeenth century, national unity had been built on religious foundations, and when proponents of Enlightenment thinking cast their doubts on the divine sanction of Protestant governments it was also natural to critique the bonds between states and their officially sponsored churches. Historian Hugh McLeod has traced the origins of secularization in Western Europe and points out that this process came as a result of intentional activity by political actors to bring about such a transformation. Furthermore, he asserts that it was not a foregone conclusion that society would develop in a secular direction, but that this result was the outcome of a heated debate between religious as well as anti-religious groups over the appropriateness of religion in public. Religious motivations for revolution were evident among political actors in Germany, France, and England prior to 1848, and the fact that each of these regions chose different trajectories to achieve secularization weakens the notion that such a development was inevitable.[64]

The connection between churches and states was perhaps nowhere as synonymous and direct as in the Nordic countries, where in each country, a single national Lutheran church operated as a branch of the government, was subordinate to the crown, and fully integrated into the fabric of public life and the national mythology. These bonds had been firmly established after the Reformation, and solidified during the subsequent age of absolutism (1660s–on). Absolute monarchs demanded unity (*enhet*) in matters spiritual and temporal, and this unity produced a homogenous religious culture in the Church of Sweden, referred to as *enhetskyrkan* ("church of unity"). State churches presided over a *de jure* religious monopoly and served the crown in administrating the education and morality of the people. These monopolies created starkly homogenous religious environments, where dissenters remained underground or faced punishment. Citizenship in Sweden was synonymous with membership in the state church, and dissenters risked not only social marginalization, but even formal disenfranchisement and loss of civil rights.

Although this religious monopoly lasted for several hundred years, the religious atmosphere was not always so tightly unified in the region that would become Sweden. Christianity had come to the region rather late compared with the rest of Europe, in a long process of mission activity between the 800s and the 1000s. Even in the early part of the medieval Catholic era, a *de facto* pluralism existed, as Norse religious customs persisted alongside Christian life. The Catholic era introduced a much more centralized form of religion than had existed previously. Norse religion had central cult sites, including Uppsala, but the shamans and chieftains did not enjoy nearly as extensive or centralized power as existed elsewhere in Europe. Religious authority was intertwined with temporal power in the pagan era, but the Catholic era would bring this partnership to new heights. In becoming Catholic, Sweden had inherited the relationship of church and state that had long existed to the south. This was the so-called "Constantinian union" between the Catholic Church and the state, a model for church-state relations that had originated in the fourth century with the precedents set by the emperor Constantine. The Lutheran era in Sweden was a continuation and intensification of this Constantinian arrangement. Whereas the

Reformation in several of the German countries and elsewhere in Europe had reintroduced religious pluralism by creating schisms and competing religious worldviews, in Sweden the Reformation meant an intensified religious monopoly in which the church was subordinated to the crown and became an arm of the state. This was not the only possible outcome, as by contrast, Brandenburg-Prussia, demonstrated an example of the coexistence of two churches, one Reformed and the other Lutheran, both sponsored by the state.[65] Though the Reformation had reintroduced degrees of pluralism in other parts of Europe, this would be deferred in Sweden until the mid-1800s, when Pietism gained a firm foothold.

George Scott. Engraving by J. Thomson after a painting by W. Gush. Used by permission. Kungliga biblioteket, The National Library of Sweden. KoB Sn. 1.

Pietism is a term that can be used to indicate either a general trend of piety in a religious movement, or to specifically identify a strain of piety within Lutheranism.[66] When capitalized, Pietism is generally identified as a specific Lutheran school of thought, beginning in the early 1600s with the German theologian Johann Arndt, and continuing through such figures as Phillip Jakob Spener, August Hermann Francke, and Nikolaus Ludwig, Count von Zinzendorf. These theologians and the movements surrounding them are sometimes also referred to as "classical Pietism," to differentiate it from later movements. The emergence of these religious revivals in Sweden in the early 1800s was directly inspired and informed by classical Pietism, through the wide readership that these German Pietists gained in Scandinavia.[67] Other religious impulses from Great Britain and elsewhere in Europe were also decisive,[68] but even the Methodist evangelist George Scott directly invoked the Pietist tradition when he founded a religious newspaper in Sweden and named it *Pietisten* ("The Pietist") in the 1840s. Rather than promote Methodism, Scott's brief work in Sweden was characterized by an attempt to build on organic, Lutheran revival traditions, hence Pietism. After Scott was driven from the country by threat of mob violence, his successor, Carl Olof Rosenius, emerged as a much more palatable revival leader due to his preference for reform of the state church, and his clearly stated opposition to separatism. This posture had typified Pietists in other Lutheran countries, who had established themselves as "churchly Pietists," in that they remained loyal to the state church despite their criticisms. Rosenius and his contemporaries conducted their evangelistic efforts out of a wing of the Church of Sweden called *Evangeliska Fosterlands-Stiftelsen* (the Evangelical Homeland Foundation, EFS), which had been established in 1856, largely inspired by Rosenius. In such organizations they thus attempted to contain the revival within the boundaries of the state church. There were also plenty of separatists who were also inspired by Rosenian Pietism, but when they broke away from the state church, they came to abandon the Pietist identity in favor of other international denominational brands, such as the Salvation Army, and the Baptist and Methodist churches.[69]

There were also attempts to prevent this disintegration of Christian unity, notably evident in the work of Waldenström. After Rosenius's premature death in 1868, Waldenström, who had been cultivated as his successor, assumed responsibility for the publication of *Pietisten*, managing it until his death in 1917. Waldenström's popularity as an evangelist produced a separatist movement of sorts when his activity inspired the creation of the Swedish Mission Covenant (SMF) in 1878, mentioned already. This was seen by many of the Rosenian Pietists as a betrayal of the spirit of Rosenius, who had preferred the traditional model of internal reform.[70] Even friends had urged Waldenström to back away from such a drastic departure from the loyal posture of the EFS, among them Amy Moberg, the indispensible secretary for *Pietisten*, who was devoted to Rosenius and well versed in theology in her own right.[71] Perhaps in part to defend his Rosenian credentials, Waldenström maintained a sense of loyalty to the Church of Sweden despite making severe criticisms of that church. The result was an ambiguous relationship between the SMF and the Church of Sweden. While the SMF functioned as an independent church organization, most members also retained their membership in the Church of Sweden. Thus, Waldenström clung to classical Pietism and perennially denied that the SMF was anything more than a "mission society," even though it did indeed assume the shape of an independent denomination.[72] The SMF and its sibling church in North America, the Evangelical Covenant Church (established as *Svenska Missionsförbundet i Amerika* in 1885), demonstrated complicated identities. They were each denominations in their own right, but also crystallizations of a specific Lutheran Pietist mindset, which had preferred a culture of decentralization and ecumenical cooperation. Ecumenism has historically been valued by these churches, demonstrated in the formative period of the SMF, and in the ways in which its members sought to influence the religious and political life of Sweden in general. (This spirit of ecumenism has also continued to be relevant, as the Mission Covenant, Baptist and Methodist churches in Sweden successfully merged and established one denomination in 2012, called *Equmeniakyrkan*, with the very name of the new institution invoking their common ecumenical roots.[73])

The history of Pietism is closely related to the Enlightenment as it emerged in Sweden. Pietism had made its first notable entry in Sweden in the 1730s, when Zinzendorf and the Moravian Brethren directed missionary efforts there. The return to Sweden of prisoners of war taken captive during Karl XII's Russian campaigns also laid the basis for local Moravian movements, as these prisoners of war had encountered Pietist texts during their captivity.[74] From these first appearances of Moravianism in Sweden, the hallmarks of the movement have been a personalized devotional life and the elevation of lay people as religious leaders. The site of religious life shifted from the parish church to the home, from the priest to basically anyone, educated or not, men or women, young or old.[75] Decisions regarding the interpretation of scripture were now being made by anyone who could read a Bible, and perhaps sometimes by people who could not. These drastic changes appeared to the established Church of Sweden as open threats, which resulted in efforts to outlaw the meetings of Pietists and other dissenting groups, called "conventicles," in a series of edicts, most famously in 1726. This strict suppression of Pietism lasted through the mid-1800s, when such measures became more impossible to maintain. It was formally overturned in 1858.

Amy Moberg. Photo from B. Wadström's *Ur Minnet och Dagboken; Anteckningar från åren 1848-1898.* 65.

Both the Enlightenment and Pietism represented an affirmation of democratic values, although to differing ends. While the Enlightenment often focused its attention on dismantling church and state for the purposes of decreasing the role of religion in society, Pietism criticized the church with the purpose of increasing the role of religion. Both movements asserted the independence of individual opinion, a decentralization of power, and increased democratic governance. It is no surprise that these two movements informed one another and even can claim some of the same people in their respective spheres of influence, people as diverse as Henric Schartau, Carl von Linné, or Emmanuel Swedenborg.[76] Both spheres can also be credited with some of the same major political breakthroughs in the 1850s and 1860s, when Sweden's government was finally changed from the four-estates model and the anti-conventicle laws were relaxed. As religious movements were allowed to blossom, another question came into play. Whereas Pietists and Enlightenment thinkers had previously shared a mutual dislike of absolutism and a preference for pluralism, once steps toward pluralism were achieved, the question became how to manage the consequences of this new environment. As religiosity was privatized it also morphed into political movements as actors in the revival became politically interested and engaged with causes, such as the temperance movement. It is in this period, from the late 1860s to the first decades of the twentieth century, that the ideals of Pietism and the Enlightenment diverged markedly. Secular humanism came into heated confrontation with three flanks of Christianity, the "high church" faction of the state church (articulating formal visions for institutional continuity, whether reformist or conservative), the "low church" faction within the state church (advocating a reform agenda in the spirit of leaders like Rosenius), and the organizations that operated independently of the state church, the so-called "free churches" (whose reform agenda was more in line with the ideas of Waldenström). Some of the foremost representatives of secular humanism were to be found in the emerging Social Democratic party, and this political group would find itself at odds with both the Pietists and the Liberal bourgeois establishment, sometimes conflating the two.

This renewed environment of pluralism in the wake of the Enlightenment has sometimes been termed the post-Constantinian era by historians.[77] This designation identifies the end of a marriage between church and state that dates back to the reign of the first Christian Roman emperor, Constantine (reigned 306–337), and which set a trend for church-state relations throughout Europe. The post-Constantinian era entailed a number of changes to the relationship of religion to politics and public life. Some characteristic assumptions of this era include the idea that churches should be privatized, that religion itself should be confined to the personal sphere, and an expectation that society was destined for secularity and that religion was headed for extinction. The history of religiosity in Europe could be roughly categorized as being divided into three periods: pagan, in which pagan religiosity, often pluralistic or syncretistic in nature, informed society; Constantinian, in which the Christian institutions were co-opted with the state; and post-Constantinian, in which public life became secular and religiosity took its place as one worldview among many in a pluralistic environment.[78]

"Post-Constantinian" is somewhat misleading, in that while suggesting a new form of Christianity, it actually in many ways was *a return* to the way that Christianity was organized in the first four centuries; in other words decentralized, pluralistic, and unconnected to the apparatus of government. Furthermore, Sweden differs from the general experience of Europe in two ways: 1) there was no pre-Constantinian period to speak of, since Christianity came to Sweden already packaged in a Constantinian form and the transition from pagan- to Catholic-endorsed governmental structures took place directly; 2) the Lutheran era represented an intense form of church-state relations, which eliminated the diversity of religious expressions present in the Catholic era and created a church under the crown, whereas the Catholic Church had been supranational and distinct from the Swedish apparatus of state. For instance, the Catholic Church, with its various orders, had actually represented more options for religious expression, particularly for women, than would come to be the case in the Lutheran era.[79]

What made the conflict so dramatic between religion and secular humanism in the nineteenth and early twentieth centuries was the fact that Sweden had been virtually isolated from religious competition for hundreds of years. The influx of "foreign" religions (in the 1800s, these were almost exclusively Protestant) and secular political ideologies presented Swedes with a religious and ideological marketplace that had not been imaginable to previous generations. For the Church of Sweden, this diversity presented a crisis, due to the fact that the apologetic muscles of the church had atrophied since its first phase of life. Christianity had first been born in a pluralistic environment, and its survival was dependent on the ability to explain itself (to "apologize") to practitioners of other religions and ideologies. After being established as a Swedish branch of the Catholic Church and later reformed into a Lutheran state church, the Church of Sweden had developed expectations of monopoly, and had developed a climate of strict orthodoxy that made communication with dissenters and outside groups difficult or impossible.

In order to succeed in the new religious market that developed in the nineteenth century, all religious leaders needed to reinvent themselves. For those clergymen and preachers who remained in parliament after the reforms of the 1860s, these leaders needed to be able to create new understandings of how they represented both the church and the state simultaneously. Religious motivation would continue to be important in informing Swedish politics, even if it was not to be done by a clearly delineated Estate of the Clergy. Waldenström's career in parliament demonstrated one of these new pathways that a religious leader could take in attempting to inform contemporary politics. His politics represented deeply held religious and moral convictions, but he did not officially strive to represent any specific church institution, but rather Christianity generally speaking. Sweden would continue to be a "Christian nation" on the books, but the reality was that one could no longer appeal to this identity in the same way that one could before. The public sphere in Sweden had become a *de facto* secular space, and the proponents of the various free churches risked having their voices silenced unless they discovered a way to reformat their convictions to fit these new expectations. Religious views had to be presented in the context of general discussions of the public good and as one option among many. Language had to be modified in order to participate in this common discussion. Waldenström's success as a leader of a popular movement can be attributed to the degree to which he was able to define a new mode of religious and political engagement that was better suited to this post-Constantinian period than that of the dominant religious establishment.

Carl Olof Rosenius. Engraving by G. Forssell, from photograph. Print.

By virtue of the fact that Waldenström had inherited Scott and Rosenius's journal with its title "The Pietist," he also had to continually grapple with the identity that these men had forged.[80] This heritage was by no means a superficial label, and profoundly impacted his worldview concerning religion and politics. Waldenström was a product of the churchly Pietism of his mentor, Rosenius, but he also cultivated and perpetuated this identity in new ways. Perhaps most evident in his theology is the tacit application of the motto used by the Moravian Pietists and Count von Zinzendorf, *"In essentials, unity. In non-essentials, liberty. In all things, charity."* What this slogan had meant for Zinzendorf and others who had employed it, was an assertion of the importance of truth regarding a core set of agreed upon values, and a relaxation on peripheral matters, and a preference for dialogue when various people come into conflict with one another over the interpretation of truth. It was a slogan indicating a galvanized, missional direction for group activity, while also understanding the validity of opposing views and the necessity of tolerance whenever disagreement occurs. It was an attempt to safeguard against the negative effects of absolutism and to encourage moderation in public debates.[81] Certainly, however, there always remained the potential for heated arguments over what constitutes essential and non-essential issues. Rosenius and Scott had asserted that even within the bounds of the Church of Sweden, an ecumenical spirit could blossom.

> *We love to understand pietism as something, which belongs to the whole world, and not just part of it, as something common and accessible for all confessions, which hold themselves to Christ the head. And this opinion makes our own confession all the more dear to us. For we should certainly fear and tremble, if devotion for this same confession involved some necessity to be prejudiced against all other confessions, or even to suspect their capability to serve as a means to draw their adherents into the one sheep fold.*[82]

This emphasis on ecumenism and unity was passed on to Waldenström, but would be overshadowed by the controversy sparked by his bold and liberal-minded interpretation of scripture, which caused him to become a lightning rod for disapproval by the clergy in the Church of Sweden. The doctrinal controversies that he thrust himself into in the 1870s became a critical opportunity for him to experience first-hand the dizzying and chaotic arena that surrounds the pursuit of truth. That he survived with his career intact is nothing short of remarkable. Though wary of relativism his entire life, he had his own moderate approach to truth-seeking that came to affect his biblical interpretation, the administration of his church denomination, and the political causes that he adopted.

This experience with intolerance and polemical arguments no doubt gave new meaning for Waldenström to the second part of the Moravian motto: "... *In non-essentials, liberty* ... " The school of Pietism that had gathered around Rosenius had perpetuated many of the priorities of Zinzendorf and the Moravians. Rosenius deferred to Lutheran doctrine, but within these boundaries, he found unconventional ways of explaining these concepts. In contrast with the academic sermons of his contemporaries, Rosenius's sermons prioritized subjective explanations of faith. For instance, if the concept of the day was God as "Creator," Rosenius would explain what this meant in the life of the believer; that he or she could participate in a relationship with a God who was intensely present and intimately concerned in all the details of the individual's life. If the concept was the fellowship of believers, then Rosenius would focus on giving examples of what it was like to participate in this community, highlighting all of the struggles inherent to successfully building relationships of mutual dependence, nurture and spiritual upbuilding. Understanding God and faith was a two-fold process; immersion in the reading of scripture, "The Word" (*Ordet*), and then testing these concepts out through daily life, experience (*erfarenheten*).[83] Rosenius did not expect his readers to accept doctrine blindly, but rather exuded confidence that believers would be able to taste and see for themselves that doctrine put into practice confirmed itself, and furthermore did so in a diversity of ways. Careful explanation of doctrine remained important, but as the main emphasis of Rosenius's preaching was to bring about tangible changes in the individual and the community, experience was almost equally important. Rosenius's reform strategy was to behave as a good Lutheran, and as such he intentionally distanced himself from the kind of bolder style of questioning official church doctrine that Waldenström would engage in (namely, questioning the Augsburg Confession). While Rosenius's attitude of deference to Lutheranism was embraced by many within the Church of Sweden's Evangelical Homeland Foundation (EFS), this same community came to see Waldenström as having betrayed the spirit of Rosenius, that he was not Rosenius's rightful successor, and should not be editor of *Pietisten*.[84] In what can certainly be read as a statement of loyalty to the late Rosenius and protest of Waldenström, both the EFS and the Swedish Augustana Lutheran Synod in North America published commemorative bound sets of *Pietisten*, including only the years in which Rosenius served as editor.[85] Many others identified with Waldenström's exuberant and often elegant defense of his views, and especially identified with his democratic understanding of scriptural interpretation and congregational life.

Waldenström had done more than start a doctrinal argument. He had contributed to profoundly weakening the authority of the clergy to be the sole source of interpretations of faith. The consequence of this was that now anyone with a talent for public speaking and an attractive message could try their hand at leading the faithful or starting new religious movements. Thus, the polemical spirit at times could be strong, and Waldenström's attempts to calm the situation he had instigated resembled a kind of dilemma not altogether unlike the one faced by Martin Luther during the Peasant Wars of 1524. Waldenström's push for reform was resulting in a splintering of the revival movement, particularly when many of his followers, now dubbed "Waldenströmians," had begun discussing the formation of a new organization, the Swedish Mission Covenant (SMF) during the so-called "preacher meetings" of 1876–1878. Concerned that this would result in a break with the EFS (and thus the Church of Sweden), Waldenström attempted to mitigate this by initially remaining on the sidelines of the discussion to form an independent denomination. When it became clear that such a church was to be formed, he then was outspoken in urging that this new organization not be a "denomination" (*samfund*) but a mission "society" (*förening, förbund*). This strategy attempted to reclaim the Rosenian spirit of ecumenism as much as possible. As a result of his ambivalence, when the SMF was formed in 1878, Waldenström was not its first president, a position that would be held instead by Erik Jakob Ekman. Furthermore, Waldenström attempted to straddle the divide by personally retaining his ordination in the Church of Sweden until 1882, and it was not until 1904 that he would formally assume leadership of the SMF. Nevertheless, he continued to be one of the central inspirations to the growth and direction of the SMF, and his hope of keeping the SMF as a mission society rather than a denomination has become a guiding philosophy of that organization well into the twenty-first century. Overall, one assertion that should be made regarding Waldenström's Rosenian heritage is that there is more continuity than difference between the two in terms of the spirit and concepts of their messages. The main difference is in terms of practice, that Rosenius represented the working model of the last generation of Pietists within the Constantinian age, while Waldenström represented the first generation of the Post-Constantinian age.

CHAPTER 4

Print Media and the Mobilization of Reform

DURING HIS VARIOUS PREACHING tours in North America, Waldenström also gave topical lectures on history and current events. In a speech on Swedish history given in the United States in 1910, Waldenström gave a long presentation of statistics and characteristics of contemporary Sweden for his Swedish-American audience. Among the claims that he made was the bold assertion that in no other Lutheran country had there been such popular involvement in church life as in Sweden.[86] While this may have been overstating the case, Waldenström was quite accurate in pointing out the ways in which religious life in Sweden had been radically decentralized and democratized. At the beginning of the new century, the "free churches" in Sweden were growing in number and influence. These congregations were not only centers for religious devotional life, but also testing grounds for democratic forms of church governance, as well as sites for societal engagement at the local, national, and global levels. Missionaries were sent out to foreign countries, particularly China, Alaska and the Congo region of Africa, and free-church members made their entry into politics. Neither the persuasion of the state church nor the law of the land forced this participation. Democratic engagement and discussion were central in this new era, and authority and leadership in the revival came from popular preachers and grassroots reformers whose success in leading was measured by the degree to which the population resonated with their message. Instead of the previous generations of religious leaders who influenced religious life in Sweden by virtue of their state-mandated authority, the newer generations of leaders were dependent on popular support. If a revival preacher demonstrated himself to be a poor public speaker or alienated people with too many unappealing opinions, he was simply not invited back to speak. Members of the revival voted with their participation. In the midst of this volatility, a critical mass of successful leaders managed to inspire and mobilize thousands of individuals to engage in ambitious voluntary community activities. The religious awakening featured individual initiative and engagement as one of its hallmarks, but was far from individualistic when it came to congregational life. This chapter will explain one important aspect of this mobilization, which is how print media was utilized to reform the laws related to religion.

The religious awakening was called *"folkväckelsen"* (the "national" or "popular awakening") and is one of the three main social movements (*"folkrörelser"*) of the 1800s. What was new about these movements was the frequency with which great segments of the population, particularly the lower classes, were engaged in regular discussion and organized activities to address social problems. The term *folkrörelse*, used to describe a wide variety of movements of the nineteenth century, can be analyzed on two levels. "*Folk*" reflects the size of the groups involved, as these were wide sections of the population. "*Folk*" is also descriptive of the fact that these actors were common, everyday people, which was part of the novelty. It was not simply the elite and well educated directing these movements. When great numbers of people had been mobilized before in history, it would likely have been seen as a mob exploding with pent up frustration. In such cases, the capacity for rational, concerted action was questioned, or deemed impossible due to lack of resources. It was the noble obligation of the privileged to think for the rest of society. Large-scale movements, such as the expansion of empires, wars, and crusades, were mostly directed by brilliant princes. In both of these cases, the potential for rational, directed action was credited to the few. The identification of "folk movements" on the other hand, places the agency for the movements with a large, indefinite, anonymous group of actors. "Movements" are typically seen as being steered by a great number of participants, presumably working in unison to accomplish a common goal. In the discussion of popular movements such as this, the focus of study is to understand how such great endeavors can be coordinated. The importance of "great men" and "great women" is sometimes diminished in favor of emphasizing the importance of decentralized participation. At the extreme, even inanimate objects and phenomena can be given credit, as can be seen with the near reification of print media and other forms of communication that appears in some scholarship on social movements, or the materialism associated with Marxism. Nevertheless, to understand popular social movements as such, it is still necessary to identify key actors such as

Waldenström, who coordinated these movements and gave them theoretical and theological expression.

Covers of *Pietisten*

In order to be a religious leader in this era, a person needed to be able to express himself or herself through the vehicle of print media. By the late 1800s, there was a wealth of both national and local religious newspapers, as well as secular newspapers with religious content. Sometimes the mixture of content in these papers makes it difficult to classify them as wholly religious or secular. Many of these papers were privately owned, giving them the flexibility to propagate the editors' opinions. *Pietisten* was privately owned, first by George Scott, then Rosenius, then Waldenström.[87] *Pietisten* began as a monthly journal, with the content primarily being essays on diverse scriptural topics. Harry Lenhammer has summarized the six main categories of the content as follows: 1) a leading article of a spiritually-upbuilding character, 2) a short biographical profile of a historical person who has modeled faithfulness, 3) news and letters, 4) miscellaneous anecdotes and ads for newly published books, 5) relevant commentary on societal developments that concern the faithful, and 6) reading for children.[88] Time-sensitive news was not the main focus, and as such, a majority of the essays and sermons lent themselves well to being republished in a variety of formats. One could also buy budget editions of the essay material (whether recent or from years past), organized in installments by month. If desired, one could collect twelve such installments and then take them to a bookshop to be bound together in volumes by year. Comprehensive pre-bound collections of the essay material were also published. These were usually grouped by the editor, such that all of the Rosenius years are together in one set, with the Waldenström years in separate sets. The abundance of volumes of *Pietisten* that one encounters in antique bookshops today are typically these collectors' editions, rather than the original printings. In 1908, after forty years as a private journal under Waldenström's editorship, it was decided that the Swedish Mission Covenant (SMF) would assume ownership of *Pietisten*. After this merger, the journal came out twice a month, and assumed more the character of an institutional organ, rather than primarily a devotional publication. In this phase, the journal retained its character as a source for upbuilding spiritual essays, but also gave increased room to news related to the various institutions and activities of the SMF, as well as photography and illustrations.[89]

In addition to *Pietisten*, Waldenström regularly communicated with several other newspapers, writing articles, sending letters to the editors and travel letters from his preaching tours. These papers included *Svenska Morgonbladet*, *Jönköpings Posten*, *Svenska Missionsförbundet*, *Ansgariposten*, *Gäfleposten*, *Norrlandsposten*, and *Stockholms Dagblad*. In North America, Waldenström frequently sent letters to *Missions-Wännen* and *Chicagobladet* in Chicago, *Minneapolis Veckobladet*, and *Canada Posten*. The sheer amount of these articles and letters gave Waldenström a constant media presence from 1868 until his death, as there was hardly a month that passed during these forty-nine years where readers could not find some word from "P.W." Often the same letters were addressed to more than one newspaper. To get a sense of how extensive this coverage of the Swedish print media outlets was, it is noteworthy that *Pietisten* alone boasted a circulation conservatively estimated to be 10,000 in the 1860s (generous estimates assert 18,000).[90] Thus together with the other papers mentioned, this was a large piece of the overall national newspaper circulation. Even in the 1920s, after the awakening had begun to decline, the combined circulation of "free-church" publications amounted to an estimated 140,000 copies, which was not all that far behind the labor movement at a combined circulation of 180,000.[91] It seems entirely reasonable to conclude that these subscriber numbers can be interpreted as being proportional to the relative size of these movements. Much has been made of the role of print media in the breakthrough of democracy, liberalism, and general conventions in public opinion building in the early nineteenth century. Prominent among the papers mentioned is *Aftonbladet*, for instance. However, in 1870, none of the daily papers (including

Aftonbladet, Dagens Nyheter, Stockholms-Tidning) had circulations larger than 10,000 households.[92] Thus *Pietisten* seems to have managed to reach a comparable number of readers as these secular papers and even eclipsed some of them!

Waldenström reading the newspaper *Svenska Morgonbladet* in the park at the seminary in Lidingö. Used by permission of Svenska Missionskyrkans Arkiv, Stockholm.

So what did the editors of *Pietisten* wish to accomplish with this influence? Despite the fact that newspapers in this period could be quite polemical, outspokenness had historically gotten the Pietists in trouble. George Scott had set a precedent with the beginning of the journal in 1842 that the content would be decidedly non-polemical, and this was continued by Rosenius.[93] Readers might inherently take issue with the general premises of the journal, but it would not be because they encountered an angry or belligerent narrator. As evident in the statement the editors made about Christian unity included previously, their goal was to boldly assert an alternate view of Christianity, but to do so while creating an inclusive atmosphere of "the more-the-merrier." Readers could take or leave what they had to say, but they were cheerfully encouraged to join the community. Joy was the overwhelming emotion that the reader encountered in *Pietisten*. In his explanation of scripture, Rosenius appears to be like some wise uncle with a great secret that he cannot wait to share. In discussing the difficult sides of life and faith, such as trials of doubt or judgment, these concepts seldom loom as impending threats, but instead as avoidable pitfalls; the reader only has to try out this advice and experience it to validate its trustworthiness. This choice of narrative voice is not a superficial question. By setting a welcoming and inclusive tone, the editors rejected previous waves of revivalism that had stressed judgment or had lobbied for separatism, and thereby communicated exclusivity. The joyful tone of *Pietisten* communicated a sense that a reader was more than simply a passive consumer of opinions. The reader was entrusted to be a participant in a discussion. Joy is an effective motivator, more so than guilt. A reader who experiences sincere joy in reading will likely keep reading, and furthermore want to be a part of whatever activities the editors are proposing. The editors spoke as though they were tutors, who established their equality with the reader, and offered to guide the reader in a conversation about faith. The ultimate goal was that these readers would mature into agents of revival and be able to offer these services to others.

Returning to the six different kinds of material in *Pietisten* as outlined by Lenhammer, one could go further and develop a theory about what these indicate about the strategy that the editors had as they sought to mobilize their readers. In trying to understand how mobilization worked, perhaps the most important question is to ask "what is the reader doing?" in each category. The most straightforward of them is category 1, the leading article. These were usually expositions on books of scripture, treated systematically as a series. Take for example Rosenius's lengthy series of commentary on the book of Romans, or Waldenström's series on Isaiah 53 or the Psalms (both of which were later published as stand-alone books). Here it is essential to note that although these series are systematic commentaries, they are not written for an academic audience. They are written in as plain speech as possible and with the intent to clarify difficult concepts and make them accessible to the lay reader. As the author models biblical interpretation for the reader, the reader in turn *is referred* to the scripture text itself, and *follows* the conclusions that are being made. After routinely reading these commentaries, the reader *gains experience* mimicking this process, and eventually *extrapolates* this process to interpret scripture in general, without the editors' assistance. One should point out that this is a departure from the academic traditions within Lutheranism, primarily in that Scott/Rosenius/Waldenström not only explained, but they encouraged the reader the freedom to extrapolate. In category 2 (the historical bios) there is a similar process of extrapolation at work. Here, the reader *sees* how historical figures were influenced by their own encounters with the scripture texts, which brought about tangible changes in their lives. In the ideal scenario, the reader *witnesses* this testimony of the historical person, *identifies* with the person, *expects* similar results in his or her own life, and *acts* in a similar way (*emulates*). In categories 3 and 5 (news and letters, and commentary on society), the editors now juxtapose contemporary events with the historical people and scripture analysis already discussed. Because of this juxtaposition, the reader can easily *make connections* between ancient scripture, historical people of faith, and their own present-day situation. The reader *conflates* past and present as being part of the same story, and *views* contemporary news as an opportunity for their own action. In category 4 (ads for books) the reader *sees* opportunities for further reading and personal development, but is also encouraged *to spread* this information to friends as an important way to participate in growing the revival. The Pietist movement was, after all, started and fueled by the activity of itinerant booksellers (colporteurs), and here is an opportunity for any reader to *become* a colporteur. In category 6 (reading for children) an inter-generational connection is made, once again underscored by juxtaposition with the previous material. The reader *realizes* that just as he or she has had a certain reading experience as an adult, so too can the reader *assume* the role of teacher and *pass on* these insights to his or her children. This is not completely new to Lutheranism, as since the Reformation there had traditionally been an emphasis that the father serve as a spiritual teacher to the rest of the family. What is new is that the parents (now more often including mothers) have new reading strategies to pass on. The parents read differently because the reading goals have changed. The primary goal now is not simply to understand Lutheran doctrine correctly, but rather to become an agent of societal transformation. I have italicized all the verbs in this paragraph to point out that *Pietisten* was designed by the editors to be a sort of exercise regimen to cultivate active readers. The reader is empowered to be a voluntary, free agent in a movement, not taking orders from above, but extrapolating this reading experience into their own ambiguous and complicated reality.

Waldenström broke the spell of congeniality to some degree in 1872 when his sermon on the atonement directly attacked church doctrine. However, this was an exception. In general, he continued the precedent set by Scott and Rosenius that *Pietisten* would not be a place for polemics. When one compares the content of *Pietisten* before and after 1872 (as well as before and after 1908), it is clear that even if the format changed, the journal retained its general philosophy of being a place for upbuilding devotional material, not heady theology or partisan politics. But as Waldenström himself was engaged in national politics and the politics of reforming the Church of Sweden, it is natural that he would articulate himself directly on these issues, as well. The solution to this conflict of interests was that he chose to segregate his writings into several avenues. *Pietisten* would remain on a pedestal, and strive to remain a model of ecumenical conversation. Just like in his sermons, political views have no place here, and they seldom show up. Perhaps as a way of keeping politics separate from devotional material and theology, Waldenström seems to have compartmentalized his writings in what can be seen as at least three groupings or streams: 1) devotional material, which was upbuilding in spirit and non-polemical; 2) doctrinally oriented writings, which took sharper stances on points of theology, such as his atonement theory or his defense of Lutheran baptismal practices; and 3) political speeches (live and reprinted), which were clearly identified as "speeches" (*fosterländska tal, föreläsningar, föredrag*) not "sermons," and journalistic writings in other newspapers and his travel literature on North America, China, and the Near East. It is in the second and third streams that Waldenström's personal political opinions are most clearly articulated, and he can even be surprisingly candid and unrestrained. By creating such a threefold hierarchy, this suggests that *Pietisten* and his many devotional books represented the prioritized content regarding faith and congregational life, and that the second and third streams were less essential. Whether readers always understood this differentiation or not is debatable. But it seems likely that this differentiation was intentional. Here is also a reflection of the Moravian understanding of "essentials versus non-essentials"; Waldenström's upper category concerned the essentials of Christian unity, whereas his lower categories were an outlet for discussion of non-essentials. Christian movements are sometimes subject to the accusation that their worldview is otherworldly and apolitical. In this case, the reasons for it can be seen not as a desire to withdraw from the world, but to attempt to differentiate between when and how it is appropriate to discuss politics, especially when it becomes as divisive as it was in the 1880s–1910s. Sermons are no place for politics, because sermons are an occasion for proclaiming "essentials." Politics for a Rosenian Pietist is about application and extrapolation of those essentials into the fractured, complicated reality of the world. Opinions about politics were treated as "non-essentials," not because they didn't matter, but because if all of these myriad subjective convictions were allowed to be treated as essentials, they would wreck the whole enterprise and thwart any hope of transforming society.

Now that the different streams of print media have been established, it is worth a look at the type of "non-essential" information that Waldenström chose to discuss. If *Pietisten's* readers had matured into active agents of reform, what practical changes could one expect from them in society? Evangelization and Christian ministry were organized into two compartments, "inner" or "home" mission (Sweden, and sometimes even Swedish-America, were in this category), and then "outer" or foreign mission activity (everywhere else). Since Waldenström was most affiliated with the Mission Covenant (SMF), it is natural that his sympathies would be strongest with its activities. However, even after *Pietisten* became an official organ of the SMF, it remained rather ecumenical in its content, including information on happenings in a variety of independent mission organizations, as well as those of the Church of Sweden. Waldenström's articles in all the papers included reports on meetings of all mainstream Christian organizations in Sweden, as well as whatever caught his attention in places like North America and Germany. These organizations needed two things, participants and financing. Waldenström demonstrated himself to be a skillful fundraiser, and dedicated regular space in *Pietisten* and other articles to celebrating congregations that were able to pay off their debt for such expenditures as building projects.[94] He is also credited with being responsible for doubling the income of the Swedish Mission Covenant after assuming leadership in 1904, and was the driving force in raising the funds to pay for its seminary on Lidingö.[95] His speaking tours in North America often collected an offering or entrance fee, something which financially benefited the activities of the church (Waldenström was quick to point out that he did not receive this money, even though his critics would suggest that he did). His travel letters would frequently identify potential building and mission projects, such as to support the seminary and missions in China, and Waldenström even saw himself as a defender of North Park College in Chicago when it faced criticism from Swedes in America.[96] Proposals for fundraising and collective action fill the pages of Waldenström's travel books. In the narrative of his journeys through the United States, Canada, and China, Waldenström compares the institutions that he observes to those at home in Sweden. What emerges in these accounts is a type of report on "best practices," in which Waldenström encourages his readers to reflect on the successful practices of these hospitals, schools, orphanages, pension plans and homes for retirees, temperance organizations, tuberculosis treatment facilities, emigration politics, and political philosophies, and to think of ways that these institutions can be supported, reformed, or imitated in other places. As the free churches were independent organizations, unlike the state church, everything had to be done from scratch with volunteer labor or donated money.

Individualism has been one aspect of the religious revivals that has been seen as a negative trend, often connected to individualism of biblical interpretation, personal salvation, and faith. This individualism has been protested from two sides. From the perspective of the Church of Sweden, the church's self image was distilled through the seventeenth and eighteenth century notions of *enhetskyrkan*. The church reinforced Swedish society with a sense of social unity and solidarity. The individualism of the free-church movement came as a logical threat to that unity. From the perspective of Socialists, the individualism of revival Christianity was perceived as a threat in that it could undermine progress toward addressing class injustices. However, what has less often been pointed out is that this very individualism often introduced the ability for a person to engage in corporate activity on a voluntary basis, reflective of the emphasis on volunteerism so typical of the Anglo-American religious experience.[97] In the past, hierarchical forms of religion had reinforced traditional social networks, and hierarchical governments commanded the obedient service of their subjects. Contributing to the common good was not an option but a duty, and furthermore the decision of what constituted the common good was dictated to the public, who largely had no say in the matter. The democratization of religious life meant that people were free to make their own allegiances and to choose their own causes based on the perceived benefits of membership. These benefits were not only for the individual, but also for the community. In the democratic culture of the revival, people could choose their allegiance from a spectrum of alternatives, as well as change affiliations if they lost incentives for membership. These were highly social enterprises with implications for both the individual and the community.

Cover for "Through North America's United States," (1890) one of the outlets for Waldenström's surprisingly candid discussion of politics and church life in Scandinavia and North America. Contrasted with the focused devotional content of *Pietisten*.

DET GEMENSAMMA SEMINARIET I KINGCHOW INVIGDT I DECEMBER 1909

The Common Seminary in China, one of many ambitious fundraising opportunities for Mission Covenanters in Sweden and North America. Photo from *Missionsförbundets Minneskrift, 1885–1910.* 150

An inherent consequence of the democratization of religion was that the privileged role of the Church of Sweden would be called into question. The separation of the state church from the state had long been a goal of both secular and religious groups, but even after the reforms of the 1860s, this progressed slowly. Various dissenting religious movements, who wanted to leave in order to start new church institutions more in line with their consciences, expressed this as *freedom of religion*. The secular argument became a matter of *freedom from religion*, as an increasing atheist minority preferred other worldviews. Where once attendance in church was mandatory, the relaxation of this practice in the 1800s had created the effect that a large segment of the population no longer identified with the rituals of the church.[98] It therefore became all the more a conflict of conscience for those people who found themselves forced to be married and buried with rituals that belonged to this estranged worldview. The struggles for "freedom of religion" and "freedom from religion" saw their first real significant period of confrontation in the 1880s, although precedents had existed long prior. Addressing this conflict of conscience and dismantling the state church monopoly is one of the more common topics of Waldenström's editorial commentary.

Waldenström emerged as an early voice for the separation of the church from the state, beginning in 1868. When the *Riksdag* was reorganized from its medieval four-estates structure into a bicameral legislature in 1866, this had resulted in the creation of the Church Assembly, to compensate the clergy for the loss of its previous representation. It was in this forum that matters related to the state church could be discussed apart from the normal business of the *Riksdag*, with certain veto privileges over the *Riksdag* in matters of religion. The delegates to the meetings included not only representatives of the clergy, but laymen from each diocese. Although Waldenström was ordained in the Church of Sweden, he was elected as a "layman" representative to this first meeting in 1868, as well as in 1908, 1909, and 1910. The Church of Sweden increasingly found itself attacked on two fronts, by free-church members and by secular citizens, who each by and large called for the complete separation of the church from the Swedish state, including limiting the church's influence over legislation and the financial support it received through taxes. The vocabulary that Waldenström used in making his case presented this separation as being part of a necessary "Reformation" within the Church of Sweden in order to become a genuine church in the biblical meaning, rather than a state institution.[99] Torsten Bergsten, in his history of the ecumenical movement among the free churches, points out that as long as Waldenström was alive, there was division among the free churches as to how to address the separation of church and state. While objecting to the "folk church" model of Manfred Björkquist and the "young church movement" (which gained momentum after 1905), Waldenström proposed a similar alternative to Björkquist's attempt to preserve the public role of the Church of Sweden. The bands between the church and state should indeed be severed, Waldenström thought, but as the state church had profound historical and cultural ties to the people as a whole, he was also in favor of the idea that the Church of Sweden should retain some of its place as a national institution.[100]

Waldenström's surprising defense of a public role for religion can be interpreted as a fear that religion would be strictly confined to the private sphere and as such, all religious groups would face a new era of disenfranchisement, after having only recently emerged from a long history of oppression by the Church of Sweden.[101] This stance also demonstrated the persistence of the traditional "churchly" Pietists' relationship to the Church of Sweden, which retained a deference to Lutheranism and an aversion to separatism (identified earlier as the Rosenian strategy). As Waldenström articulated his views on this issue for his readers, he also encouraged these readers to join him in this concern that religion not be relegated to the private sphere and instead to act and vote in the political sphere in such a way that will counteract this trend. On this issue, his nuanced understanding of the role of religion in public life left him between the stools; he was neither fully at home in the Church of Sweden, nor fully accepted in his own church, the SMF. This has made it difficult to place Waldenström solidly in one camp. Three assumptions have traditionally been made regarding

Waldenström, which need to be suspended in order to understand his point of view. First is the assumption that because he did not firmly take a side on the issue that he was therefore not consequential. This has led to a general neglect of Waldenström's long career in the Church Assembly and *Riksdag* related to these issues. This is evident in the Church of Sweden's histories of the church-state debates, in particular, which has neglected renegades like Waldenström. The second is a general assertion that the free churches acted out of self-interest, while the secular movements were the true champions of pluralism. Ture Nerman's account of Branting's involvement in achieving religious freedom bears a strong flavor of this assumption.[102] A certain amount of self-interest and self-preservation can be expected to characterize all efforts in the interest of personal freedoms. It is natural that those who are negatively affected by governmental practices would most enthusiastically fight for their correction. Secular advocates of religious freedom were certainly also inspired by self-interest in their attempts to leave mandatory religious practice. The third assumption is that religion is purely a private matter, and should be cleansed from the public sphere, a viewpoint that has been advocated by secular and religious groups alike. However, the relegation of religious worldviews to the private sphere is an assertion that can no longer be assumed to be common sense, as recent identity politics has demonstrated. Of all the messages that have been communicated by the movements for gender and sexual equality, for instance, one of the most profound has been the assertion that "the private is public." There are aspects of this train of thought that are present in Waldenström's writings, and his complicated understanding of the role of religion in public is evidence of this.

Religious ideology was understood by Waldenström as one ideology among many. Exterminating religion from public life would come to have negative consequences for all religious communities, as well as Swedish society as a whole, in that it would hinder the development of a truly pluralistic public sphere. In the context of Swedish society at the turn of the century, the political spectrum was leaning toward a decidedly anti-religious tone. In both radical and moderate Socialist circles there was open discussion of eliminating all influence of religion from public life, evident in the statements by Viktor Lennstrand and Hjalmar Branting (treated later). Waldenström's concern that religion would be marginalized was not paranoia. It was actually a keen observation that the direction of public life in Sweden was not necessarily destined for pluralism, but could also very easily trade a Lutheran state church for a *de facto* atheistic civic religion inspired by Marxist socialism. If certain elements triumphed within the Socialist party who were most vocal in their campaign to cleanse the public sphere of all religious influence, this could easily become a reality. In this environment, the only way that religious interests would continue to be represented in public discourse would be if those interests maintained their seat at the table. Allowing the Church of Sweden to continue to exist, not as a state church, but as an independent, para-organization to the state, would be one way to safeguard against this trend. In this light, Waldenström's defense of the Church of Sweden's right to exist was not simply due to sentimentality, but actually can be seen as an example of calculated realism. In his view, it did not serve the interests of the free churches to try to undermine the Church of Sweden, beyond untying the basic bands of church and state.

Although in protest of many aspects of established Swedish Lutheranism, Waldenström nevertheless remained invested in the successful reform of the Church of Sweden long after he formally resigned his ordination in 1882. Some of the motions he introduced not only served to create freedoms for religious dissenters, but lobbied the Church of Sweden itself to become more democratic in its structure. In 1868, this included a motion to allow laymen to participate in the election of bishops (which was passed that year, and then reintroduced by Waldenström and passed again in 1908).[103] This motion was accompanied by several others seeking to expand the ability for laymen to conduct worship services and distribute communion without the presence of a priest. These were concerns that were deeply held by Pietists, so much so that the prohibition of these practices would be determinative for the establishment of the Swedish Mission Covenant in 1878. It was also at this meeting that Waldenström made the first of several motions for the introduction of civil marriage. His reasoning here (as later in 1885 as a representative in parliament) was first and foremost a defense of the Church of Sweden's ability to decline service of marriage due to conscientious dissent on the part of the priest. At the time, the Church of Sweden was legally bound to perform marriages as a service to the state at the discretion of the state, thus forcing even proclaimed atheists and members of other faiths to be married in a Lutheran ceremony, as well as second marriages for divorced couples, which was hotly contested.[104] This issue was symbolic for Waldenström of the overall danger of the state dictating the interpretation of scripture on these matters. Civil marriage was an option after 1880, but only for those who had formally left the Church of Sweden (most Mission Covenanters maintained dual membership). As members of parliament, both Waldenström and current Covenant president, E. J. Ekman, petitioned for allowing all people, even members of the Church of Sweden, the option of choosing civil or churchly marriage.[105]

In 1908, Waldenström brought forward a motion that the baptisms conducted by laymen in the free congregations be acknowledged by the Church of Sweden. In 1896 the Church of Sweden had acknowledged this with a notation in the church recordbook that read "baptized by a layman," but had since amended the notation to simply read "not baptized by the Church of Sweden."[106] While this may seem like a minor point, it is important to remember that the Church of Sweden's record was the official national record, referred back to whenever anyone applied for marriage or sought certain public offices for which baptism was required.[107] While this was on one hand an effort to force the Church of Sweden to acknowledge other churches' legitimacy, it also served to underscore the hypocrisy that the state would require and acknowledge one church's baptism, but not the others'. While freedom of religion, and even freedom from religion, were generally accepted principles in the *de facto* secular society of the time, the legislation on the books demonstrated the church-state philosophy of a much earlier age. It was not until 1951 that citizens were able to leave the Church of Sweden without entering another state-approved denomination. It was also not until 1951 that Waldenström's request for acknowledgement of baptisms outside the Church of Sweden was acknowledged in the church record books.[108]

In three consecutive Church Assemblies, 1908, 1909 and 1910, Waldenström brought forth motions to separate the Church of Sweden from the state. All three times the motions were defeated (it would not be until 2000 that the church would separate from the state, and even afterward there were still ties that remained, mostly financial). Although he was not surprised by these defeats, Waldenström re-articulated his motion each year, urging the Church of Sweden to realize the inevitable divorce that was coming between the church and state, and the fact that the church would be able to negotiate the most favorable terms if it took a proactive approach.[109] In addition to outlining the inconsistencies already mentioned above, Waldenström focused his attention on the problems of conscience that were posed by a union between spiritual and temporal authorities. Many priests, he pointed out, were troubled by the fact that they were forced by law to carry out marriages, baptisms, and confirmations that otherwise would have been objectionable to them.[110] Religious instruction at the secondary and post-secondary level was frequently marked by tendencies toward so-called "liberal theology," in which the divinity of Christ and other central points of doctrine were dismissed outright as fables.[111] At the time, the national school system was an arm of the Church of Sweden under the authority of the state. In the 1909 and 1910 Church Assemblies, Waldenström pushed for changes that would allow parents to remove their children from instruction that undermined faith or contradicted their understandings of faith. Such privileges were currently allowed for members of other recognized denominations, but not allowed for members of the Church of Sweden, who were technically not "dissenters" and therefore not covered under the dissenter laws.[112]

A crucial aspect in understanding Waldenström's view of religious freedom and pluralism is that it was flexible and based on practical considerations of the present needs of society. There can be no permanent solution to such questions, since as society changes, the expectations that society would place on the Church of Sweden would change as well. Waldenström's view was evolutionary in that it saw the Church of Sweden as needing to determine what the age required of it. What society expected from a church in ages past, is not a role that the church can perform in the present without becoming oppressive and engendering resentment. Waldenström also demonstrated a common belief of the time that religion was essential to the functioning of a moral society.[113] While the Church of Sweden could not be allowed to continue to function as a religious monopoly, he saw that it still had a role to play as long as the Swedish state was constitutionally defined as a Christian nation. If circumstances changed, and Sweden were to redefine itself as a secular nation, then the Church of Sweden would have to privatize more completely. But even in this hypothetical later condition, Waldenström still foresaw the Church of Sweden functioning in a consultant role to the Swedish state.[114] While the separation of church and state was a main concern of Waldenström, he only pushed for it directly in the Church Assembly, not in the *Riksdag*. He wanted the initiative for separation to come from the side of the church.[115]

Through the print media outlets that Waldenström chose and the way he utilized them, he was able to cultivate readers who were engaged in a movement for reform. These readers regularly heard his opinions on various reform proposals and were encouraged to make these reforms happen. Because of the egalitarian emphasis of his particular tradition of Pietism, there was a differentiation between "essentials" and "non-essentials" which Scott, Rosenius, and Waldenström strove to pass on to their readership. Waldenström demonstrated in the way he compartmentalized his various publications that he did not expect that his own political opinions would be binding for his readers, but rather informative. Furthermore, as he commented on the various missions enterprises of the free churches, encouraged fundraising efforts, and advocated political engagement to change the laws of the land, he was modeling for his readers that there was a connection between the spiritual transformation of an individual and the societal transformation that individuals could and should enact.

CHAPTER 5

Religion in Public: "Private Matter" or "Matter of Conscience"?

EVEN IN THE EARLY twenty-first century, "common sense" would recommend that when one is in mixed company such as at a dinner party, one should avoid bringing up topics like sex, politics, or religion. Doing so is asking for trouble, as there are sometimes assumptions that these things are nobody's business, or a "private matter," and can be avoided. However, in the late 1800s in Sweden, religion was everybody's business and unavoidable because everyone was a member of the state church, and though many people wished that they could leave, this was for many different reasons and inspired by conflicting ideologies. Though most participants in the debate about religion in Sweden could agree that society was changing, they had great difficulty agreeing on what this meant and how to re-order society to come in line with these changes. A number of conflicting viewpoints collided, which when taken together resulted in the unique trajectory that Sweden has taken in the past century, toward greater individual freedom of choice in the exercise of religion. Waldenström's opinions about the role of religion in public were not forged in isolation, but instead drew inspiration from public debates about these issues from a variety of perspectives. The opinions expressed by prominent figures in the political arena were alternately inspired by and shaped Waldenström's views in the matter, and his pronouncements and political actions related to religious pluralism were often reactions to these opinions. This chapter will explore the views of three people in particular who articulated opinions about the role of religion in public, including Viktor Lennstrand, Hjalmar Branting, and Kata Dahlström, as well as trace their interactions with Waldenström.

When the question of the role of religion in public was most heated, it was usually a result of challenges from the Socialist movement. The fact that Socialists frequently called for the removal of all religion from the public sphere caused many within the various church denominations to view this as an inherent result of the atheistic orientation of Marxism. This was confirmed when zealous members of the party did in fact propagandize with the intent to eradicate faith. Few carried out this mission with as much energy as Viktor Lennstrand, whose speeches and books aimed to convert Christians from their delusions. In 1888, Lennstrand founded the "The Utilitarian Society" (*Utilistiska samfundet*), which had the expressed goal of combating "false religious beliefs and superstitions" (*religiös vantro och vidskepelse*).[116] When many Christians, including Waldenström, made reference to the atheistic element of socialism, it was no doubt due in part to the work of Lennstrand.

The great irony of Lennstrand's story is that not only had he begun life in an enthusiastically evangelical home, but that one of his primary Christian mentors had been none other than P.P. Waldenström. Lennstrand was apparently a man of extremes. As a youth, he had been the most confident in his faith of his siblings, and had even requested that Waldenström, who was one of his teachers at *Gävle Högreläroverk*, would organize a Bible study for him and some of his peers. This met at Waldenström's house. (Waldenström's popularity and influence in Gävle was extensive at this time. Interestingly, Swedish-American labor leader Joel Hägglund, "Joe Hill," also appears to have attended Waldenström's church in Gävle during his childhood). After entering the University of Uppsala and initially becoming heavily involved in the Christian student organization at the university, Lennstrand eventually made an about-face, and instead took on a decidedly anti-church posture. The rest of his life was spent as a missionary in an effort to undermine Christian beliefs, denouncing them as fables and holding well-attended speeches in which he painted a picture of a future where religious superstition would no longer be allowed to hold back human progress. When he returned to Gävle in 1887 to hold a speech in the packed hall of the "Gävle Workers' Society" (*Gävle Arbetarförening*), his old spiritual mentor was there seated in the front row (Waldenström was active in this organization[117]). According to one account of the meeting, Waldenström, in an apparent attempt to suck the wind out of his sails, requested a word before the speech began, in which he spoke on the piety of Lennstrand's parents, as well as insinuated that Lennstrand as a student had not been all that bright. Perhaps anticipating that such an accusation would be made, Lennstrand had come prepared, and circulated a copy of his outstanding grades among the audience. There is no word on how Waldenström responded to this, but one can imagine that a comeback would have been difficult. Lennstrand gained a reputation as a debater with a razor-sharp wit, regularly leaving his opponents speechless, "fumbling and spinning about as though they were flies who had lost one wing," as related by the Norwegian writer Bjørnstierne Bjørnson.[118]

His zeal took its toll and he died from poor health at the age of thirty-four. In one of his last letters he summed up his cause against religion.

> *I am dying, content in the belief in a happy people of the future, who will live without ill will, prejudices and superstitions, and a society where goodwill and goodness prevail. To work for this people and this society is the highest religion, although it certainly will take centuries, even millennia, before the ideal is realized.*[119]

Lennstrand represented an extreme swing between two poles that existed in Swedish society at the time, revival Christianity and secular atheism. In the way that Lennstrand himself portrayed his conversion, this was a movement away from a worldview that was dominated by religious doctrines and ignorance, toward a worldview that was enlightened, liberated, and secular. It was progress, and it was an unavoidable outcome of the expansion of the scientific method and the spread of Enlightenment thinking. However, others would point out that the narrative as told by Lennstrand had its weakness, namely in that he demonstrated the very type of overconfidence and dogmatism that he accused his opponents of having. Lennstrand, in the eyes of his critics, had merely replaced a religious form of absolutism for a secular one. The debate had a range of nuanced viewpoints, and in that great middle ground, both Lennstrand's opponents and his friends were busy fighting over a definition of pluralism, in which there was room for a multiplicity of views. Although Lennstrand was closely connected to several people within the Social Democratic party, his absolutism quickly became a liability for not only the party, but also the project of pluralism in general.

Hjalmar Branting was one of these friends who realized this most acutely and took steps to distance the party from Lennstrand's rhetoric. In a sympathetic, but critical obituary in November 1895, Branting explained some of the problems with Lennstrand's worldview.

> *Utilitarianism as an anti-religious sect movement will follow Lennstrand into the grave. [. . .] Especially when fighting the dominant religious faith, we socialists prefer a less high-handed method; we expect the increasing prevalence of the enlightenment of natural science and above all, we do not share orthodox*

utilitarianism's absolute, ahistorical view on these matters. It is a late-born plebian daughter to the aristocratic rationalism of the past century. On the contrary, for our part we do not see this successive procession of religions as merely or primarily a heap of lies, but instead frame the question this way: which historical and social conditions have created these ever-changing divine fables, into which our forefathers deposited their assumptions about what they did not know? By posing questions this way the battle against religion loses its sting, or more accurately, it is directed not at the consequence: a certain religious superstition, but toward a cause: social injustice, from which human beings are forced to flee, at least in fantasy, to a better, more just world than the one that surrounds them. To the degree that this now abundantly flowing spring of religiosity is stopped, religion will become defeated in a much more radical way than with the often downright superficial utilitarian criticism of the Bible: it will die off as an organ, that no longer has a function, will fall to indifference, apathy, not through disputation and debate.[120]

While Branting agreed with the idea that religion was a superstition, he disagreed with the anti-religious strategy of Lennstrand. Science, he held, would eventually expose all superstitions on its own, provided that society could be ordered in such a way that allowed for pluralistic debate about the truth. Lennstrand's anti-religious approach was unacceptable for the very reason that it precluded such an open debate. Neither did Branting have all that much respect for the free-church religiosity of the Waldenströmian variety, and he took many opportunities to weaken the position of Waldenström by referring to him as a hypocrite. Despite Branting's attempt to also characterize Waldenström as an extremist, a clear difference existed between Waldenström and Lennstrand, in that the former was actively engaged in brokering a compromise on the issue of religion in public (in parliament and the Church Assembly), while the latter's primary mission was to evangelize against Christianity and thereby eliminate one whole side of the debate. Branting's relationship to Waldenström will receive extensive treatment in Part III, but what should be said here is that these two opponents were actually in agreement when it came to many aspects of pluralism. Both saw the extremism of Lennstrand as a danger to pluralism, and furthermore, Waldenström's association of Lennstrand's anti-religious agenda with the Social Democratic party put pressure on Branting to address this negative trend within the party. Branting's criticism of Waldenström should be read as evidence of a calculated power play, rather than simply a confirmation of Waldenström's extremism.

A Socialist agitator named Kata Dahlström adds yet another layer to the discussion of pluralism. Dahlström was one of the most articulate and conscientious members of the Socialist movement on the issue of religious liberty, actually urging a union between faith and socialism. In her writings and in her participation in the discussions of the Social Democratic party, she advanced the idea that although religion was a private matter, to be determined by an individual's conscience, socialism should not define itself exclusively as atheistic. A long-standing question in the party was how to define itself in relation to religion. The established church was traditionally described by Socialists as an enemy to the movement, in that it reinforced the position of the propertied classes. The weakening of the church was assumed to be a necessary part of the advance of the working class and their interests. However, Dahlström saw the animosity among some in the party toward religion to be both a breach of individual conscience and a policy that could later become a new form of ideological oppression if not checked. She therefore made a passionate case against anti-religious rhetoric.

> *Christian doctrine has nothing, absolutely nothing in common with the dogmatic faith that is presented as "Christianity" by both priests and the state—and which is forced on the defenseless children of the people.*
>
> *Therefore we must demand that our children are no longer poisoned by this false dogmatic Christianity, which is antagonistic to education. As lofty, beautiful and compassionate as the teachings of Jesus are, so too this false Christianity is low and wretched and antagonistic to humanity's teachings of brotherhood, and which have been presented to humanity ever since the state and the church (the Christian) were joined together in the time of Constantine the Great.*
>
> *The state has made the church into its assistant in the cause of hindering the development of humanity.*
>
> *They have made our struggle to reach light and clarity more difficult. Therefore we must combat this falsified Christianity, which has been forced on us against our will by state and clergy, which now is pressing the people to the ground like a nightmare.*
>
> *But the teachings of Christ, the gospel of compassion and brotherhood, let us in the name of every good divinity not fight this teaching!*[121]

Dahlström's pleas for toleration of religion were met by stark opposition by some within the party, who wished to see the secular political arena cleansed of all religious influence. A common terminology that was used at the time to this end was the phrase "religion is a private matter" (*religion är en privatsak*). Dahlström represented a contingent who feared that by making religion a private matter and excluding it from having a place in the party's discussion, this would actually result in a new form of ideological oppression. By making religion private, that meant forcing people to make it invisible, which was not pluralism at all.

Being a spiritual person herself, Dahlström had written a number of books on religious topics, one of her most famous being her numerous attempts to merge Christianity with socialism, perhaps most notable in her praise of Leo Tolstoy's accomplishments in this area.[122] What Dahlström urged the Social Democratic party to do was to affirm that the *choice* of religion should be a private matter, not that religion should be private. Her main goal in the various reforms that she proposed was that the state would cease misusing religion. Thus the role of the Social Democratic party in its campaign against the established church should not be to abolish religion, but simply to eliminate its official enforcement by the state.[123] Religious instruction in public schools should not be abolished, but simply reformed to be instruction *about* the religions of the world with emphasis on ethics, rather than instruction in the doctrine of Christianity exclusively.[124] Dahlström faced criticism for her soft approach on religion by others in the party who were more intent on eradicating religion from public view. One of Branting's biographers, Ture Nerman, noted that Dahlström's defense of religion was a half measure that served to extend the influence of the church into the late twentieth century and prevented the establishment of a truly secular public sphere. He approved of Hjalmar Branting's strategy, which was to indirectly undermine religion by ignoring it, but he also criticized Branting for not pursuing a more direct attack on the state church.[125] Nerman preferred August Palm and Axel Danielsson's more aggressive attempts to ban religiosity from the party's ideology.[126]

Branting had been raised by Pietist parents who were involved in the EFS. Within this religious context, however, he had made radical acquaintances including the sons of clergymen, Per and Karl Staaff and Efraim Rosenius.[127] When his continued participation in EFS activities began to sour during his adulthood, his radical inclination increased. By the mid-1880s Branting was involved in the creation of a "Society for Religious Freedom" (*Förening för religionsfrihet*). While assuming a decidedly radical position in terms of wanting to decrease the role of religion in society, this association made its primary goal the dissection of the church from the state. What is perhaps most interesting is that the organization called religion a "matter of conscience" (*samvetssak*) rather than a "private matter" (*privatsak*). This significant distinction demonstrates more the line of thinking of Dahlström, in that it does not identify religious expression as something to be abolished from the public sphere. Instead the focus was simply on ensuring that this affiliation or non-affiliation was the individual's choice. The language of the organization's constitution spelled out its strategy as follows:

> *In the observation that religion as a matter of conscience may only be decided by free conviction and that worldly powers consequently may not place hindrances in the way of spiritual freedom or intervene in the religious sphere, the Society shall seek, through the means of meetings, lectures, petitions and other expressions of opinion, as well as through influence in the elections of members of parliament, to repeal all of the laws, decrees and institutions that together make up the bands of the state church . . .*[128]

Even so, Branting himself sometimes also used the term "private matter" to refer to religion, but this was done in a way that intended the elimination of the state church's influence over the individual's religious orientation, not the elimination of religion in public. As the years progressed, and as Waldenström took up the issue of reforming the Church of Sweden's relationship to the state in the Church Assemblies of 1908–1910, Branting's criticism of this relationship increased.

> *All of this development away from religion by force is founded on the more or less apparent acknowledgement that* religion ought to be a private matter. *In keeping consistent with this, this principle cannot be united with the concept of the state church. But with such a far-reaching reform as the dissolution of the state church it is clearly of great importance to proceed with these questions in order, so that the civil state does not simply loosen the band, with which it holds the church. The state must stand ready in everything to meet the consequences of this new order and be well prepared against the power-grab, which will almost certainly be attempted by certain obscure denominations. The Waldenströmian, all too commonly repeated songs of praise for the Catholic Church, which never bowed to the power of the state, but mightily ruled over millions of souls, demonstrate clearly enough where the "Popes" of our Swedish free churches find their idols. They have already openly recommended the separation of the church from the state "in time," that is to say while the former can have the position to take with them from this divorce the resources of power, which an enlightened and vigilant people should never leave in such hands.*[129]

Branting was here alluding to Waldenström's speculations about the future of the Church of Sweden after it separated from the state. As part of this discussion, Waldenström had suggested that the Church of Sweden should take notes from the Catholic Church in envisioning its future, in that it needed to find new ways of being engaged in public life outside of the official channels of a direct relationship with the state—"The Catholic Church has been indomitable in regard to defending its freedom from the state. The Protestant churches, on the other hand, have a weak spine, like pliable saplings."[130] Branting here ignored the fact that Waldenström was also calling for separation of church and state, and instead focused only on his suspicion that this "free-church pope" would try to fill the void left when that separation occurred.

Branting and Dahlström positioned themselves as opponents to Waldenström, as is evident in the derogatory way they referred to him and the "Waldenströmians." Here it is important to remember that the climate within socialism at the time was such that any sympathy for religious worldviews was held suspect and needed to be qualified. It was therefore essential to Dahlström's and Branting's credibility for them to take their stabs at Waldenström whenever they could, regardless of whether they disagreed with him or not. Such posturing has historically been read at face value, and has served to obscure those instances when Socialists and Christians saw eye-to-eye on issues of pluralism. Nevertheless, they were often competing for the same audience at times, which necessitated exaggerating their differences. Dahlström was a popular speaker, and as she herself was a spiritual woman, she often directed her speeches at reaching those in the religious sphere with the Socialist message. In one such instance, she was in a town called Elmhult, which she identified as a "bastion of Waldenström."

> *In Elmhult there was a tremendous discussion. One of Waldenström's worst bastions is there. Despite the most inclement weather, the location was full of people, and they had traveled there from both Onsby and Hästveda. There were almost exclusively religious people there and the most remarkable utterances were made by these people—against false Christianity and dogmatic faith.*[131]

Dahlström's surprise at the ability of these presumed Waldenströmians to entertain ideas of pluralism borders on patronizing. She was either unaware of Waldenström's similar thoughts in the matter, or she was intentionally ignoring that fact. She, like Branting, found herself in a delicate balance between trying to mend the divide between Socialists and Christians and expand the party's constituency, while at the same time undermining a political opponent, Waldenström. Such a balance of power is bound to cause mixed messages and misunderstandings. Similarly, Branting's suspicion of Waldenström's motives in separating the church from the state should also be read in this light. In his actions in the Church Assembly, Waldenström had expressed hope that the Church of Sweden could thrive as an independent organization from the state, while still maintaining influence in society and cooperating with the state wherever that relationship was deemed fruitful. While Branting criticized this as an aspiration of Waldenström to become a "free-church pope," he thus refused to admit that Waldenström was asserting that the Church of Sweden, like any other of the free churches or ideological organizations, should have the right to be able to exist and participate in a pluralistic public debate. In his effort to undermine his political opponent, Branting neglected to acknowledge where he and Waldenström agreed, which was on the question of the right for dissenters to exist and be visible. It is clear from the language that Branting used in this quote that his focus was on the balance of power between the religious and secular camps. He seems to have missed the central element to Waldenström's motion, which was the necessity of separating the church from the state. On this point, they were in agreement, even if they differed in their motivations.

Despite Branting and Dahlström's opposition to Waldenström's particular worldview and motivations for separating church and state, their courting of religious voters demonstrated that they thought they needed to take Waldenström and religion seriously. The fact that they distanced themselves from Lennstrand's openly anti-religious tack is a clear example of this. As leader of the party, Branting expressed not only the hope that the church and state would separate, but also that the influence of religion would decrease. Dahlström on the contrary had no interest in defeating religion, and quite the opposite, worked to increase not only the participation of religious voters, but also to defend, reform, and enrich the spirituality of society. An example of the tension between them came in 1897, as the Social Democratic party leadership discussed its relationship to religion. At a meeting that year, party member Carl G. Schröder had encouraged the party to transition from simply declaring religion to be a private matter (a defensive posture), to declaring an offensive position against all expressions of religion that contradicted science. The language he suggested was "The combating of the public expressions of religion, which stand in contradiction to science and the development of society toward a socialistic order." (*Bekämpande av de offentliga religionsyttringar, som stå i strid med vetenskap och samhällets utveckling till socialistisk ordning.*) Not even the more measured Hjalmar Branting opposed this. Branting even suggested more absolutist language, adding that the party's statement should extend to eliminate "superstitions of all sorts" (*all slags vidskepelse*). Dahlström, on the other hand, argued against such language, pointing out that this could easily be misused by the party and would actually limit the very ideological freedom and scientific inquiry that party members were trying to encourage. However, Dahlström found herself the lone voice in opposition to this direction, for which she was harshly criticized.[132]

Schröder's opposition to certain "public expressions of religion" is an aspect of this debate that raised important questions about the relationship of the party to religion in general, namely the question of the degree to which religion can be "public." If "public" is defined as an officially-sanctioned state opinion on religion, then this definition would have been agreeable to the majority of free churches of the time (including Waldenström) who were in protest of the Church of Sweden's position of power in dictating these matters. However, if "public" is defined more broadly as "in the party meetings" or even "audible to others in public," then this becomes a new form of ideological oppression and a breach of pluralism and freedom of speech. At least this was the danger as Dahlström identified it. In the long view, it seems that although she was in the minority at the time, the party eventually developed in her line of thinking and veered away from this antireligious policy. Branting's support of Schröder's suggestion seems to have been an exception. Overall, he was more in agreement with Dahlström, not Schröder, and he remained for the most part committed to a strategy of decreasing the legal connections between church and state, rather than attempting to directly attack the church. As cited earlier, he hoped that religion would simply shrivel up and die on its own as a result of scientific progress and did not need to be exterminated.

In fashioning the Social Democratic party in Sweden, Branting had taken a great interest in the development of German Social Democracy. This extended also to the question of that party's relationship to religion. At the time of its founding in 1875, the German Social Democrats had included a statement in their founding documents that religion was a private matter, something that Branting attempted to replicate in the Swedish model. However, Ture Nerman has made the distinction that there was a notable difference between the way that the Germans interpreted this principle and the way that Branting did. The Germans, he argued, had taken "religion as a private matter" to be a foundational principle for the state (*en statens grundval*), in contrast to Branting. Nerman's evaluation of Branting was that he was lax on this principle, and Nerman preferred August Palm and Axel Danielsson's more aggressive attempts to ban religiosity from the party's ideology as well as the functioning of the state.[133] Assuming that Nerman was correct in his evaluation of Branting's stance, the reasons for such a stance were perhaps due to the fact that Branting thought the strength of religious interests in Swedish society were too strong to risk alienating. Or, perhaps Branting was convinced by others like Dahlström that the goal of the party should be to establish religious pluralism—not to root out all forms of religiosity from the public sphere. A combination of both reasons is also possible.

The intense debates over the role of religion in politics during this time forged new understandings of notions of "public" and "private." While there was wide-spread criticism of the Church of Sweden's privileged position from both secular and religious groups, there was great disagreement over the solution to this uncomfortable relationship. The issue was more complicated than simply dismantling the church-state legal bureaucracy. The role of religion in public had to first be defined in order to ensure that the new political apparatus did not simply fill that void with a new oppressive system of ideological beliefs, religious or secular. A pluralistic public sphere would not automatically emerge in the absence of a state church. Pluralism had to be defined, established as a cultural value and then vigorously defended. Waldenström's understanding of pluralism developed during these heated debates and he took an intense interest in the questions of when and how religion should be private, and when it should be allowed to inform the public sphere. Waldenström seems to have feared that the new situation of religious pluralism involved two perils; on the one hand it could devolve into polarized conflict that would create a new absolutism, or on the other hand, if religion was defined as a private matter, it could be excluded from the public sphere. Both of these extremes were to be avoided in that they risked replacing the old Lutheran monoculture with a new secular atheistic one.[134] The ideals of pluralism that were brewing since the Enlightenment could easily be compromised and lost if any ideologies, religious or secular, were wholly restricted from public life. Both Dahlström's and Waldenström's vigorous defenses for a public role for religion have in the past been seen as marginal, conservative perspectives. However, in analyzing their debates with Branting and Lennstrand, it becomes clear that the understanding of the role of religion in public could easily have developed on another trajectory. Due in part to the protests of dissenters like Dahlström and Waldenström, the view that did come to dominate was that the choice of religion should be a private matter, but to demand that expression of any ideology should be restricted to the private sphere bore serious threats to pluralistic values and the democratic project as a whole. Thus the preference that came to dominate was that the state would safeguard the choice of religion as a matter of conscience, rather than define it as a private matter and forcefully exclude religion from the public sphere.

CHAPTER 6

On Conscience and the Rights of Dissenters

ONE AREA WHERE THE sponsorship of religion by the Swedish state had traditionally been the most influential and apparent was in the national school system. The relationship between the church and the schools had evolved over hundreds of years. In the wake of the Reformation, catechetical instruction was established by law, and by the 1840s, the church was given the charge by the state to establish parish schools to create a universal education system (*folkskolan*). The central role of the Lutheran church and clergy in the educational system of the nineteenth century is difficult to overstate. Education in the precepts of Christianity was a mandatory part of a student's overall education, and was watched over by the clergy, who made sure that it was in line with the official teachings of the Church of Sweden. As religious pluralism increased as a result of the revival activity and the introduction of "foreign" denominations, this curriculum was one of the first social institutions to be questioned. Waldenström had early on been one of the prominent voices who were critical of the nature of religious instruction. Because society was changing so rapidly, the nature of this debate also changed between the 1860s and the 1910s, during the time that Waldenström was active in the debates. He, like the society around him, adjusted his argument to correspond with the changing reality. In the beginning, his emphasis was on criticizing the monopoly that the Church of Sweden had in religious instruction, and finding ways to allow room for dissenting members of the free churches to be able to opt out of the instruction provided in school. In other words, the goal was for parents to be able to remove their children from this instruction, due to matters of conscience and ideological conflict. He agreed with the notion that Christian education should be a part of the education of good citizens, and there was little in the 1860s to suggest that a formally secular Sweden was a likely possibility in the near future. After the turn of the century, however, the speculation about a possible secular, "post-Christian" Sweden also finds its place in Waldenström's discussions. This chapter will outline the evolution of this discussion, focusing on how conscientious dissent was defined. Though dissent was specifically related to this issue of religious instruction, it is relevant to the general discussion of pluralism and the protections that dissenting minorities could expect to receive in this new environment.

Gävle Högreläroverk, upper secondary school where Waldenström taught classical languages and religion. Photo from N.P. Ollén's *Paul Peter Waldenström: En Levnadsteckning*.

Waldenström's first major opinion piece on religious instruction appeared in 1867 with an article that he published in the journal *Pædegogisk tidskrift*. This was later republished as a booklet with the title "On Bible Reading in School" (*Om bibelläsning i skolan*) written for a larger audience. This booklet took up the question of reforming the philosophy of religious instruction, and his criticism focused on the general philosophy behind teaching religion. In his view, religious instruction should first and foremost be directed at encouraging spirituality and cultivating a sense of independence in the students so that they could read and interpret the scriptures for themselves. Waldenström criticized the methods of instruction, which he saw as placing too little emphasis on primary source material and too much emphasis on secondary sources. In other words, the students were reading textbooks about the Bible rather than the Bible itself.

> *By doing this, won't the students learn to think that the word of the Bible is comparably less important than the confessional system of doctrine? [. . .] Instead of the textbook being a key to the correct understanding of the Bible and as such accompanying the reading of the Bible, now the Bible must be content with the honor of accompanying the textbook, so that for example dicta probantia (proofs) are inserted here and there from the Bible.*[135]

This was the case to varying degrees in all grade levels. Those students in the elementary grades were especially taught by rote memorization, which Waldenström saw as ineffective from a pedagogical standpoint.

Even worse, however, was the probability that this type of memorization served to engender resentment among the students, rather than to inspire interest in Bible study. The lack of encounters with primary sources led to the extreme consequence that the students risked seeing these exercises as being impersonal and irrelevant for their own lives.

> *But biblical history is just as unable to replace the Bible, as illustrations of plants can replace the living plants themselves. They are good together, as long as, for instance, biblical history is only used as a guide to the concise summary [of the Bible], but it cannot become the Bible, any more than illustrations can become nature.*[136]

Another consequence of the focus on textbooks was that Bible passages were lifted out of their contexts and used to explain the Lutheran creeds. In objection, Waldenström pointed out instead that "The Bible does not exist for the sake of dogma, but dogma for the sake of the Bible" (*Bibeln är icke till för dogmatikens skull, utan dogmatiken för Bibelns*).[137] In some cases this was not problematic, but in other cases it could easily be the case that these passages were used as static proofs of doctrinal minutia, thereby losing their dynamic vitality and obscuring the nuanced meanings that could be gained from them when read in their context. This method was flawed in that "one begins and builds upon the concept, the abstract, dead unity, instead of from the living, concrete, and observable diversity" (. . . *man börjar med och utgår från begreppet, den abstrakta, döda enheten, i stället för från den lefwande, konkreta och åskådliga mångfalden*).[138] As an educator, Waldenström saw this as being in contradiction to the natural way that human beings develop and grow. Children naturally begin learning by being immersed in all of the various aspects of life, and gradually come to understand it. They begin learning by making observations about the world in which they find themselves. Only after these observations, aided by their parents and teachers, can children come to understand things in terms of categories, systems, and laws.

Waldenström may have overstated this *a posteriori* nature of learning in his effort to correct the negative tendencies that he saw in the educational system. However, by his comparisons of other disciplines, he was able to provide some rather progressive educational principles that were current in the general debate about the Swedish school system. One of these was a criticism of instruction by rote memorization. In Waldenström's ideal classroom, the students would remember religious principles because they were well read in the scriptures, and possessed a deep knowledge built up over years. This would be in contrast with the current situation, in which the students were consuming and regurgitating boiled-down principles, which they were not able to explain in their own words. The other important aspect of Waldenström's criticism was that the way that religion was taught was in contrast with many other subjects, such as the Classics. As teaching classical languages was Waldenström's primary occupation, he was drawing on first-hand experience for these comparisons. In the Classics, he argued, any good teacher would not content himself to teaching about the texts, but would prioritize in-depth reading of the primary sources by the students. If this was taken as common sense in the field of Classics, then why did the teachers of religion not prioritize the reading of the most primary of primary texts, the Bible?[139] Waldenström's educational philosophy was thus experientially-based and communicative, in that the goal of the teacher was to teach faith, not teach about faith, by allowing students the latitude to engage directly with the texts and make it personally relevant. This could be expected to be far more effective than for a teacher to simply teach a list of what is true and false. A teacher should bring the subjects to life, and not just be some kind of conduit for transmitting a presumably objective set of principles. This could be achieved by the teacher modeling faith, through a demonstration of personal grappling with the complexity of the scriptures.

There were naturally negative reactions to Waldenström's philosophy within the leadership of the Church of Sweden, which held that if teachers were allowed to teach from a personal perspective at all it would lead to a subjective and one-sided presentation—and likely an unorthodox viewpoint.[140] As if to pacify these concerns, Waldenström assured his potential critics that even this seemingly unorthodox method of teaching religion would not be detrimental to the orthodoxy that they wished to protect with the current curriculum and practices. He expected that orthodoxy would, on the contrary, be strengthened if it were communicated in a more healthy way.[141] Furthermore, Waldenström held to the line of thinking that subjectivity is in the eye of the beholder, particularly if the beholder is invested in the established paradigm. Education was not inherently "value free," so it should not pretend to be. Whether it is the Bible or the confessional books or a textbook, anything could be presented subjectively. The best solution to this dilemma was for educators to try to mitigate the tendencies toward subjectivity by presenting plenty of primary sources from an early age and relating their own experiences with the texts in the hope that students learn to read for themselves. The students would thus learn how to search for a faith that they could own.[142]

Since primary texts were essential in Waldenström's educational model, he also made fervent pleas for modern translations of the original Greek and Hebrew texts into Swedish. It was not practical for the students to be expected to master these classical languages. The next best thing was to have them translated regularly to keep pace with developments in modern Swedish. It should be a priority for the Church of Sweden to keep the translation of the Bible in current speech.

> *Our translation is written in a language, that has received the name "church language" and which is prayed with a piety as if the Spirit of God hung upon these old case endings and German word order [...] If the apostles had thought, that church language would be a language that no one spoke or wrote and few understood, they would never have written in the Hellenistic dialect.*[143]

Waldenström deemed the Bible translation then currently in use as outdated and accused the Church of Sweden of sitting on its hands for the past ninety years as they tinkered with test translations without coming to any concrete result. Without a fresh translation of the Bible, teachers of religion were forced to waste a great deal of time "translating the translation" for their students, explaining what the outdated vocabulary meant.[144] He applauded the Norwegians, on the other hand, for their successful translation of a "folk Bible."[145] Waldenström later took this project on himself, publishing his own translation of the New Testament with commentary.

Waldenström's critique of Christian education continued in 1900 with another treatise on the "Reform of Christian Education at the Upper Secondary Schools." This was submitted as a report to the State Council and the Head of the Royal Ecclesiastical Department and then published for the general public. In keeping with his earlier criticisms, Waldenström took issue with the central textbook in confirmation itself, Luther's Catechism. Both the short version, known as the "small" catechism, and the full version were ill-suited pedagogically for children, due to their famous question-and-answer format which was nothing more than rote memorization.[146] This collapsed presentation of theology even contained some mistakes, as some Bible passages were taken out of context in order to serve as proofs for doctrine.[147] Furthermore, Waldenström thought that there were many instances when children would be better served by reading the Bible itself to learn doctrinal points. The catechism only confused these concepts, when the Bible, he thought, was often simple enough for children to understand directly.[148] Waldenström even recommended that the catechism be delayed until the third class, as he thought it would be better if the students in the first and second classes were able to focus on the reading of the Bible and Christian history.[149] This history should, furthermore, be taught in such a way that it did not focus on the obscure details of Old Testament kings, but rather on the central storyline of the Old Testament, which reveals the nature of God; "the most important task of religious instruction is that the students would come to know God." (. . . *religionsundervisningens viktigaste uppgift är att lärjungarne må lära känna Gud.*) [150] Christian history should not be taught as a long list of facts to be known, but as it relates to explaining the origins of faith as it existed in Swedish society. National church history, which had until then played a very small part of the curriculum, should be emphasized far more, as this recent history had the most direct relationship to the students and helped them understand their own context.[151] Globalization, even if it had not yet been defined as such, had already become quite apparent to Waldenström. He explained that changes in the availability of transportation and increased travel would cause Swedish citizens to come into increased contact with the surrounding cultures and religious worldviews. In order to be able to make sense of this plurality of viewpoints, they deserved to be taught about those religious worldviews, as well.

> *As modes of transportation are developing and thereby even the contacts between the various parts of the world and the peoples, it seems to me that religious instruction at the higher levels ought to include the task of communicating to the students a short overview of the most prominent heathen forms of religion, such as Brahmanism, Buddhism, Confucianism, Shintoism, forms of religion that have proven themselves formidable enough to create a comparably high culture. This type of education ought to be much more in demand as the Christian mission among the heathen peoples grows year after year in scope and energy. It should also be of a much greater significance in the expansion of the students' spiritual perspectives than that, which they now receive, and which therefore could well be replaced to make room for this one.*[152]

Later on, as a representative of a dissenting denomination, Waldenström increasingly developed the concern that the individual have the right to follow his or her conscience. This evolved out of a self-interested concern that the religious instruction as it was taught by the Church of Sweden compromised the efforts of free-church parents to be able to instill faith in their children in line with their own consciences. However, Waldenström was both a dissenter in relation to the Church of Sweden, as well as being invested in the successful reform of that institution. It is not, therefore, accurate to dismiss these suggestions for reform as solely based in ulterior motives. He remained in practice a sincere Lutheran in many ways, and his reform agenda rests on an assumption that other sincere Lutherans will agree with him. Furthermore, his defense of dissenters can easily be extended even to his ideological opponents, namely the secular Lutheran parents who wanted their children to avoid being taught religious concepts that they identified as narrow-minded dogmatism, or parents who were atheists and wanted their children removed from religious instruction altogether.

Waldenström found himself fighting a battle on two fronts. On the one side was his critique of the conservative education given by the Church of Sweden, which he identified as having relied on flawed curriculum and practices, such as using Luther's catechism instead of regular and thoroughgoing reading of the Bible. On the other hand, he found a much worse alternative, which was that within the system as it existed, there was a growing frequency of teachers who undermined faith itself by teaching an extreme rationalism. This rationalism posited that there was no room in the modern era for superstitious belief in divine interferences in human history. Instead, such teachers presented all such accounts in the Bible as instructional myths, including even the central miracle of the resurrection of Christ. These fables were taught as only having value as moral tales, and were written by humans as a sort of poetic instruction in morality, having no literal basis in history. God was the author of the Bible only as an indirect source of inspiration, or a type of muse—not as a direct author. According to Waldenström, such a hypercritical presentation of faith to children at a young age was not respectful to the children themselves, who were not allowed to immerse themselves in the source material and begin to be able to make up their own minds. It was also not respectful to their parents, who were expecting that their children were being given a foothold in the faith of their ancestors. Faith was precluded before it could ever be given a start. Finally, this trend was a contradiction of the nation's constitution, as the constitutionally-established state church was essentially poisoning itself at the root.[153]

In a heated debate in the newspaper *Stockholms Dagblad* in 1912, Waldenström defended himself against the criticism of a certain lektor Åhfeldt, who complained about Waldenström's support of the right for Christian parents to remove their children from public instruction in religion.

> [. . . I] shall never cease to fight for the constitutional rights of parents to demand from the school a biblical, Christian religious instruction for their children. With this right is included the ability to remove children from an education, which goes in the opposite direction. For that reason, as a consequence, it is not implied that there are any such rights for rationalists, materialists, etc. to remove their children from a bible-believing education, as long as the Swedish people legally confess their allegiance to the Lutheran Reformation, the origin and foundational principles of which are the authority of the Holy Scriptures as an infallible norm for Christian faith, life and worship. The situation will be completely different, if that day comes, when the Swedish state crosses out the Christian religion from its program. Then it goes without saying that Christian education would be altogether set aside in the state's schools and on its perch replaced with a general, "objective" history of religions, where Buddhism receives precisely the same rights as Christianity and Madame Blavatsky is placed with Christ on the one side and Muhammed or Confucious—not to mention Joseph Smith—on the other. [. . .] If, for example, Methodists and other dissenters have the right to free their children from the school's religious instruction, on the grounds that it is not a Methodist one, etc., then it would certainly be surprising, if the Church of Sweden's members would in the end be denied the same right in protest of an education, which undermines that church's own founding principles.[154]

It is clear that what was taking place in Waldenström's mind during these later years was that he was realizing that it was likely, if not inevitable, that Christianity would be officially abandoned from the state's agenda at some point in the future. While he makes an apparently contradictory claim that religious parents should be able to remove their children from religious instruction that goes against their consciences, but not allow that same right to "rationalists" and "materialists," his main point here is that religious instruction needed to be consistent with the law of the land. Reform needed to be done in a certain order; first introduce a legally enforced pluralism, then reform education. His complaint was that this was being done in reverse order, which was an assault on faith from the rationalists and materialists, whose goal was not pluralism, but the very extermination of faith altogether. The current situation was such that the Church of Sweden was in a highly compromised position in which it was serving to dig its own grave.

A key ingredient in Waldenström's counteroffensive to this trend was defining the nature of "dogma." Opponents of religion in public frequently presented religion as being the enemy of reason and objectivity, as is evident in the statements of Lennstrand, Branting, and Dahlström, mentioned in the previous chapter. Church dogma was considered the perfect example of this, and it was common for opponents of religion to portray religious instruction in school as a mindless, brainwashing activity where children were force-fed lies. To this claim, Waldenström responded with a clarification that all ideological paradigms, whether religious or not, were made possible by spelling out their beliefs in the form of dogma. He responded to lektor Åhfeldt's similar criticism with this claim.

> *Lektor Å pronounces a harsh judgment on the large catechism. At the same time he speaks of dogma and religion as though they were in some respects opposites. He ought not do that, however fashionable such speech may be. For Lektor Å knows full well as anyone else, that no religion can exist without dogma. As soon as I say to a child, that there is a God, I am speaking dogma. As soon as I say, that this God loves the world, that he made the world, that he sent Jesus in order to save the world, etc.—then I am teaching dogma. If it is true, that the essence of religion is belief in God, it is then just as true that all faith in God puts forward beliefs about God.*[155]

Waldenström furthermore did not see dogma as a static set of unquestionable beliefs, but instead used scientific language to describe how over the centuries theologians in the various denominations had been in dialogue with both the scriptures and dogma to fine tune their theories about the supernatural, much along the same lines as scientists proposed, defended and challenged their theories about the natural world.

> *It sounds so beautiful, when one says: "We have the Bible, that is enough, therefore we do not need any dogma." That is altogether as if someone said: "We have nature, and as such do not need any teaching about nature." Only crude ignorance can speak like that.*
>
> *[. . .] It remains relevant then to continue to study the Bible in order to adjust, correct, and complete one's dogma, just as it remains relevant for the scientist to all the more study nature in order to come to an even more complete and richer understanding of her.*[156]

The type of pluralism that Waldenström was calling for was a climate that allowed for this conversation to continue. He viewed his opponents as wanting to end the discussion altogether, which would effectively defeat any real hopes of religious pluralism.

As demonstrated in the discussion of parents' rights to remove their children from objectionable instruction, defending conscience became a red thread through all of Waldenström's discussion of pluralism. The defense of the individual's conscience is central in his theology overall, and his explanations of the tension between truth and conscience remain one of his most enduring contributions. Furthermore, without understanding this one principle, many of Waldenström's seemingly contradictory stances in the political arena will not make sense. Protecting people's rights to express their dissent was a natural concern for the free-church leaders, who in recent history had received censorship, fines, and arrests for breaking with the doctrine and practice of the Church of Sweden. In addition to education policy, the main legislative issues where Waldenström made appeals to conscience were in reform proposals to protect those who dissented from the state's practices and requirements for baptism, marriage, and burials, all of which were under the centralized control of the Church of Sweden. For religious dissenters, this was not a question of whether or not these practices should take place, but how. For the growing segment of the population that was opting out of religious participation, the very idea of the state enforcing these things at all was thrown into question.

Since the aspect of Waldenström's career that has been most extensively researched are the religious protests leading up to the departure of the Waldenströmians from the Church of Sweden in 1878, this will not be treated here.[157] These protests related most directly to the rights of members of the Church of Sweden to meet for worship, communion, and mutual education apart from the supervision of ordained clergy. Instead, the focus of this book is on understanding the political repercussions that developed from these earlier religious protests, which continued through the beginning of the twentieth century. What began as the request of a minority of religious dissenters to follow their consciences out of the state church and into their own private gatherings evolved into a much wider national discussion about whether the state should be involved in religion at all. As Waldenström remained in the debate from the 1860s until his death, he evolved with it as it changed, amending his own philosophies of pluralism to help answer the new questions that were raised.

One of the most famous occasions when Waldenström made a defense of conscience was during debates about the expansion of civil marriage in 1885. At the time, civil marriage was possible for those people who had formally left the Church of Sweden in order to join a state-approved alternative religious denomination (it was not until 1951 that members could leave the church of Sweden without joining another religious group). Erik Jakob Ekman, a close friend and colleague of Waldenström, as well as then president of the Swedish Mission Covenant (SMF), had just presented a motion to the *Riksdag* to expand these rights even to those members of the Church of Sweden who, for any reason, could not or did not want to leave that church. This affected both members of the SMF, many of whom retained dual membership with the Church of Sweden, as well as atheists and other dissenters who were prevented by law from leaving the church. Waldenström, who was participating in his first *Riksdag* as an elected representative, stood up to defend the motion, giving what would become one of his most interesting political speeches, with the provocative title "Was the Apostle Peter legally married?" In order to demonstrate the ridiculous situation that dissenters found themselves in, Waldenström focused his speech on the theme of conscience, framing the debate in terms of the consciences of the men and women wanting to get married, as well as on the conscience of the clergyman performing the ceremony. Regardless of whether a person was a Christian or an atheist, the fact that this ceremony was forced on all parties presented an undesirable situation for everyone.

Erik Jakob Ekman. Photo from Ekman's *Den Inre Missionens Historia*. Frontispiece.

> There are members of the Swedish state church, who do not believe in Christ, indeed, not even in God. They are atheists or materialists, and as such they despise and scorn both the church, her faith and her clergy. Such is not at all an isolated occurance. Now, say they want to get married. They must then send for a priest and then let him read over them those prayers and that blessing, which is contained in the churchly wedding ceremony, which they in their hearts and souls despise. As a Swedish priest, I have married people with such a disposition, and it has always been so repulsive to me that I have wished that I was a thousand miles away. For whom can it well be a blessing to force on such people the churchly blessing? Can it be for the party in question themselves? No, for them it must be in the first place offensive. By this they are galvanized in their hatred. Can it be for the church or the state? To answer 'yes' to this question were the same as saying, that a lie can be a blessing to the state or the church.[158]

Waldenström then went on to explain how it was inconsistent that the current system allowed civil marriage only for those who had transferred to other denominations and left the Church of Sweden. For many people who objected to the idea of a church marriage, the best alternative was to join any other denomination at random, be married with a civil ceremony, all with the intention of leaving that denomination as soon as possible. Such instances benefited neither the state nor any of the churches. Coincidentally, Hjalmar Branting was one of many people who had done just that, having joined the Methodist Episcopal Church in 1884 in order to be married in a civil ceremony, apparently with no intent of continuing to participate in that church after the wedding.[159] Although it was E. J. Ekman who introduced this motion in 1885, Waldenström would later come to reintroduce this motion in the *Riksdag* in 1890, 1891, 1892, 1896, 1898, and 1900.[160]

Baptism was another central issue where conscience played an essential role. Baptism was a prerequisite for many of the privileges that now are considered civil rights, including the ability to hold certain public offices, as well as to apply for marriage. The issues surrounding baptism during this period have typically been viewed from a religious perspective, in which the question of when, how, why, and by whom a person was baptized were theological matters. Conscience factored into these questions primarily as it related to the interpretation of scripture and the legal ability of a person to follow his or her conscience in regard to those interpretations. It was also an important issue of pride for the free churches to be able to have their own respective forms of baptism acknowledged as being equal to the baptism offered by the Church of Sweden, instead of being looked down upon as an inferior practice. However, a more important question was that if a baptism is a prerequisite for public office, then that would reduce the spiritual significance of the event or even make it sacreligious. For instance, many of the Christian traditions in Sweden at the time placed a strict taboo on multiple baptisms, including Waldenström's church. Thus if an infant was baptized in a denomination outside of the Church of Sweden, and then that person was forced to be baptized later in life, this would potentially create a crisis of conscience for the individual. For some people, this would be a difficult decision to be re-baptized, simply as a means of satisfying a spiritually-meaningless bureaucratic requirement. Waldenström argued for years that the Church of Sweden acknowledge in their records (the "church books," which were also the state's official population records) that the baptisms performed by free churches also be indicated. There was opposition to such an acknowledgement within the Church of Sweden. Instead, if a person was baptized in one of the free churches, but not by the Church of Sweden, the notation would simply read "not baptized by the Church of Sweden." Waldenström had suggested that it could at least be noted "baptized by a layman." While there were no doubt deep emotional desires among many in the free churches for different forms of baptism to be considered equal, Waldenström focused his argument on the practical value of establishing a legal equality between these practices, which was framed as a civil right.

> *If we can come that far—and we shall arrive there, there is no doubt—then we have won everything that we need, as long as a person's civil status can in any regard depend on, that it can be strengthened by him being baptized.*[161]

It is interesting to note that Waldenström was not interested in advancing a campaign of "baptism equality." His spoke out against an attempt by the effort behind the so-called "Gullberg-Hamrinska" motion to amend baptismal and burial practices, which would make the free-church practices equal to those of the Church of Sweden. His main reason behind his rejection of this motion was that it would "make the free-church pastors into some kind of new state church clerical order, if only of a lower level (but, so to say, half-official). May God protect us from that."[162] Even though the church books read "not baptized by the Church of Sweden" (*icke av svenska kyrkan döpt*), which he found unsatisfactory, this was still a minor victory in that it indicated that the issue had been investigated and that there would be proof of a lay baptism elsewhere in the citizen's file. It was thus an implied admission of lay baptism, which would hopefully satisfy the bureaucratic requirements for baptism on the part of the state. Waldenström thus urged the free-church congregations not to request that the *Riksdag* do anything more than what would secure their civil rights. Otherwise they would bring the state into issues that were best kept separate.[163]

On the whole, the fact that Waldenström chose to frame the discussion of the dissenters' rights as a matter of conscience is profound. It would be natural for a dissenter to insist on his or her own rights, but it is not always a given that dissenters in one segment of the population will acknowledge the equal rights of other dissenters with whom they do not agree. By framing the issue as a matter of conscience, Waldenström made the discussion about the universal experiences of dissenters, rather than simply about the experiences of a specific group. Despite his own inconsistencies in acknowledging the validity of his opponents' complaints at times, his preference for defending conscience was quite consistent. Furthermore, this consistent defense of conscience can serve as a significant basis for various contemporary ideologies, religious or secular, to be able to find common ground in this heritage.

CHAPTER 7

The Limits of Democracy in the Kingdom of Christ

There can be little question that the reorganization of religious life that took place at the prompting of preachers like Waldenström served to democratize the way that Swedes of various confessions participated in religion. Both in the free churches, as well as in the Church of Sweden itself, there was a marked shift from leadership by the educated few to leadership by the rank and file members. The churches developed more sophisticated institutions for incorporating lay input in the governance of the local churches and the denomination. Public opinion, often expressed in newspapers, criticized the leadership of clergy and politicians alike. Although working to different ends, a host of critics from outside and from within the churches thus pushed a common agenda of democratization, and created a pluralistic environment in society in general, as well as an increased level of pluralism within Christianity itself.

However, the degree to which this pluralism and democracy could be asserted within Christianity had natural limits. For one, Christianity bore then, and continues to bear now, the essential nature of a monarchy with Christ as king. This is a designation that goes far beyond simply the medieval, feudal language that pervades all of Christian theology and hymnody. Any theistic religion has a snapping point where democracy can only be stretched so far. Submission to a deity entails the idea that the deity ultimately must be obeyed. Even if this worldview is democratized to its extreme, there still remains the reality that the religious participant stands as a subordinate to the deity, even if all of the participants are equal to one another. The other complicated aspect of Christianity is that while Christ is the virtually undisputed king, he is an absentee ruler and his dictates need to be interpreted. In coming to terms with this absentee situation, Christians invariably have to cope with the reality that they serve a "once and future king," in which the only guidelines they have to interpret his will are his recorded sayings and the promise of his final return. In the great void between these historical moments, the participants have to be satisfied with "seeing through a glass darkly." Full confidence is elusive in this kind of pursuit of the truth, in which the individual negotiates between a belief in an inherently objective God, who is only able to be known to the individual through a two-directional approach; on the one hand, through identifying and interpreting revelations from God through the subjective filters of human experience, and on the other hand, by rationally organizing and explaining observations about the physical world and human history.

In the era of absolutist orthodoxy (1600s–on) this was not as acute of a problem, as spiritual leaders could establish consensus on the truth and prevent challenges to those claims (through scholastic argumentation and established precedents for interpretation). In this period in Scandinavia, one factor that made this possible was the commonly held belief that the truth was unified and that the truth could be known. Once this belief in the unity of truth was weakened, however, an unstable environment appeared, in which participants now have the increased ability to choose whether they will submit to a deity or not, and which interpretation of the deity's wishes they accept as having a claim on their lives. If the individual develops a distaste for submission, or if he or she disagrees as to what the will of the deity is, there exists the option to exit the religion, choose another affiliation, or cease to participate at all. Within Christianity, although Christ may be king, and his will may be communicated through scripture, there is still the potential for different denominations and preachers to interpret this will differently. Thus there is a limitless number of possible ways to organize Christians under their king. As apparent in *Squire Adamsson*, this tension is something that Waldenström's theology did not try to resolve, but instead to explore and explain as a potentially productive experience. His answer remained that the best response to this confusion was to promote a culture of tolerance, where flexibility would allow conflict to be able to be managed and made productive, rather than destructive. This strategy demonstrates a hybrid heritage, from both the subjective devotional experience of Pietism and the Enlightenment's insistence on the freedom for scientific inquiry and debate. These traditions have their differences, to be sure. However, they also have something tremendous in common, which is that they each represent the two different, but related, approaches to empiricism; respectively, discernment of truth based on personal experience, and the discernment of truth based on experiment and observation. Both traditions elevated the empirical, though Pietism retained its deference to the essentials of Christian doctrine. Enlightenment thinkers increasingly sought to free themselves from the weight of binding theories and doctrine. Pietists chose to minimize the number of theological doctrines that were binding, but to embrace the ones that were deemed "essential." Truth be told, the Enlightenment thinkers also had their own essential doctrines, though they chose not to think of them as such.

Rosenius in the Pulpit at Bethlehem Church in Stockholm. Photo from Ekman's *Den Inre Missionens Historia.* 431.

The Pietists were in effect introducing a version of Christianity to Sweden that had never existed there before, although it had existed elsewhere in Christian history. This version of Christianity was structured as a democratized, constitutional monarchy. Because it came in the midst of the previous culture of absolutism, this was bound to create a crisis of authority. If all citizens of this kingdom had the equal right (more or less) to read, interpret and speak about matters of faith, the net result was bound to be chaos. The strategy developed by Rosenius to counteract this negative trend was to affirm the idea that all Christians have the equal right to speak, but at the same time to temper this by developing a culture of humility, in which the individual learns how and when it is appropriate to defer this authority to others and keep silent. Because everyone in principle had an equal claim to authority, no one should ever expect to have an exclusive claim to it or to have a monopoly on the interpretation of the truth. As an indication of when it was time to speak formally, Rosenius recommended that one needed an invitation. A person should not get up in the assembly without having received a request from the others to do so. This was an external calling, which also needed to correspond with an inward calling, whether due to pangs of conscience or a revelation from God. Also, just because a person was called once, does not mean he or she is always called, and furthermore, it is not everyone's calling to leave a secular occupation to become a full-time preacher. Some laypeople should not seek to be ordained.[164] This reflects Rosenius's personal opinions, as it was the course that he followed in his own life. He was deliberate in his choice to not be ordained as a minister, and to attempt to follow a principle of only speaking publicly so long as he was invited to do so. In this way he used his life to model what he saw as a lifestyle that, if everyone followed this example, the community could avoid unnecessary conflicts over authority. Admirable as these principles may be, there is a great risk that some people will never be asked to speak, and thereby will be marginalized. However, Rosenius seems to indicate that the desired culture is one in which all people are welcomed to speak and given the latitude to explore the nuances of the truth ("the non-essentials"). If they seek to abandon "the essentials," they simply won't be asked to speak again or at least not as often. This is not a utopian community, but a practical strategy to minimize (not eliminate) disagreement by allowing as much diversity and latitude in the common conversation as possible. Non-essentials may be discussed in a democratic fashion, but certainty about non-essentials is deferred to the distant future (i.e., when the monarch returns).

As Rosenius was not only a preacher, but also an author, one might also wonder how an author can be "invited" to speak. At a basic level, this occurs as often as the reader continues to turn the pages. Readers vote their approval by buying books, subscribing to journals, and by sending letters to the editor. Rosenius as an author intentionally cultivated a narrative strategy that deferred authority to his readers. He speaks, and yet it is the reader who grants him the right to speak. The persona that he adopts in his authorship is never as an expert (he is after all a *bona fide* layman), but as a guide on an equal footing with his reader. At times he points to the Word (the revealed, objective truth of Scripture), at other times he holds up the importance of the confirmation of truth through subjective experience. By doing both, he makes theology into an activity that anyone can participate in because everyone has experiences that can potentially be related to the topic at hand. The objectivity of the essentials is a vertical axis (in which God reveals truth), whereas the subjectivity of the non-essentials is a horizontal one (in which the faithful are granted the latitude to be able to engage with the implications of this truth without jeopardizing their right to citizenship in the kingdom). This idea that Rosenius sought to be an "author without authority" is similar in some ways to the pronouncements of Kierkegaard on this concept.[165] Though the two differ greatly in their approach to theology, it should be little surprise that they bear similarity to one another on this point, as Kierkegaard is also profoundly influenced by Moravian Pietism. Kierkegaard's elevation of subjectivity goes to greater extremes than Rosenius ever dared to go, but reflects a similar realization that Christianity in the modern era needed different strategies to establish authority. The modern human being would not be content simply to receive the objective truth passed down by clergy who acted and spoke as absolute monarchs, but instead would increasingly demand that subjectivity be given space to be explored and validated within a more democratic conversation.

Waldenström may have departed from full adherence to the strategy of his more cautious mentor. He was ordained and held advanced academic degrees, whereas Rosenius was a layman through and through. The saintly Rosenius waited to be asked to speak; the bold Waldenström seemed always ready to share his opinions, whether or not they were invited. As a politician, he did not shy away from getting his hands dirty in national politics, or from making his own pronouncements on opinions concerning nonessentials. But the differences between the two are perhaps more a matter of personality. At the core, there is the philosophy common to both of them, that authority is not the private domain of the spiritual leader, but should be deferred to the group as a whole, whose task it is to share in the project of discerning truth in a collaborative process. An important test of the limits of this worldview came in 1904, as Waldenström came into conflict with his close colleague, E. J. Ekman, then current president of the SMF. Ekman had published a book on the eternal punishment, raising the idea that God ultimately would redeem the entire human race, thus even rescuing the damned from Hell.[166] This was an emphasis on God's grace taken to its absolute extreme. Waldenström identified this as an unacceptable interpretation of the essentials of the faith, and worked to have Ekman ousted from his post as president. However, also demonstrating the Rosenian line of inclusivity, Ekman was not treated as a heretic, but remained a member in the SMF. One apparently had the latitude to have questions even about essentials, though it was going too far to assert these opinions from an official post in the church.

Another point of tension between Christianity and democracy is the traditional role that Christianity has come to serve in many periods during the history of Europe, which is to support and endorse the actions and laws of earthly governments. In Sweden, as elsewhere, the Lutheran church endorsed the legitimacy of the Swedish kings as God-given rulers. This ruler was to be obeyed as a representative of God, a prominent feature in Lutheran sermons that was backed up with sources in the gospels. As a result of this relationship with the government, the Church of Sweden and the free churches frequently defaulted to this position when trying to dissuade political reform groups from challenging the legitimacy of the government. Waldenström, especially in his confrontation with the Socialists, took this traditional approach to dissuade Christians from participating in "anarchistic" movements. This is the primary area where Waldenström has been criticized and accused of being conservative, particularly toward the end of his career, when debates about the establishment of universal suffrage coincided with an intensified Socialist call for a dramatic revision of the political order. His brand of classical liberalism, forged during the 1860s and informed by the humble Rosenian piety of the revival, now seemed hopelessly dated, as well as too deferential to the Swedish establishment.

A skillful depiction of E. J. Ekman as Saint George being defeated by Waldenström as the Dragon. "Sankt Göran och Draken." Edvard Forsström. *Puck*. 10 March 1904. Reproduction: Svenska Missionskyrkans Arkiv.

Erland Sundström, in a concise but eloquent explanation of the contradictions within Waldenström's political philosophy, emphasized the great deference that Waldenström had for the traditional Lutheran perspective on obedience of the citizen to the government. Sundström also pointed out the fact that while Waldenström urged obedience to the temporal authorities, when it came to obedience to the Lutheran church itself, Waldenström was far from obedient. Sundström made reference to a dissertation by William Öhrman, which made the interesting hypothesis that Waldenström's strong support of the Swedish government was a sort of compensation for his radical rebellion against the Church of Sweden.[167] Sundström also pointed out that while Waldenström discouraged any revolutionary challenge to the Swedish government, this did not mean that he was an anti-reformist.

> *Waldenström was very Lutheran in the area of social ethics. Even so he saw boundaries to submission [to the governing authorities]. When the authorities place themselves over the laws of God and restrict freedom of belief and conscience, then the Christian has the right to civil disobedience. Further it applies that the Christian citizen has the right to use legal means to replace a bad authority with a better one. A Christian is in general responsible for the development of his society. It is a Christian civil duty to use political means to introduce Christian values in legislation and reforms.*[168]

In short, Waldenström was evolutionary in his understanding of reform, which is a theme that frequently appears in his explanations of politics. No drastic, overnight revision of the social order was advisable. Both in the context of religion and in the context of political activity, the best way to ensure stability and protect the individual from the dangers of absolutism was to identify a limited number of "essential" principles and prioritize those principles while using existing channels to pursue reform of those aspects of society that needed reform. Once again, the "unity in diversity" principle as expressed in the Moravian Pietist motto manifested itself in very practical ways in Waldenström's philosophy. In the case of the reform of the church, the defense of essential principles involved defending the scriptures themselves by freeing them from the weight of the Lutheran creeds so they could be engaged with in a living process of interpretation by all Christians. In terms of political reform, Waldenström identified other texts which he thought needed defense, namely the national constitution (*grundlagar*), which provided the only proper channels through which Swedes could reform their government.[169] He treated these secular texts as though they too contained a set of essential principles that had to be conformed to as long as they were the accepted constitution of the state (more on this in Part III).

Part II—Separating Church and State

In Part II, the focus has been on the ways in which Pietism informed the transformation of religious practice in the direction of increased strategies of pluralism. In the next section, the focus will turn toward understanding how these religious changes went far beyond religious reforms, and impacted the development of pluralism in the secular, political arena, as well.

PART III

Brokering Confrontation and Exchange: Pietism and Socialism

> *Now since we have a tendency to either lean to one side or the other, then is quite healthy for us to keep company with brothers who have the opposite opinion from us. It is healthy to listen to both Paul and James, though it can cause us to be conflicted within ourselves. [. . .] Let us with this great unity in mind, look past all of our differences and, as siblings for eternity, support one another during our mutual struggles on this journey to our common homeland and our Father's house in heaven! Amen.*[170]

—Carl Olof Rosenius, *Pietisten*, 1859

CHAPTER 8

Pluralism as Productive Tension

THE RELATIONSHIP BETWEEN SOCIALISM and Christianity has historically been a tense and complicated one, and was especially so during the late nineteenth century and beginning of the twentieth. In these years, the proponents of Socialist ideas were still fighting for acceptance in the political and social establishment, and in Sweden, this showdown reached a climax around the turn of the century. Relative to the rest of Europe, Sweden was "behind," both in terms of democratic reforms of government, as well as the representation of laborers' concerns. Historian Berndt Schiller has identified the period from 1906–1914 as "years of crisis," based on the tense relationship that existed between political parties in the *Riksdag*, which he classified as being the most reactionary government in Europe, "surpassed only by the Prussian Landtag."[171] Although historians after the second World War, like Ingvar Andersson, would maintain that these political confrontations " . . . were conducted with the general welfare as a guiding star and with marked feeling for the value of things uniquely Swedish . . . ," Schiller by contrast saw the period as more perilous. While addressing suffrage questions on a superficial level, conservatives and Social Democrats made great gains in terms of parliamentary seats, each at the expense of the Liberal party.[172] The result was a polarization between conservatives and radicals, as resentment of bourgeois power on the one hand and fear of anarchistic Marxist socialism on the other hand drove a wedge between the members of the Liberal party and threatened to split it in two.

From Schiller's evaluation it follows that despite the potential for Sweden to be viewed as a miraculous middle way between political extremisms, there were never any guarantees that Sweden would avoid falling into a Socialist revolution in the wake of the Great War, nor escape a reactionary wave of conservatism as occurred elsewhere in Europe. Although the identification of the period as "tense" is unquestionable, what has remained elusive in accounts of the period are explanations of the exchange that took place between these camps. While the political landscape was polarized between Conservatives, Liberals, and Socialists, these groups did not remain unchanged by their confrontations. The tension of the period does not need to simply be interpreted as a negative confrontation, but also can be seen as a productive tension that caused each side to adapt and incorporate the criticism of the other. This exchange can rightfully be seen as productive for a couple of reasons. First is the fact that open conflict never escalated past minor episodes of violence during strikes and protests. Second, while Socialists lost ground to Conservatives between 1906–1914, they managed to survive and grow in number, so much so that by the 1930s they were able to set the national political agenda for the rest of the century—all without ever eliminating their political opposition. Swedish Social Democracy was a hybrid creation, forged in the productive tension of an exchange between opponents, based in part on compromises struck between parties, as well as adaptations made by each side in response to the challenges of opponents. For this to be a productive exchange, instead of a stalemate and a devolution into extremisms, it was essential that the political arena preserve a climate where pluralism was valued as a common ethical good. This chapter will propose some answers to why pluralism came to be defended and valued in the political arena during this period, as well as explain Waldenström's role.

In these confrontations, religious figures and institutions of all shades have often been identified as firmly part of the conservative establishment. Acknowledgement is made of the fact that many in the working class were often involved in the religious awakening, but the assumption is that this religiosity served to diffuse and delay the march toward social justice, due to the conservatism of churchgoers and the antagonism of the preachers. The free-church movement is seen as incompatible with the labor movement, because these religious groups had little understanding or sympathy for socialism.[173] A few self-identified Christian Socialists, such as Kata Dahlström and H. F. Spak, were vocal in their support of socialism and a rapprochement between that movement and Christianity. Beyond these exceptions, there has not been much discussion of the ways in which Swedish Christianity was in a constructive dialogue with socialism. This is no doubt in part due to the seriousness of the Social Democratic party's struggle to attain a secure position in parliament in its early years. Although Socialists under the leadership of August Palm had established the Social Democratic party in 1889, it would not be until several years into the twentieth century that the party would gain a firm foothold in the *Riksdag*. The first Social Democrat in the *Riksdag* was Hjalmar Branting, who was elected in 1896, but even then it was on a Liberal party ticket. For Socialists engaged in this uphill battle, it was deemed necessary to identify the elements of society that played the role of the "establishment" that prevented their success, which often included the various church denominations.[174] The Church of Sweden was one element that often took a conservative stance in regard to socialism, as did the members of the various free churches. This opposition was due to many ideological factors, but paramount among these was the tendency of Socialists to endorse an atheistic worldview and a rejection of religion, at least religion in any traditional sense. Christianity in general became seen as representing the interests of the bourgeois classes and the monarchy. Despite the fact that Christianity in Sweden was also tensely divided between the state church and the pietistic free churches and mission societies, differentiations between these groups were not often made and Socialists in the press frequently presented them as being united in their conservatism. Socialism, too, was by no means united in the formative years of the 1880s, and even though the party established in 1889 described itself as "Social Democratic," there were sharp divisions over the direction the party would take. Orthodox Marxists resisted collaboration with the Liberal party, while democratically-minded party members like Branting sought a fusion of political ideas and pursued collaboration with the Liberals. The conversation that developed between the adherents to various Socialist and Christian perspectives in this period was thus a multi-faceted conversation between several poles: Liberals versus Conservatives, Liberals versus Socialists, radical Socialists versus Social Democrats, the state church versus the free churches, and liberal theologians versus conservatives in both the state church and the free churches.

As a member of the *Riksdag's* lower chamber, and as a standard bearer for Pietism in Sweden, Waldenström was engaged in this conflict in a public manner. His discussions with Socialists and other elements within Swedish politics reveal a great deal about this cultural confrontation and present valuable insights on the nature of the exchange that forged the political climate of the twentieth century. This section will focus on Waldenström's relationship to his contemporaries and evaluate the role that his particular brand of Pietism played in this critical dialogue over the nature of pluralist democracy. Whereas this conflict has often been seen as a stalemate, the discussion here will analyze the ways in which the opposing sides critiqued each others' program, and ultimately contributed in the development of each others' values and worldviews. Specifically, it will be suggested that Waldenström's critiques of the labor movement were significant in the development of the labor movement and for the development of Social Democracy.

A good place to start a discussion of Waldenström's relationship to socialism is a quick visit to one of the climactic moments of the "years of crisis" described above. In contrast with the current political situation of Swedish society, which is famously stable, the political landscape of a century ago demonstrated ripples of all the social unrest that typified the rest of Europe. The summer of 1908 witnessed one of the more highly charged episodes in the Swedish labor movement, and also was an occasion when Waldenström presented a public critique of socialism, as well as an exhortation to pluralism. An explanation of these comments in light of their context is key to understanding his political agenda and relationship to socialism. Throughout 1908, Socialist agitators had been busy harnessing the discontent of workers into organized strikes. Each strike was seen as a forerunner of a coming "Great Strike," which would unite the working class, bring the bourgeois class to its knees, and usher in a new era of equality. A great strike did in fact come the following year, although with much less success than organizers had hoped. Nevertheless, the tensions between classes during 1908 were marked. Throughout the decade, employers had been organizing a counter-offensive to the strikes, orchestrating large-scale lockouts in order to maintain the upper hand in negotiations. The hatred felt by many workers toward their employers can be read in the incendiary language used in the Socialist newspapers. Columnists such as Hinke Bergegren drew on prophetic, Marxist imagery and revealed anarchistic aspirations that included visions of bloodshed and the overthrow of the present order. Within the young Social Democratic party, leaders with cooler heads attempted to reign in extremists like Bergegren.[175] Violence was feared on all sides.

On the night of July 11 these fears were partly realized. In the harbor town of Malmö in southern Sweden, a bomb exploded on a ship named *Amalthea*. Due to the strikes in Malmö, employers had brought in English workers to break the strikes and keep production moving. When these strike breakers began receiving threats against their lives, it was decided that they would be housed onboard the ship for their protection at night. Then came the bomb attack, which blew a giant hole in the side of the ship. One unfortunate worker was killed, twenty-three others were injured. A group of radical anarchists led by Anton Nilsson were arrested for the crime. In this sensational trial Nilsson received a death sentence, which was later reduced, becoming a highly charged symbol of the conflict.

The Amalthea Incident (*Amalteadådet*), as it was known, became a focal point of public debate. Among the people who weighed in on the discussion was Waldenström, who made a speech a month later in the city of Karlstad. Although Waldenström had formally left elective politics after his defeat in the 1905 parliamentary elections, he continued to write political speeches and commentary in the newspapers for the rest of his life. The main message of his Karlstad speech was clear: *don't vote for the Socialists in the coming elections*. According to Waldenström, the stability of Swedish democracy depended on a balance between parties and a healthy climate of pluralism. The rhetoric of the Social Democratic party was alarming proof to him that the party was antagonistic to parliamentary practices and, if granted a large enough platform, would stifle debate and drive out opposition. The Amalthea Incident, with its direct inspiration from Bergegren's anarchist rhetoric, was for Waldenström a clear sign of the threat that this rhetoric posed to pluralist democracy.[176]

For anyone familiar with Swedish politics in the twentieth century two things will likely come to mind when presented with Waldenström's dire predictions. One is that beginning in the 1930s the Social Democratic party did come to dominate Swedish politics for the majority of the century. The second is that this rise to power was accomplished without a bloody revolution. Rather, this power shift has been celebrated for its preference for reform over revolution, and in comparison with other countries where Socialist movements ushered in dictatorships and violations of civil rights, Sweden seemed to manage to find the golden mean between capitalism and communism. The predictions of revolution and societal collapse made by politicians like Waldenström have thus been discredited as alarmist and not given much treatment by political history. They have also been used to reinforce the idea that the Pietist movement was solidly conservative and anti-reformist, most notably by the contemporary Socialist press.

In the past decade, however, the political dominance of the Social Democratic party has been challenged, which has also prompted a re-evaluation of the dominant historical narrative that was sponsored by this party and which helped make its dominance possible. As a result of this current transition period, new insights have been able to be made into what happened in the formative years of the Swedish welfare state in the first decades of the twentieth century. Waldenström's political philosophy can now be revisited in light of these new findings, and suggestions will be offered here as to how the activity of this Pietist politician may be interpreted as having influenced the preference for pluralism in Swedish politics. The focus will be on the general philosophy that guided his approach to politics, and will highlight some of the specific issues that Waldenström took up in his career.

Waldenström's lifetime (1838–1917) was a period of rapid social, economic and political reforms. The kingdom of Sweden in the mid-nineteenth century was sometimes referred to as a "fortified poorhouse." Sweden, like other Nordic countries, had the trappings of other Western European kingdoms, but the majority of its population remained agrarian and poor, and while usually receiving a basic education, nevertheless enjoyed limited political representation in comparison. Industrialization also came late to

Sweden. As the cities swelled and standards of living declined, the working class began looking to their fellow workers in Denmark and Germany for inspiration in methods of organization. But even in the 1880s, the labor movement was still weak and impotent against the captains of industry, making for several uneasy decades of political conflict.[177] Politically speaking, Sweden was a constitutional monarchy with a long tradition of a democratically elected parliament, the *Riksdag*. This representation, however, was limited, and it was not until the mid-1860s that the *Riksdag* was reformed from the antiquated four-estates model which it had since the middle ages. The new two-chamber parliament introduced in 1866 was an improvement, but even this new system quickly became criticized for favoring the propertied classes. As debates for universal male suffrage began in earnest in the 1890s, it was pointed out that only 5–6 percent of the population was actually represented in the *Riksdag*. The reason for this was that suffrage was limited by a minimum income requirement, which the vast majority of urban workers could never meet.[178]

Genuine party politics were also established rather late and it was not until 1917 that true parliamentarianism made a breakthrough.[179] When Waldenström entered the *Riksdag* there were a few interest groups that referred to themselves as parties, but they functioned more along the lines of "old boys' clubs" without real party procedures.[180] However, the basic interest groups that would develop into the standard five-party spectrum were present even in the 1880s: the loosely organized interest groups that gradually congealed into parties were the Agrarians (*Lantmannapartiet*, 1867, divided in protectionist and liberal camps between 1888–1895), Conservative or "Moderate" (*Allmänna valmansförbundet*, 1904), and Liberals (*Liberala samlingspartiet*, 1900) and those on the left were the Social Democrats (*Socialdemokratiska arbetarepartiet*, 1889) and the Communists or "Left" (*Vänster*, 1917, 1921). Thus the time that Waldenström served in parliament was a period that was both formative and rather unstable for Swedish politics.

Waldenström was a member of parliament for over twenty years, from 1884 to 1905. It is not surprising that the members of the church he had inspired, the so-called Waldenströmians, would become a driving force in electing him to parliament; he represented the city of Gävle in the lower chamber of the *Riksdag* through a remarkable seven terms. In relation to these political parties, Waldenström remained deliberately non-affiliated with any one political party throughout his career. He was jokingly referred to as a party unto himself by the newspapers, something which he himself liked to repeat. Although maintaining the image of a maverick, the politics of this one-man "Waldenström Party" most often resembled those of the Liberal party. This is after all where the majority of the Mission Covenanters of the time found their political home.[181] During the time of Waldenström's political activity, the concerns of the Liberals generally included the expansion of voting rights, and the maintenance and defense of individual freedoms, such as freedom of speech and freedom of religion. This emphasis on these classical liberal values was particularly important for the Mission Covenanters and other pietistic groups, who remained focused on disentangling the apparatus of the church from the state.

In the great showdown between Liberal and Socialist politicians that began in the turbulent decade of the 1880s and continued through the 1910s, Waldenström demonstrated himself primarily as a Liberal, although after the turn of the century he began identifying frequently with the Conservatives. This move to the right was directly related to the rhetoric used by Socialists. This rhetoric, in Waldenström's mind, was dangerous for one main reason, that it contained anti-democratic elements and the potential to undo all of the Liberal reforms that had been achieved in the development of the Swedish constitution and parliamentary practices since the 1860s. Swedish democracy was still in its infancy and there remained no precedent to gauge how a Socialist revolution could be carried out in a way that could be reconciled with democratic principles. The violence of the Paris Commune of 1871 was still fresh in the minds of many Swedes. What was alarming to those in the Liberal side was that such revolutions were a source of inspiration for some Swedish Socialists, including even moderates within the Social Democratic fold such as the future prime minister Hjalmar Branting, but especially anarchists like Hinke Bergegren and Anton Nilsson.[182]

Thus, when Waldenström rose to give his speech in Karlstad in 1908, just weeks after the bombing in Malmö harbor and with the next elections approaching, his fears of the collapse of the Swedish democratic project were perhaps at their highest. And so he repeated his cautionary tale about the dangers of extremism, and urged those in the Liberal and Moderate parties to do their part to provide balance in the *Riksdag*. It was at this occasion that he communicated his tale of the coachman and the cart (included in Part I).[183] Since Waldenström was one of the more prominent opponents to socialism, columnists and cartoonists had a field day whenever he made pleas for moderation. Images like the ones he employed in the Karlstad speech were seen as proof of Waldenström's reactionism and his opposition to reform. As the tensions mounted between Liberals and Socialists as to who would define the next chapter of Swedish political reform, the attacks on Waldenström's personality also increased. In the campaign years of 1902 and 1905, the Socialist press led a concentrated campaign to remove Waldenström from office, which finally succeeded in 1905. Due to these personal attacks, he glided further to the right, alienating himself from many within the Mission Covenant, who remained firmly in the Liberal camp.[184] Reconciling this later conservative period with his earlier radicalism has been rather problematic in defining Waldenström's overall political philosophy. His legacy has been contested between those who have largely dismissed him as a conservative and those who have tried to identify Waldenström as essentially radical throughout his career (most notably historian Ragnar Tomson). However, this seemingly eccentric political activity can be explained without resorting to defining him as either a conservative or radical. In reading his political speeches and commentary even during his later career, it is clear that his main motivation was not a particular party ideology, but he was instead guided by a vigorous defense of democratic pluralism; maintaining balance between parties in the *Riksdag* was a top priority.

As mentioned already, recent work in Swedish political history has called into question some of the assumptions about the nature of the political confrontations of the early twentieth century. Political scientist Sheri Berman has suggested that Social Democracy as it emerged in Sweden was not a triumph of socialism over liberalism, but instead was a hybrid creation that was achieved through a dialogue between them. Thus neither ideology remained unchanged by this process; Social Democracy was produced by the confluence of both.[185] Similarly, another Swedish historian, Åsa Linderborg, has explained that Swedish history has been written from a decidedly Social Democratic viewpoint, which emphasized its radicalism and triumph, but has not acknowledged the ways in which it was affected and changed by its confrontation with liberalism.[186] If Swedish Social Democracy can indeed be seen as a middle way, it would be to the degree that Swedes were able to maintain an atmosphere of pluralism where diametrically opposed ideologies were able to coexist and influence one another in an ongoing political dialogue.

Such themes of balance and a positively defined pluralism are everywhere in Waldenström's speeches. In the Karlstad speech, social progress is presented as a wagon traveling along a road with deep ditches on either side. In order to navigate the hazards of extremism on the right and to the left, the driver needs to navigate a course somewhere in the middle. This middle course is not simply a lukewarm position or a retreat from taking a firm stance, but can in fact be identified as a stance in its own right. Waldenström can be seen here attempting to translate his role as a preacher into the political sphere by preaching a sermon on political ethics to his audience of Swedish voters. The ethical good that he is attempting to promote is an approach to politics in which voters anticipate the rise of divergent viewpoints, and then attempt to compensate for them through political power sharing and strategic re-affiliation. Recall Arend Lijphart's "consociational" model of power sharing, or George Weigel's view of pluralism as an intentional, active strategy, both discussed in chapter 1. If opposing viewpoints can confront each other, while at the same time sharing the public sphere, they can navigate a healthy trajectory of social progress. The net result of this struggle is, in Waldenström's view, a positive outcome and a desirable tension.[187] While this may seem simplistic, it should be pointed out that this is the strategy that many so-called "swing voters" employ regularly in modern politics, and also why these swing voters are so aggressively courted. They are unpredictable and can make the difference between a left or right victory.

It should also be underscored that Waldenström was articulating this strategy at a critical point in the development of Swedish democracy, right before the suffrage reforms that were passed in 1907 would be used for the first time in 1909. In other words, many would-be voters had no experience voting before, and one might imagine that some would be anxious and receptive to advice. Voter participation in Sweden was very weak until the end of the 1880s, and even in the early 1900s actual election campaigns were still a new concept. (Liberal Karl Staaff is credited with this innovation.)[188] The newness of political campaigns meant that the politicians themselves were not used to politicking outside of the *Riksdag*, and needed to develop the means to communicate with constituents on a national scale. Newspapers became critical for this, and there was a flurry of new political papers founded around the turn of the century. For the Social Democrats, for instance, there were twenty-some new papers founded in the 1880s and 90s.[189] Hjalmar Branting, in parliament since 1896, spoke from the platform of one of the most prominent of them, *Socialdemokraten*. It should be no surprise then that a politician like Waldenström would succeed as long as he did. He had been a newspaperman and national figure since the 1860s, and for him the use of print media for generating public opinion was "old hat." Waldenström's success in politics was certainly due in great part to his being ahead of the game in terms of using print media.

The vocabulary that Waldenström used time and again in his speeches and articles draws from themes of openness, freedom, and liberality. It is open discussion that leads to progress, not ideology-driven dogmatism. A key word that he returns to frequently in his speeches is the term *frisinne* (translated as "openmindedness," "freedom from prejudice," or "liberal-mindedness"). This is a complicated term to define, as on the one hand it was associated with a progressive wing of the Liberal party (*Frisinnade landsföreningen*, 1902), in which even a number of free-church members were active. On the other hand, Waldenström seems to have co-opted into *frisinne* some of the much more radical meaning of the term *fritänkare* (or "free thinker"), which was used in Socialist circles and could have strong anticlerical and atheistic implications. Waldenström appears to have been indiscriminate in his understanding of these two terms, perhaps reflective of a rhetorical strategy to conflate them and suck some of the wind out of his opponents' sails. Nevertheless, it is remarkable that he urges his listeners to search for a true *frisinne*.

> True liberal-mindedness attempts to understand the perspective of those who think differently. It offers reasons and demands reasons. If it finds that the opponent has a better explanation than it was able to offer, then it is not ashamed to change its position and opinion. On the contrary, in a situation like this, if it were to stubbornly hold on to an earlier position, that is obstinacy, that is stubbornness in the ugly sense of the word. Such a person is pigheaded, and that is indeed no pleasant title. May we therefore be in truth liberal-minded thinkers. May we seek to understand the perspective of those who think differently than we do, and the reasons, which they have to defend their opinion, and judge them accordingly.[190]

While Waldenström could often make pleas like this on behalf of pluralism, he could also work against it. The Socialist press often identified him as having been one of the most negative influences in the culture wars between the Socialists and the Liberal/Conservative opposition, and his steady protest of socialism clearly had consequences for ideological exchange.[191] However, he redeemed himself at some key moments. For example, in 1889 a controversial law was proposed in the *Riksdag*, called the "muzzle law" or "gag rule," which was designed to limit the revolutionary and incendiary speech of Socialist groups. Waldenström was one of the representatives to stand up in opposition to the motion, citing the fact that while the speech of the Socialists might in fact be harmful to law and order, the principle of free speech could not be sacrificed. He also, appropriately, compared this to the injustice that Pietists themselves had faced due to the restrictive policies of the Church of Sweden only decades earlier.[192] Despite his distaste for socialism, on this occasion he was big enough to recognize and acknowledge publicly that they had common experiences of being discriminated against, and that such discrimination could not be tolerated in Swedish politics.

It is clear through the extensive treatment in the Socialist newspapers that Social Democratic leaders were aware of Waldenström; he was one of the central targets for political cartoonists during the first decade of the twentieth century.[193] Although he presented himself as an obstacle to the party's rise to power, his critiques also forced the party to confront the fringe of radical anarchists that discredited the movement as anti-democratic. Since its inception in 1889 through the outbreak of the first World War, the party leadership was in a struggle between orthodox Marxist leaders like August Palm and moderates like Hjalmar Branting. Such incendiary language used by radicals like Hinke Bergegren that inspired the bombing in Malmö were easy targets for people like Waldenström and therefore a liability. In short, the party had to clean house if it was going to be taken seriously by the electorate and be able to succeed in cooperating with the other parties in the *Riksdag*. It is in response to such concerns that Hjalmar Branting took the lead in having Bergegren banned from the party conference for a second time in 1908.[194] Even after Bergegren and the "Young Hinkes" (*Unghinkarna*, as his followers were known) were discredited officially in the Social Democratic party, there continued to be tension within the broader Socialist camp through the 1920s. Radicals and anarchists would remain a specter that haunted Swedish politics: Conservatives and Liberals exploited these fears to gain an edge over their opponents, and Social Democrats had to deal with the uncomfortable reality that the politics of anarchists often aligned with their own. Even the following year, 1909, there was an anarchist scare in Stockholm, as the visiting Russian Tsar was subject to an unsuccessful attempt on his life. Another Swedish general on the scene was not as fortunate and was shot to death. Branting was portrayed by the impatient radical wing of his party as representing a sort of "bureaucrat socialism."[195]

In the process of responding to critics and successfully dealing with this persistent public relations problem, Branting demonstrated that he was an advocate of democracy and reform, rather than revolution, who would set the tone for the transformation of socialism into a truly "democratic" Social Democratic party. One can easily draw a line between Waldenström's protest of anarchistic socialism and the responsive actions of Branting, in which the latter was forced to rearticulate the Social Democratic agenda in such a way that it could be incorporated into mainstream Swedish political life. Branting's own comments on Waldenström after his death reveal a glimpse of how formidable Waldenström had been as a political opponent and underscore the influence this one-man party wielded: " . . . his death will not pass without our salute to an exceptional warrior, a strongman of uncommon proportion." (. . . *vid hans död skall icke saknas vår honnör för en stridens man som få, en kraftkarl utanför det vanliga måttet.*")[196] One common political strategy that Waldenström and Branting shared was an ability to transcend party ideology when it was deemed necessary for the overall success of democratic pluralism. Branting, while retaining an ideological liberalism, engaged himself in the leadership of the Socialist party with the goal of democratizing it.[197] Alternately, Waldenström retained his liberalism while making common cause with the conservative party in order to protest the anti-democratic nature of socialism. It was the showdown between these two viewpoints that forged the Social Democratic party as it emerged in the subsequent decades. Today Branting is widely praised for his genius; Waldenström, on the other hand, has rarely been studied with these questions in mind.

"Hjalmar Branting tries to scrub clean Hinke Bergegren, who proves to be the devil himself."
"Brantings Storbyk." Oskar Andersson. *Söndags-Nisse*. 1906. Reproduction: Kungliga biblioteket.

Historians have traditionally asserted that the religious revivals sparked by Pietism functioned as "lessons in democracy" for lower- and middle class Swedes who were transitioning from their traditional, agricultural, and patriarchal society.[198] However, this connection has largely been left abstract, and these religious movements tend to be seen as having prepared the Swedish people for participation in the development of the modern welfare state, but not necessarily as having directly participated in the political process. Pietists are rather assumed to have remained on the sidelines. Instead, what becomes evident through a close analysis of Waldenström's career is that the Pietists were not just a prelude to the activity of later Social Democrats, but instead seem to have been rather influential in the creation of the emergent social and political paradigm of the twentieth century. In line with Sheri Berman's thesis, the Social Democratic party in Sweden can be seen as having been shaped by the criticism that it received from the Liberal and Moderate parties. To her thesis it seems appropriate to add that the "Waldenström Party" and other participants in the religious awakenings also threw their weight in this direction. The social-critical activity of Waldenström was directly absorbed into the overall societal paradigm as it evolved through fierce public debates. The defense of pluralism and democratic processes articulated at key moments may ultimately have helped to foster a more pluralistic environment than would have been the case if only one party had been allowed to predominate.

CHAPTER 9

Branting v. Waldenström: The Debate to Define Absolutism and Moralism

THE EVENTS OF 1908, as described above, introduce many aspects of the dialogue between Christianity and socialism that warrant further discussion. In seeking to trace the dialogue between Waldenström and the Socialists, it is necessary to focus on specific people with whom he was in dialogue. Perhaps most significant of these people in terms of his position in society and influence was Hjalmar Branting. Although they maintained a distance from one another in public and were by no means friends, Branting and Waldenström were two political opponents who became decisive in each other's political careers and influenced one another in profound ways that have not been seriously explored. As is the practice of many politicians who do not wish to draw too much attention to their opponents, both men avoided making direct reference to one another, choosing instead to focus on the issues themselves. However, in the statements that they made on these issues as well as in the passing commentary that they did make on one another, they revealed an acute awareness of the other's positions. Even in their derisive statements, they communicated their critiques to one another, which they each needed to address in the interest of their political survival. This chapter will present some of the exchange that occurred between them, particularly regarding their discussion about the nature of a specific type of absolutism, moralism, and the threat that moralism poses to pluralist democracy.

Lina Sandell-Berg and C. O. Berg. Photos from B. Wadström's *Ur Minnet och Dagboken; Anteckningar från åren 1848-1898*. 161.

As Sweden in the late 1800s was a small country, the various circles of elites in Swedish society in the period were closely interwoven, with dynamic interaction between various ideological groups. Leaders in the various political and social movements often knew one another, and in many cases had gone to school or church with one another. Such was the experience of Social Democratic leader Hjalmar Branting, who was particularly well connected in multiple circles. Although not religious later in life, Branting had been involved in the religious awakening in his youth, participating in the religious activities organized by C. O. Berg, an active participant in the Evangelical Homeland Foundation (EFS) and husband to the iconic newspaper editor and hymnwriter Lina Sandell-Berg. In the course of his participation in the religious awakening, a distaste for religion had developed for Branting, which had caused him to view religion as irrational, judgmental, and overly moralistic.[199] Thus when Branting came into conflict with leaders of the awakening, he had somewhat of an insider's perspective into the language and ideology of the movement. Branting leveled one critique in particular at the movement, that religion was moralistic and as such, posed a threat to pluralism and to a rationally constructed democracy.

This discussion of moralism that developed between Waldenström and Branting had wider implications than simply an opportunity for political mudslinging. The discussions about moralism became a moment of exchange, when each side was forced to reflect on and correct negative tendencies in their respective movements. On several occasions, through the vehicle of his newspaper *Socialdemokraten* ("The Social Democrat"), Branting's critiques of Waldenström became opportunities to correct negative trends in his own party. In a lengthy obituary for colleague Viktor Lennstrand in 1895, Branting pointed out that Lennstrand had begun as a student of Waldenström, who "as of then had not been revealed as the hypocrite he was." Lennstrand's enthusiasm for his free-church upbringing had once inspired him to dream of becoming a missionary to spread the Christian faith, but in losing this faith later in life, it had been replaced by the same zeal for socialism. He thus did become a missionary, Branting pointed out, although spreading a message *against* Christianity and instead promoting a so-called "utilitarianism" (*utilismen*) through his own organization "The Utilitarian Society."[200] Branting first praised Lennstrand for his contribution and legacy, but then issued his stern critique of Lennstrand's overzealous approach.[201] With this observation, Branting explained a defining characteristic of his political worldview, which was a resistance to "absolutism" and "moralism" whenever it appeared, even the secular version represented by Lennstrand. Religion needed to be defeated in the political arena not simply to the extent that it was a "lie," as Lennstrand found it to be, but because it so often could manifest itself as an uncompromising, conservative force and prevent necessary reforms. In his commentary concerning Lennstrand's campaign against Christianity, Branting noted that such a campaign was counterproductive and unnecessary. Scientific inquiry would lead to the inevitable result that religion would become irrelevant, as the societal causes of misfortune and inequality would be revealed by science and societal progress. Furthermore, this type of absolutism and moralism could come in the form of party ideology, as well. As a figure linking the Social Democratic and Liberal parties, Branting would experience this absolutism on several levels.

As newspaper editor, Branting found the opportunity to comment on literature and other cultural trends. Among these, Branting criticized August Strindberg's controversial *Blå bok* ("Blue Book") from 1907, seeing in him a similar animosity toward modern science and Darwinism, comparing him to both Waldenström and the evangelical newspaper *Svenska Morgonbladet*.[202] In a negative review of Selma Lagerlöf's novel *Jerusalem*, Branting also found cause to invoke Waldenström's name. In the novel, Lagerlöf had explored the psychological mindset of the religious revivals that occurred in the small parishes of central Sweden, and at one point in her fictional account, directly connected this type of spirituality to Waldenström's influence.[203] Branting's critique was along the lines of style, echoing the observation of literary critic Oscar Levertin, that Lagerlöf had attempted to elevate the "Waldenströmian simplemindedness of the pious farmers" (*waldenströmsk bondeenkelhet*) and present it in the form of high art, which it was not.²⁰⁴ On the occasion of the politician Karl Starbäck's fiftieth birthday in 1913, Branting took the opportunity to congratulate Starbäck as the man who finally succeeded in taking Waldenström's parliamentary seat several years earlier in the *Riksdag* in 1905. In doing this, Starbäck had, according to Branting's judgment, managed to drive back "the advance of the free-religious horde and the extreme absolutists" (*frireligiösa och extremt absolutiska anloppen*). In 1922, on the fiftieth birthday of Fabian Månsson, a left-leaning politician with free-church connections, Branting again commented on absolutism. In reviewing his political opinions in the "Tariff Debates" (*tullstriderna*), Branting said that Månsson had an absolutist's and moralist's perspective on the toll question, but despite that handicap, Månsson was nevertheless able to channel that negative impulse into a beneficial scientific approach to political questions, through a meticulous collection of data in making his arguments.²⁰⁵ Branting's presentations of Waldenström and anyone even remotely associated with the free-church camp thus often focused on identifying them as an example of absolutism and moralism. This also demonstrates important developments in Branting's own political philosophy, particularly the role that ideology should take in a pluralist democracy. Here he makes the implicit claim that all ideologies should be hindered from evolving toward their logical extremes, in the interest of maintaining space for criticism by other ideologies and dissenters.

Branting apparently never acknowledged that Waldenström held a similar understanding as he did of the importance of restraining ideological extremism. Waldenström's hard line against the Socialists was primarily due to his fears that the movement was driven by an uncompromising ideology that was opposed to democracy, and if allowed to be unchecked, would spell disaster for the democratic project. In this perennial face off, he and Branting both forced each other to explain why their own ideology, at its best, was *not* dogmatic and was instead compatible with democracy and parliamentary procedures. The references that Branting made about Waldenström are most interesting because of how he used them. He used these references not to critique Waldenström himself, but instead to critique *other people*, including people in his own party who exhibited these negative tendencies. In these instances, there are clear indications that Branting heard Waldenström's warnings about the dangers of undemocratic strains of socialism, internally acknowledged their validity, and addressed these concerns by targeting prominent people in the Liberal and Socialist folds who exemplified these same negative traits. At the same time, Branting weakened his political opponents by publicly presenting Waldenström as an idiot and extremist.

It is in these impressive acrobatic maneuvers that Branting demonstrated rhetorical and political brilliance.

Nevertheless, the public version of Social Democracy that Branting presented often bore little acknowledgement of the internal divisions and currents of extremism that were present in the party. Such is his evaluation in December of 1908.

> *Our Swedish socialist labor movement has a program that is happily free from theoretical doctrinairism and therefore also has stood not only unshaken but also uncriticized within the party itself for more than 11 years now. In our political praxis we have also proven ourselves to be happily free from the intransigent doctrinairism, which in its inflexibility sacrifices the possibility to accomplish* something, *because it is not possible to get* everything *or at least the* most *immediately according to our thinking. With an increasing authority there now follows a duty to continue in this same path. We have promised the working people of Sweden in these elections to do what we can in order to promote their wellbeing. Then it is also our duty as a party to with integrity, do our part to seek to bring about a left party such that the way is prepared this time for a genuine democratic breakthrough. Personal feelings or antipathies must in this work give way for the greater objective perspectives.*[206]

Branting's claim that the party was "happily free from theoretical doctrinairism" was in fact in direct contrast to the realities of that year, as the Amalthea Incident had taken place only months before, as had the banning of Hinke Bergegren from the party for the second time. The direction of the party was far from uncriticized then, and would continue to experience much more turmoil, as the extreme left remained critical and eventually separated to form its own party in 1917. At other times, Branting argued against the radical elements of his party who called for an immediate transfer of power. Branting maintained that the time was not right for such a takeover, as the Social Democrats and the others on the left were only united in their desire to win the election and lacked a coherent plan as to what to do once in power.[207] Branting's public presentation of the political situation in these decades can be seen as more prescriptive than descriptive, as he is a political leader attempting to inspire a certain vision for the party's future. There is therefore little use for him to acknowledge the role that was played by outside protesters like Waldenström, who drove these concerns about absolutism to the foreground, and thereby forced the Social Democratic party to distance itself from extremists.

Waldenström's criticisms of the Socialists also seem to have resonated with a wide segment of the population, which had connections to both the Social Democratic party and the free-church movement. The influence of Waldenström and his criticisms of socialism also set the stage for the choice of Branting as party leader over other candidates. This outcome was by no means a given, and in the formative years, there were far more radical leaders in the party, foremost of these being party founder August Palm. This struggle between Branting and Palm began during the years 1885–1887, when both men vied for control as the editor of the newspaper *Socialdemokraten*. This contest involved one of its more famous moments in the notorious episode called "The Scuffle" (*Slagsmålet*) in Stockholm in 1886, when a meeting of the Workers' Association (*Arbetarförening*) to discuss the future direction of the party erupted into a large-scale fist fight. Historian Ivar Sundvik identifies the reasons for the workers' eventual preference of Branting over Palm as being dependent on the fact that Branting identified with the values that pervaded this demographic. Though bitter battles raged over the question of leadership and party direction, in the end the workers were quite simply more heavily influenced by Liberal values and other social movements than they were by the worldview of Karl Marx. Sundvik summarizes the origins of this choice thusly:

> *The majority of the representatives in Social-Demokraten's contracting party were certainly that sort of social democrats. They were reformists, without revolutionary disposition, still residing in the liberal and open-minded thought patterns inherited from their homes, acquired in the handcraft-influenced labor unions, in the free churches or the Good Templar movement. Perhaps ideologically [they] belonged more there than with Marx. It was this type of worker in the contracting party who lifted Branting to the chief post in Social-Demokraten and wanted to have him as leader in the struggle for a better society.*[208]

Sundvik here suggests that those members espousing Liberal values in the end simply outnumbered the members who embraced more revolutionary variants of socialism. If this is true that many Social Democrats who had roots in the free-church movement retained this earlier influence, then Waldenström's protests of absolutism within the party would certainly have had a residual influence. Historian Hans Falk also points out that publications by Marx were not readily available in Swedish at the turn of the century, which explains the preference of the workers for Branting over the more Marxist-inspired leaders like Palm.[209] They simply had more chances to read other authors than they had to read Marx. For many of these people in the working class, this list of authors would have undoubtedly included Rosenius's and Waldenström's books and newspaper articles. Furthermore, Waldenström is known to have been involved in the worker's society in Gävle (*Gefle Arbetareförening*), having directly represented their interests in the tariff debates in 1886, enjoyed their endorsement in the election of 1901 for city council (*stadsfullmäktig*), and even donated books to their library.[210] As pointed out before, Waldenström enjoyed a readership that surpassed the readership of other leading secular authors, such as Levertin and von Heidenstam. If Marx was not readily available in print, as Hans Falk suggests, then it is no exaggeration to suppose that Waldenström had a wider readership among Swedish workers than did Marx. At any rate, the influence of the dominant political ideology of the free-church movement was far reaching.

While Waldenström and Branting each argued against and distanced themselves from absolutism, they did this in different ways. When Branting addressed absolutism, he very often used "moralism" as a synonym, pointing his critique mainly at religiously inspired moralism, but also, as evident in the commentary about Lennstrand above, addressing secular absolutism in his own party. In the political arena, Waldenström focused on addressing political absolutisms, usually using the term "anarchist" as a synonym. Also, while Waldenström and Branting publicly portrayed each other as representing the absolutist's stance, in practice their arguments preserved space for opposition and dissent, and thus left room for one another in the public sphere. The valuable insight that can be taken from their debates is that they ultimately agreed on what the dangers of absolutism were, as well as the necessity of safeguarding the political arena from excesses.

Absolutism and moralism are distinct, but closely related concepts. Both Branting and Waldenström had occasion to define what they meant by moralism as they discussed a book published by a Marxist priest. H. F. Spak, known as the "Socialist Priest," had fused Marxism with his Lutheran worldview and became an active agitator for the labor movement, enjoying popularity as a speaker at demonstrations. The book he published, *Gammal och ny moral* ("Old and New Morality") aroused controversy for its relativism regarding morality. Interestingly enough, it was none other than Branting who wrote the foreword to this book (6 April 1910). While showing support for the author's intentions, Branting took the opportunity to express his criticism on the use of religion to inform politics.

> *As a Christian priest the author naturally sees the development of the world first and foremost with the eye of a moralist. On the contrary, Marxism's distinctive is for him that* economic development

> is the driving force of history, to the extent to which it propels or undermines the position of power of different classes, while morality quite simply expresses in its area the needs of different periods and classes and furthermore changes with these. Here we see little of these classes, apart from the present, but we read much about the doctrine of various moral teachers and the perfection of their ideas toward the absolute. Morality is therefore freed from the context of which, according to Marxism, it is a product, and hovers like a spiritual power over human evolution, leading it toward the absolute ideal, which was already given to us in Christ. It hardly needs to be added that the author does like every theologian before him, the so-called liberal minded thinkers just like the orthodox; each and every one rewrites his image of Christ to be in line with his own conception of moral perfection.[211]

As Branting indicates in this foreword and Marx encouraged in his manifesto, Spak took the stance that morality, or values regarding acceptable and unacceptable behavior, were the product of a given historical moment, and should not be seen as eternally relevant. These moral codes were instituted by the dominant classes as a means of protecting their lifestyle and interests at the expense of the underclasses. This morality then becomes a hindrance to progress, whenever societal circumstances change. The moral practices that were advantageous during one generation cannot be assumed to be advantageous in all ages and circumstances, and therefore morals can become outdated. Thus Spak identified the difference between "old" and "new" morals, and urged that Swedish society would not confuse morality with justice. This definition of morality was widespread among the leaders of the labor movement. During the Great Strike of 1909, when Socialist newspapers described the need to break Swedish laws and legal contracts between employers and workers, this was explained as an example of how "the Great Strike had a new morality" (*storstrejken hade en ny moral*). Waldenström protested this as duplicity and urged that morality not be relativized.[212]

It is remarkable that Branting would involve himself with a religious author like Spak, not least because of Spak's marginal position within both the Christian and Socialist circles. But it also could be seen as a way in which Branting attempted to court a fringe minority. Socialism traditionally had strong anticlerical tones, so Branting's close engagement with Spak demonstrates Branting's tolerance of a minority view within his party. It also demonstrates again that the socialism that Branting was arguing for was one in which pluralism and tolerance would be valued. As demonstrated by his comments, Branting adhered to a Marxist reading of history that scientific inquiry and enlightened discourse would make religion obsolete by eliminating the need for supernatural explanations to answer questions about the unknown. Moralism here was identified as the rigid adherence to codes of conduct which were designed to correct negative behavior in society. These codes of conduct would not have a place in the new order, since decisions of what was advantageous for society would be based on scientific inquiry. Moralism would become a restrictive force on progress, because it would stifle debate and undermine democracy.

Furthermore, much of Waldenström's motivation in remaining active in politics seems to have been an effort to maintain a sense of normalcy for the inclusion of religion in the public sphere, and to not let Christian politicians be marginalized as moralizers and absolutists. Branting's endorsement of Spak's book also carried with it an implied endorsement of Spak's opinion of Waldenström, which was starkly negative.

> *The modern "believers" who now so loudly confess their literal faith on everything "which is written," would altogether certainly be caught up with holy rage and fury, if they managed by accident to look up their Old Testament and could see there how violently the prophets treated the upper class of their time.*[213]

This is a direct reference to the Waldenströmian slogan "*Var står det skrivet?*" ("where is it written?"), which Spak is using as an example of how religious leaders blindly misused their literal interpretations of scripture and ignored the seemingly contradictory nature of some passages of the Bible. Waldenström, in turn, saw the danger that this accusation posed to the position of Christian groups within Swedish democracy. He responded to these types of accusations as an assault on all religion, and attempted to refute the notion that religious people were any less rational in their beliefs than adherents to secular ideologies.

> *And what is socialism as seen from the Christian perspective? As an answer I will state some of the words of one of the socialist members of parliament. He says: "To a great extent the church and the prayer house are a retreat from life. These people are just as unreceptive to common sense, truth and justice as beheaded corpses. It is just as impossible to bring such an individual to enlightenment and knowledge as it is to teach a hen to learn the multiplication tables. When religion is a hindrance in this way for the labor movement's march forward, then the party will direct its agitation not simply toward the religion of the state church or Christianity, but toward everything that can rightfully be seen as religion."*
>
> *Well, that is how it sounds, when people speak plainly. But still there are many good Christians who are not able to see any*

real danger in socialism, and even are angered by the battle cry: "Front against socialism!"[214]

In the debate about moralism and absolutism, both Pietists and Socialists used certain labels to identify when the other side had crossed the line between reasonable discussion and fanaticism. Pietists called this "anarchism" and "syndicalism," even when it was not. Socialists similarly called it "moralism" and "simplemindedness" (*enfaldighet*) and later "fundamentalism." Each thus talked about and warned against the same dangers of absolutism, but had a specific code that distanced the phenomenon from their own activities and made it seem like the private domain of their opponents. While Waldenström was painted as the epitome of blind religiosity and reactionary thinking, he responded by doing the same thing, by pointing out where various Socialists were moralizing and allowing their ideology to impinge on healthy democratic debate. One thing that Branting did not acknowledge openly, but which Waldenström did, was that secular ideologies could take on a moralizing character just as well as any religious worldview could. As evidenced in his political speeches, Waldenström cast several Socialist leaders as absolutists, namely Hinke Bergegren, Anton Nilson, and even August Palm, as he deemed their speeches to be uncompromising in their adherence to orthodox Marxism. Waldenström's case was that intolerant orthodoxy on any end of a political spectrum, left or right, poses the same threat as any other absolutism.

Waldenström instructing his "pupils" in the free-religious voting school—"Please repeat after me, boys." "I den frireligiösa valmansskolan." Edvard Forsström. *Puck*. Aug. 1902. Reproduction: Kungliga biblioteket.

CHAPTER 10

The Impact of the Free-Church Vote

WHILE BRANTING AND WALDENSTRÖM could agree that absolutism and moralism posed great threats to the progress of democracy, they represented differing perspectives as to how to achieve a balanced, but still progressive, political arena. Branting had urged cooperation between the Liberals and the Social Democrats as the way to create a strong and effective second chamber in the parliament. The first chamber was dominated by conservative interests, and therefore a coalition of left-wing parties in the second chamber was seen as an essential element in achieving reforms. This cooperation was also essential for the Social Democrats in the 1890s and 1900s, as without Liberal assistance, their entry into the *Riksdag* would possibly have been delayed for years. Alternately, Waldenström's prognosis was that the best way to ensure balance was for the Conservative and Liberal parties to cooperate, which would allow the Liberal party to maintain its position as the main progressive party. If the Social Democrats surpassed the Liberal party in numbers, that would mean that the Liberals would have to either join with the Socialist agenda in order to maintain their position at all, make common cause with the conservatives in an attempt to balance out the Socialists, or face the prospect of the party being split in two. Repeated warnings appeared in Waldenström's newspaper articles, which predicted that if the Liberals made common cause with the Socialists, they would soon be forced to abandon their Liberal values, which were incompatible with the demands of an orthodox Marxist interpretation of socialism.

While Branting's careful acrobatics in brokering cooperation between the Liberals and Social Democrats have been duly noted by historians, there is less certitude regarding the impact that religious figures like Waldenström had in parliament. In a 1975 survey of the role that the folk movements played in the decades in question, historian Sven Lundkvist implied that the free-church movement did not have that large of an influence on politics, relative to other countries.[215] This is a puzzling conclusion, considering the great number of politicians with free-church connections that were active in the *Riksdag* in these decades. In the 1880s, there were as many as thirty members of parliament in the second chamber (13 percent), which gradually climaxed in 1911, with fifty-one members (22 percent).[216] Even before the reform of the *Riksdag*, there had been politicians with clear connections to the awakening, such as L.V. Henschen and Sven Rosendahl in the 1850s and early 1860s. By contrast, historian Lydia Svärd has suggested that the impact was quite significant, and has counted at least twenty politicians with ties to the awakening, who were ushered into politics in the new two-chamber parliament in 1867. She also notes that the year 1884 was a breakthrough year for such politicians to gain prominence and influence. Among the more famous politicians who appeared at this time were not only Waldenström and Ekman, but also E.W. Wretlind, J. M. Eriksson, and Erik Nyström.[217] This also does not take into account the members who were involved in the free-church movement, but did not explicitly acknowledge their affiliation. It is important to point out that these were members of a movement, not card-carrying members of a party, so they are not easily counted and also crossed party lines. Questions of religious freedom and temperance were often important to these politicians and their constituents. However, they also weighed in on discussions of all manner of issues, and drew voters away from other parties.

It is also important to note that the highest concentration of free-church members was in the Liberal party.[218] This fact sheds a great deal of light on the question of why Waldenström was so aggressive in voicing his concern that the Liberals not abandon their traditional program in favor of that of the Socialists. Many of them were members of his church, and for that reason, this courtship with socialism was perhaps experienced like a personal betrayal. Furthermore, the fact that many members of the Liberal party resonated with Waldenström's values cannot have been overlooked by Branting. This does much to explain why, for instance, Branting chose to take seriously the more marginal religious figures within his own party, H. F. Spak and Kata Dahlström. Branting's diplomatic attitude toward religion was more than simply a demonstration of enlightened tolerance. It was also an essential strategic maneuver, since one of his main goals was accomplishing the collaboration between the Liberal party and the Social Democrats. Although Waldenström had gradually drifted to the right, thereby alienating many in his own church,[219] the degree of his influence over the

Liberal party remained uncertain. With Waldenström repeatedly warning the Liberal party not to cooperate with the Social Democrats, it therefore was quite logical for Branting to make the endorsement of Spak's book. Christians, both within the Church of Sweden and in the free churches, were voting constituencies that Branting could not afford to alienate. From this perspective, tolerance of religion in politics was less a magnanimous act and more an example of calculated realism. Waldenström's claim that socialism was absolutist and moralist thus forced an endorsement of pluralism within the Social Democratic party.

In this dance around the Midsommar pole, Waldenström is in the ring just to the right of the pole. Hinke Bergegren is the second man to his left, and Hjalmar Branting is the third. Prime Minister E. G. Boström is playing the tuba. "Två ur dansen." Oskar Andersson. *Söndags-Nisse*. 21 June 1903. Reproduction: Kungliga biblioteket.

From the founding of the party in 1889 well into the first years of the twentieth century, the gains by the Social Democrats were modest. However, by 1908, these gains accelerated dramatically. After the 1908 elections, the Liberals held 105 seats, followed by the Conservatives with ninety-one seats, and the Social Democrats with thirty-four seats. While still a minority, the Social Democrats had made a great leap that year, gaining twenty-one seats, most of which were taken from the conservatives. The 1911 elections left the Liberals with 102 seats, the Conservatives with sixty-four seats, and the Social Democrats also with sixty-four. In the special spring elections of 1914, this trend was drastically reversed, with the Liberals shrinking to seventy-one seats, the Conservatives reclaiming their majority with eighty-six seats, and the Social Democrats rising to seventy-three. The regular elections in the fall of 1914 left the numbers at fifty-seven Liberals, eighty-six Conservatives and eighty-seven Social Democrats.[220] In a matter of seven years, the parliament had thus gone from being dominated by the Liberal party to being sharply divided between the Conservatives and the Social Democrats. The Liberal votes were courted by both sides.

Table 1: Comparison of the outcome of four elections

	Liberals	Conservatives	Social Democrats
1908:	105	91	34
1911:	102	64	64
1914 (Spring):	71	86	73
1914 (Fall):	57	86	87

Long critical of socialism, in 1908 Waldenström's predictions of the negative outcome of the relationship between the Liberals and Social Democrats intensified. His newspaper articles during this time warned that if Liberals made common cause with Social Democrats and did not question this party's ideology, they would soon find themselves out of the job.

> We have had a terrible fuss during the parliamentary elections that passed during the month of September. There were horrible divisions. The openly and energetically anti-Christian socialism has taken a number of seats, due to the support of the so-called liberals. These people, for their part, in exchange gained the support of the socialists for some of their candidates. But they know full well that as soon as they have helped the socialists so far that they can manage on their own, then they will kick out their helpers. They have done this in a number of places at this year's elections especially in Stockholm where they have kicked out several liberals. Liberal newspapers who realize the danger of socialism

> *and fight against it, have complained about the "right" because it has not wanted to help them against the socialists. But at the same time the idea has been altogether foreign for them that victory against socialists could have been won in many places, if the liberals had supported the candidates on the right. But no. They have rather voted with the socialists without considering where this would lead.*[221]

After the results of the 1911 elections, Waldenström perceived that the Liberal party's current dominance was an illusion. Although some talked of a "lower house parliamentarianism," meaning that the two left parties of the second chamber would be able to overrule the conservative first chamber, Waldenström dismissed this as "humbug." Instead, he expected two things: that the Social Democrats would call the shots for the Liberal party, and that the current weak position of the conservatives would eventually be balanced out by an exodus of Liberals to the right. He thus urged that the newly-elected Liberal prime minister, Karl Staaff, make common cause with the conservatives (led by Arvid Lindman) as a way to balance out the influence of the Social Democrats and save the Liberal party. A telling insight into Waldenström's opinion of the balancing act that was necessary came in his article "*Staaf [sic] i kajutan Branting vid rodret*" ("Staaf in the cabin, Branting at the helm") from September 1911.

> *The liberal speakers have certainly tried to calm the general public. But Branting has spoken plain speech. He has let the liberals know that they will not get anywhere without the help of the socialists. Without this they stand <u>totally powerless</u>. But he has also let them know that they cannot count on the help of the socialists without extensive compensation. He has let them know that their actual task is to make way for socialism which will be the final heir. […]* ~~How long a left government will be able to hold out against socialism that will depend <u>on the right</u>.~~
>
> *Any person who has any kind of education has been able to see this for a long time. It has also been said repeatedly from the side of the moderates. Even such liberal newspapers as Aftonbladet and Svenska Dagbladet have realized this and shaken their heads doubtfully. But neither Branting's nor Lindman's words have been able to open the eyes of the liberal voters. […]*
>
> *15 or 20 years ago there were voices raised that pointed out the danger of socialism's advance. The answer was then—and I myself got to receive this answer—"What does anyone have to fear from a handful of socialists?" It was treated like fear of the dark. And now? Now the socialists' party is the dominant one in*

> the Riksdag. It is that party that will always come to make the decisions in every question, where the liberals and the moderates stand against one another.
>
> [. . .] And so it is shown clearer than day for anyone who does not cover his eyes, that talk of a lower house parliamentarianism is a big humbug. For that requires by necessity a majority party in the Second Chamber and not merely a coalition of two parties that are sharply divided against one another, whose only genuine common interest is to topple the standing government. As soon as this comes to a positive political task, then Mister Staaff may speak as much as he wants about a "productive cooperation"—Mister Branting has in a rather harsh way let him know that any other cooperation than such that promotes the interests of the socialists will not come into question. Branting can therefore at any moment that is convenient topple a liberal government, if the right does not save her. That is how the matter stands in reality.[222]

It is significant to point out that the "productive cooperation" between these two parties did lead to the rapid decline of the Liberal party. As indicated by the election results above, by the time of the regular elections of 1914, the Liberals had decreased in number, so much so that they fell behind the Conservatives. Waldenström's prediction in this regard was largely accurate. What Waldenström did not acknowledge was that the cooperation between the Liberals and Social Democratic parties would also leave an indelible mark on the program of the Social Democrats, which functioned to pull them into the mainstream. Even after surpassing the number of seats held by the Conservatives in 1914, the Social Democrats still needed to court the Liberal party if they were going to be able to establish any dominance over the Conservatives. In this process, they also needed to make their program palatable to the Liberals, which drew the Social Democratic agenda toward the center and toward compromise.

Furthermore, although Waldenström painted a picture of a close courtship between Staaff and Branting, in reality this relationship does not seem to have been all that comfortable. Historian Sven Ulric Palme has explained that the relationship between Staaff and Branting was actually far from comfortable, and that Staaff did not want to cooperate any more than what was deemed necessary. According to this interpretation, Staaff prioritized strengthening the left wing within the Liberal party, at the expense of the Social Democrats.[223] Waldenström's prediction, that cooperation with the Social Democrats would alienate the right wing within the Liberal party, certainly contributed to forcing this hand. This negative attention in the press put added pressure on Staaff to concentrate on reconciling the various factions within the Liberal party, and thus kept the Social Democrats at arm's length. As the Conservatives and Social Democrats each continued to court the Liberals during these turbulent years, the most logical result was that extremist political movements of all persuasions were simply not able to dominate in the *Riksdag*, as neither the right nor the left could afford to alienate the centrist position of the Liberals.

"The Summer Promenade of Politics." Waldenström's commentary about the direction of the Liberal party did not go unnoticed in the press. This cartoon depicts the flirtation between Hjalmar Branting and Karl Staaff, "According to Waldenström" ("Efter P.W."). On either side of the election urn are a fanatical Hinke Bergegren on the left and the conservative politicians on the right. "Politikens sommarpromenad." *Söndags-Nisse*. 28 June 1902. Reproduction: Kungliga biblioteket.

"Hercules at the Crossroads." The picture shows Karl Staaff dressed as Hercules, standing at a crossroads and testing the winds, which are coming from the leading newspapers. On the left is a cloud marked "*Svenska Morgonbladet*," in which Waldenström was a regular contributor. (In the past, this picture has been identified as Per Ollén, the editor, but this image more resembles Waldenström.) Directly opposite is Branting, blowing out of a cloud marked "*Social Demokraten*," of which he was the editor. "Herkules vid skiljovägen." Edvard Forsström. *Puck*. 1913. Reproduction: Kungliga biblioteket.

Another aspect of this balancing act between parties was that it was apparent that there were differing interpretations of how to operate under the current constitution while striving to reform it. Waldenström viewed the constitution as a binding contract, which though it could be revised, must be done in the right order and with consensus—in other words, it must be done "the Swedish way." One of the distinguishing features of Swedish democracy is a high level of preference for decision by committee. This practice has old roots in the tradition of using committees (*utskott*) in the *Riksdag* throughout the nineteenth century, but the formative period for this type of decision making has sometimes been attributed to Erik

Gustaf Boström's use of committees during his time as prime minister from 1891–1900 and 1902–1905. Historian Torkel Nyman presents Boström as having been instrumental in developing the trend of using committees to maintain control of politics in parliament. Whereas previous prime ministers had fallen from power when they had gone against the majority opinion of the *Riksdag*, Boström developed a sophisticated means of predicting the outcome of votes through discussion by a committee of strategically chosen members.[224] Two benefits came from this process: one was that the prime minister was able to test the results of a vote in advance, and second, he was able to control the outcome in favor of his own policies. The goal of these committees was to solidify political positions in advance of voting, and thereby defuse the level of conflict in controversial questions. It also allowed Boström to remain prime minister, even when representing a minority viewpoint. Waldenström came of age as a politician during these years and can be seen as reflecting the expectation that consensus is built in this kind of committee work.

Boström's legacy is multifaceted. On the one hand, he represents a conservative figure who, inspired by the model set by Otto von Bismarck, attempted to tightly control the decisions of government, even when he was in a minority position in relation to the rest of the *Riksdag*. He was also one of the last prime ministers who presided over the parliament as a royally-appointed cabinet figure. However, as Nyman points out, he was also a key transitional figure in developing modern Swedish parliamentary practice. While trying to control outcomes of voting by carefully orchestrating bipartisan committees, he eventually lost control, as these committees came to reflect a cross-section of the political landscape of the parliament as a whole. His strategy in choosing committee members was based on the political clout that these members had within their respective parties.[225] This allowed all or most of the prevailing perspectives to be represented in the committee, and they were also represented more equally than in the larger assembly. In other words, regardless of how many members of each party there were in parliament, because these committees were smaller, there was more potential for opposing views to be given equal footing. The high level of importance played by committees in this period can be seen as having ultimately diminished the threat posed by shear majority rule, as minority perspectives were ensured at least some level of representation. Here one can see an example of the style of power-sharing or consociational government advocated by Arend Lijphart, presented in chapter 1. Even if this favorable situation for a power-sharing government was a byproduct (or unforeseen consequence) of Boström's overall strategy, it nevertheless can explain in part why Swedish parliamentary procedure developed in this direction.

It is within the context of the Boström years that Waldenström served most of his time in parliament, and he also came to be a regular member on these committees. According to the *Riksdag protokoll*, Waldenström served on no fewer than sixteen committees, fourteen of those committees being during Boström's tenure as prime minister.[226] There were both standing committees and *ad hoc* committees. Perhaps the most prestigious of the standing committees was the constitution committee (*konstitutionutskottet*), on which Waldenström served in 1900, 1901, and 1902. The constitution committee comprised twenty members, who were responsible for reviewing the laws that were proposed in the *Riksdag* and determining whether these laws were in line with the national constitution (*grundlagar*), and then referring the proposed laws for further review by another appropriate committee, in the event that this was not able to be determined by the *Riksdag*.[227] This involvement on the constitution committee did two things for Waldenström's political philosophy: it galvanized his loyalty to Swedish constitutional law and the democratic processes necessary to amend and develop those laws, and it galvanized his opposition to any threat to those processes. Waldenström became one of the more outspoken champions of constitutional due process. Socialism was to be protested because, he thought, its basic tenets were anti-democratic. Waldenström took the revolutionary rhetoric of Socialist columnists like Hinke Bergegren seriously, and as a result, predicted that Socialist activity would circumvent constitutional and democratic due process. All of the "conservative" positions that he took, including the defense of the rights of the monarch, were based in this central concern that due process needed to be followed in amending Swedish constitutional law.

Due to his close association with the committee system, and thereby its architect, Boström, Waldenström was presented by the left wing of the Liberal party and the Social Democrats as a conservative and a monarchist (as portrayed in the cartoon below). Waldenström did have a relatively supportive relationship to the Swedish monarch, Oscar II, and subsequently his son Gustav V, who was active in politics as crown prince even before succeeding his father in 1907. Waldenström followed what had by that time become an established trend among Pietists throughout Lutheran Scandinavia and Prussia of cultivating close relationships with the royal courts. As the monarch was also the head of the church, this relationship was essential for the survival of Pietists during the years when there were harsh restrictions on their activity, since it was not approved by the state church. Only the patronage of the monarchs could overrule the laws of the church that restricted unofficial meetings, the anti-conventicle edicts. Even after the reforms of 1858 relaxed these restrictions, the attempts at censorship continued, as did the relationship between the Pietists and the royal court. One of the more famous episodes of this interaction between the Pietists and the crown came when the celebrated composer and performer, Oscar Ahnfelt, faced criticism for his unorthodox evangelistic message and performances. His wide popularity as the "spiritual troubadour," wowing audiences with his voice and dexterity playing a ten-string guitar, was perceived as a threat by some among the clergy, who sought to ban him from performing. When asked what he would do about this, King Karl XV responded that he needed to investigate the matter himself before deciding. Ahnfelt was summoned to the royal palace to perform, an event which has taken on the character of legend. The song chosen was an enchanting ballad, newly written for the occasion by Lina Sandell, "*Vem klappar så sakta i aftonens frid på ditt hjärta?*" ("Who knocks so gently in the evening's peace on your heart?"). Ahnfelt's performance of this strategically chosen song worked; the king was apparently emotionally moved by the "knocking of the Lord," and responded by granting Ahnfelt the right to freely perform "in both his kingdoms" (Norway and Sweden).[228] The Pietists were not quick to forget the fact that their survival had occasionally been dependent on this kind of monarchical intervention and pardon. This type of sentiment coincidentally also affirmed Geijer's Romantic view of the monarch as the defender of the people over and against the "gentlefolk," a view toward monarchy which was more problematic among the Socialists for instance.[229] Viewed from the outside by critical Socialists, the Pietists were hopelessly conservative, even if their reasons for expressing support for the monarchy were multifaceted.

"Before the Masterpiece" shows a painting of Boström, seated as an Eastern mystic, surrounded by sycophantic admirers, including Waldenström, kneeling to the right. The men in the gallery represent newspaper editors, who are saying "Look there, a painting in my taste." Per Ollén is to the far right and is holding a copy of *Svenska Morgonbladet*. "Inför mästerverket." Edvard Forsström. Reproduction: Kungliga biblioteket.

Oscar Ahnfelt. Photo from B. Wadström's *Ur Minnet och Dagboken; Anteckningar från åren 1848–1898*. 48.

The extent of the king's powers had been established by the 1809 constitution, the very constitution which Waldenström had spent years interpreting and defending through his participation on the *Riksdag* constitution committee. While the king's powers were spelled out by the constitution, by the turn of the century the Swedish political system had evolved away from the model of absolutist monarchy that had prevailed earlier in the century. By the end of the reign of Oscar II, it was no longer acceptable for the king to intervene in politics, especially to undermine the decisions of the prime minister. This came to a head in 1911 and 1914, when differing understandings of the constitution from the right and the left clashed. After the elections of 1911 had resulted in Conservative prime minister, Arvid Lindman's resignation, Gustav V attempted to form a new government with the Liberal Karl Staaff. Staaff had no expectation of simply being an appointed cabinet member to the king, and instead came with his own demands. These included that the upper chamber of parliament would be dissolved and a new election called (which would be guaranteed to result in a decrease of Conservative influence in that chamber). The king had little opportunity to refuse, since Staaff was the only logical person who could serve to form a government. In practice, this episode exposed the reality that the king's actual power had decreased. The constitution placed him above politics, but that had come to mean that he was not to directly challenge his government, nor was he to speak in any partisan conflict. When national concerns over defense had arisen and prompted calls to increase the capacity of the military, Staaff faced criticisms to the right and the left. The left thought he was too accommodating to those in favor of defense, and the right thought he was non-committal. The impatient conservatives started taking up voluntary collections in order to fund the purchase of armored ships, culminating in a demonstration of 30,000 "farmers" who marched to the royal palace in 1914. Gustav V, thinking he had the right to speak "above politics" in response to a manifestation of his subjects, effectively challenged the position of his government during his address to the demonstrators. The "Castle Yard Crisis" (*Borggårdskris*), as this event came to be called, resulted in Karl Staaff's resignation, after he had unsuccessfully requested that the king submit his speech in advance for approval. This episode resulted in a redefinition of where the actual power resided in Swedish politics, and there was an increasing understanding among Liberals that practice had outgrown the letter of the constitution. With the king thus unable to form or dissolve governments without the approval of his ministers, this development set the stage for the breakthrough of true parliamentarianism.

When Waldenström took part in the debates surrounding this crisis, he defended the monarch as merely exercising powers that were rightfully his according to the constitution. This brought Waldenström into conflict with both the Liberal and Social Democratic parties. However, regardless of any personal allegiances to the crown that he might have had, his protest of the "ultimatum against the king" after the Castle Yard Crisis was articulated first and foremost as a defense of constitutional law. In a three-part series of newspaper articles, in which he drew on his experience on the constitution committee, he sympathized with the democratic reforms that were being advocated, but explained that they needed to take place through the proper channels for amending the constitution. If the Swedish parliament and prime minister were going to make the claim that the king had no right to intervene in politics, then they needed to amend the constitution to say so. Referencing the earlier pronouncement of a certain Direktör Holmberg, he noted that common practice was to refer to the "state council" (*statsråd*) as "the government" (*regeringen*), but not include the king, who was the regent (they had abandoned the practice of referring to *kungliga majestätet* or "His Royal Majesty").

> *If one wants to be done with royal power, then rewrite our constitution, say farewell to the king and set in his place a president instead. That would be genuine, that would be truth.*[230]

In part II, which was written after the change in prime ministers, he recommended to the incoming state council a "peaceful, sensible, purposeful movement forward" (*lugnt, sansadt, målmedvetet framåtskridande*).

> We have a constitution. According to it the king is the one who rules the kingdom—the king personally, not a royal neuter or phantom. <u>Everyone</u> must acknowledge that this is prescribed by the constitution, even those who earnestly wish that it was not so. But alongside the constitution on the other hand people have put forth something that is called "constitutional praxis," which has gradually become a party slogan and "realized its breakthrough" (!) in the election of 1911. Now conflict has arisen. The king holds fast to the explicit words of the constitution, which are not denied by anyone, nor have they been refuted by anyone. The liberal party places the aforementioned praxis <u>over</u> the constitution, "This praxis," said the socialist Mr. Staffen in the First Chamber, "is the true life of the constitution, while the constitution is only a temporary expression of the understanding at a given moment. When this praxis has reached a certain development, the time will come to also change the letter of the constitution." By saying this he certainly touched on the true meaning of the left. He also expressed here with clear and true words that the present conflict is based on the contrast between the words of the constitution on the one side and a "constitutional praxis that has grown up around the constitution." And thus the remarkable situation occurs, that the king who in accordance with his stipulated duty and royal oath, holding fast to the constitution, is accused for having behaved unconstitutionally, and even "having jeopardized the constitution," while the party holding power for the time being <u>and its government, which has sworn allegiance to the same constitution as the king</u>, refuses to act constitutionally and to <u>defend</u> our constitution, when it consciously acts in conflict with its unambiguous words. And <u>Christian</u> members of parliament are even going along with this!
>
> That there are people who wish for a completely implemented parliamentarianism after the English model, where the ministers are regent and the king is a sort of secretary, who countersigns the decisions of the ministers, that is understandable. That they work toward this goal, this is their right, and no one can blame them for that. But this shall be achieved by changing the constitution.[231]

He concluded his long explanation by recommending that the party leaders Edén and Branting "not order the frying pan until the grouse has been shot" (*icke beställa stekpanna, förrän tjädern är skjuten*). In part III, he defended the act of the king as being a proper response to his subjects, when the

30,000 farmers marched on the palace to demand that he investigate the issue of purchasing armored cruisers (*pansarbåtar*) for the navy.[232] According to Waldenstrom, these farmers were operating through a traditional channel that was open to the Swedish people, particularly used by minorities, which was to seek the direct intervention of the monarch on their behalf. The monarch in turn, he thought, ought to be able to exercise his role as an intermediary. Waldenström's position aligned with the Conservatives in that he is deferring to the constitution, but he is not denying the possibility that the constitution could and should be rewritten, thereby also demonstrating his more characteristic Liberal orientation. It is valid here to interpret him as being sincerely conflicted on this issue.

Waldenström's reverence for the constitution demonstrated an expectation that in a democracy, legal precedents need to be respected, even when social expectations have changed and society is in the process of rewriting its laws. What was at risk was national confidence in the democratic project. Waldenström had interpreted the Castle Yard Crisis as a crisis of trust in constitutional democracy. The farmers who had presented their request to the king were expressing their will through one of the channels traditionally outlined in the constitution. For them to have approached the king, instead of the prime minister, demonstrated for Waldenström an example of the way in which the people had felt that their voice was not sufficiently heard in parliament. This is what political scientists might call "forum shopping." For the Staaff government to dismiss this as out of line, when the constitutional laws had not yet been amended, would undercut popular trust in the legislative process. In Waldenström's view, it was essential that these reforms be pursued within the appropriate channels, as stipulated by legal precedent. Going outside of these channels would damage trust between the elected officials and voters, as well as civility between political opponents. When this trust breaks down, then the seeds of revolution are easily sown, as he saw it.

While Waldenström's explanation of his philosophy is clear enough in these articles, his critics found plenty of evidence to convince them that he was an unreflective conservative; his expressions of patriotism and support to the king also helped to fuel these accusations. Among his articulations was a speech written about the same time as the Castle Yard Crisis, in which he praised Gustaf V as a defender of the Swedish people, and a rallying point for defending the nation. Waldenström suggested that the current king, like Gustav Vasa hundreds of years earlier, could have a central role to play as a symbolic rallying point for building up the defenses of the nation against foreign advances.[233] For Social Democrats, like Hjalmar Branting, who viewed all militarism as a plot by the ruling classes to suppress the labor movement and prevent democratization, Waldenström's patriotism was reprehensible. His status as a member of so many committees was mocked and even used to insinuate that he enjoyed elite favor.[234] By painting him as a conservative romantic, Waldenström's opponents neglected his central argument. His articles throughout these years can be seen as one long attempt to influence the free-church voters to remember their heritage of working within the Swedish constitution to accomplish their desired reforms. By warning against too many concessions with the Socialists, he was attempting to use the free-church vote to shift the national conversation in support of this kind of democratic reform. The strategy he chose was to make a defense of constitutional law, while also asserting that the establishment of a republic in Sweden was a feasible and worthy goal, provided that it took place through democratic channels.

CHAPTER 11

Majoritarianism v. Proportionalism: Making Space for Dissent

THE ROAD TO UNIVERSAL suffrage in Sweden had been a long and bumpy one, and the anticipation for these reforms was building up steadily during Waldenström's last years in parliament. Suffrage was one of the questions that came to define the elections of 1902 and 1905. The debate was a convoluted mess. Not only was there the question of whether or not to implement these reforms, there was a range of propositions as to how this should be done. Some of the proposals were based on the expected short term gains that a party could make in coming elections, and other proposals sought to exclude or limit new voters who would block pet interests. Historically, voting rights had been based on property and income. The parliamentary reforms in 1866 had established that in order to vote for a member of the *Riksdag*, a man needed to have 800 *riksdaler* in annual income or own property valuated at a minimum of 1,000 *riksdaler*. This meant that only 5.5 percent of the population could vote in national elections. For elections to the local government (*kommunalstämma*) the right to vote was open to adult men and to women who were legally declared of the age of majority, and the income threshold was 400 *riksdaler*. Furthermore, the relative weight of this vote increased on a graduated scale based on income level, in effect giving wealthier people multiple votes. Elections were counted on a majority-rule basis until the suffrage reforms of 1907–09, when proportionalism was introduced. The Liberals in parliament had initiated the push to expand voting rights already in the 1860s, which built to a crescendo by the turn of the century. However, when the reforms finally passed, the proposal had surprisingly come from Arvid Lindman's Conservative government, in which all elections to the first and second chambers of the *Riksdag* would be proportional and open to all men over twenty-four years of age (raised from twenty-one), and with no threshold income requirement. Women had to wait until 1918–21.

In the build up to the reform of 1907, there were a number of proposals on the table, which could be combined in countless ways. These can be generalized into four rough categories: 1) lowering the financial requirements for elections to one or both chambers; 2) eliminating the financial requirements and allowing all men of a certain age to vote in elections to one or both chambers; 3) instituting majority rule elections in one or both chambers (a "winner takes all" system); or 4) instituting proportional elections in one or both chambers (where all parties receiving a minimum threshold of votes gain seats in parliament based on the overall percentage of votes they received). Conservatives often blocked proposals that would allow the vote to lower-income or property-less citizens. Liberals and Socialists often preferred proposals for majority rule elections, as proportional elections were seen as a strategy by the Conservatives to retain influence even after they had lost elections. Such was the rationale for Karl Staaff's support of majoritarianism, as he hoped that this would facilitate the breakthrough of the left.[235] Of course, politicians were known to change their opinions based on when they felt they controlled the majority and when they did not. One of the interpretations of why the Lindman government came with its proposal was that the Conservatives realized that change was inevitable and wished to control this change on its own terms, hence the use of proportionalism. Waldenström's frequent expressions of support for proportionalism have thus caused him to be interpreted in a similar light as a reactionary conservative. The aim of this chapter is to revisit these pronouncements regarding voting reform from his perspective, namely to see how this support for proportionalism can be understood as independent of left-right politics, and rather fits into his broader ideas about democratic pluralism. As part of this discussion of voting rights, there will also be discussion of Waldenström's opinion about labor strikes and the dissenting strike-breakers. In his mind, these were related issues, as both situations concerned the rights of dissenters to maintain a seat at the table.

The debates surrounding Waldenström's campaigns during the years 1902 and 1905 were followed closely by the newspapers, among them *Gefle Dagbladet*, *Arbetarbladet*, and *Svenska Morgonbladet*. Central in the debates in Gävle was suffrage reform, and many in Liberal and Social Democratic camps were pushing for a straightforward introduction of suffrage for all men of a certain age. But like elsewhere, the proposals from both of these parties often demonstrated careful calculation to maintain party dominance in the short term against the resistance of the Conservatives. In other words, the reason why this debate was so hotly contested was because party survival (mainly for the Liberals) was thought to be dependent on achieving reform at the right time and in the right order, which sometimes caused politicians to change philosophy or to opt for incremental reforms rather than everything at once. The First Chamber was not a "House of Lords" in a strict sense, but as it was dominated by wealthy businessmen and members of the upper classes, it came to stand for Conservative opposition to suffrage reform. The impulses for reform thus often came from the Second Chamber, which is where Waldenström served and which had been the stronghold of the Liberals. This power struggle between the two chambers, as well as the struggle of the Liberals to maintain control of the lower house, added to the complexity of these elections. While Waldenström asserted a single-minded defense of universal suffrage and proportionalism, he came into conflict with other Liberals, who had abandoned proportionalism and opted for majoritarian elections in order to defeat the Conservatives' attempt to block suffrage reform. In his staunch refusal to deviate from his ideals in the short term, Waldenström often found himself at odds with the Liberal party, with whom he would otherwise have agreed.

Waldenström's stance became a pivotal issue in the elections of 1902 and 1905, the latter of which spelled the end of his career in parliament. In fact it is difficult to overstate the role that this played in the media's opinion about suffrage reform. Waldenström was very much wedded to the notion that the only proper way to introduce universal suffrage was to ensure that the elections took place according to a philosophy of proportionalism. As Waldenström represented the city of Gävle in the *Riksdag*, the debate was facilitated by the various newspapers in the area. He regularly sent in articles to *Gefle Dagblad*, a Liberal-leaning newspaper, as well as *Svenska Morgonbladet*, which was published out of Stockholm and was an organ for the free-church movement. In his articles and speeches reprinted by those papers as well as *Arbetarbladet*, a Socialist-leaning newspaper, Waldenström consistently took a hard line on two aspects of suffrage reform; support of proportionalism and a conviction that reform should take place by a reform of the national constitution (*grundlagar*), not the laws of the municipality (*kommun*). The reason for his rejection of the latter strategy was that he felt this was a "back door" means of achieving reform, which was more easily subject to being reversed. It also might mean that the new voting laws would retain the income requirements that were part of the local voting laws of the municipality. Proponents of reform at the level of the municipality sometimes endorsed an expansion of suffrage by simply lowering the minimum income requirements, not eliminating them.[236]

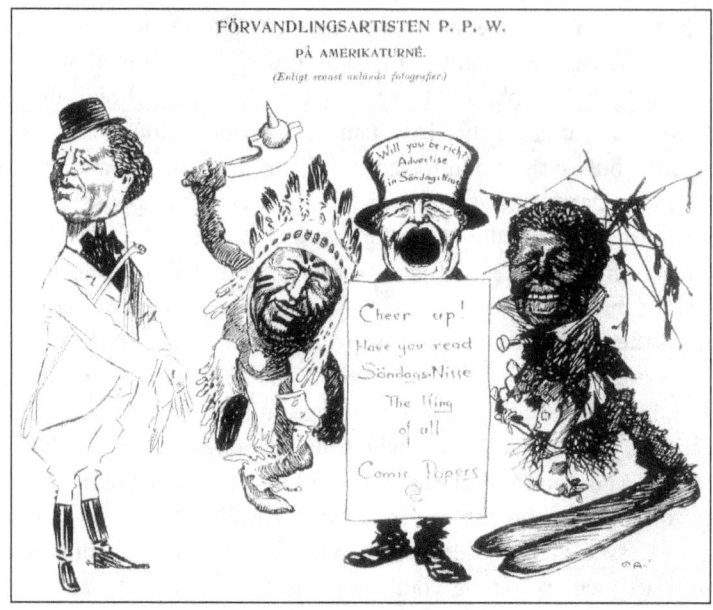

"The Quick-Change Artist P.P.W. on tour in America; According to most recent photos." "Förvandlingsartisten P.P.W." Oskar Andersson. *Söndags-Nisse*. 17 Nov. 1901. Reproduction: Kungliga biblioteket.

Waldenström remained consistent in his support of universal suffrage, but as he was committed to the idea that this needed to be done based on a proportional system and that the changes needed to originate with reform of the national *grundlagar*, he was not dependable in voting the Liberal party line. Other Liberals, as well as Social Democrats, were seeking to rally around majoritarian proposals, and were open to the idea of implementing reforms starting at the municipal level. Waldenström's independence was therefore a liability. In 1902, the Social Democratic paper *Arbetarbladet*, seized the opportunity to drive a wedge between Waldenström and the Liberals in Gävle. The editors pointed to his undependability as a party player, referred to his politics as "Waldenströmian Jesuitism," and identified him as the "greatest of flip-floppers," the "greatest enemy of culture," and "the most intolerant of the free-church apostles." They instead urged the citizens of Gävle to "throw off the weight of their Waldenströmian oppression."[237] Among the arguments used to convince their readers of this was the fact that Waldenström had played a divisive role in the campaign of 1899.

Election statistics were included, which showed that Waldenström drew votes away from both Liberal and Conservative candidates, and that he had no true home in either party. *Arbetarbladet* warned that Waldenström's politics were "kaleidoscopic," and that his presence in politics resulted in an obscuring of party lines. At the time, voters cast their ballots with two names, which they could mix at their choosing. The results of the 1899 elections were as follows:

Table 2: Outcome of the 1899 elections in Gävle

Brodin-Olsson (pure right list)	533
Lindh-Englund (pure left list)	331
Waldenström-Lindh	231
Waldenström-Brodin	171
Waldenström-Ahlström	169
Waldenström-Olsson	85
Waldenström-Jäder	32
Waldenström-Hedvall	6
Waldenström-Nordin	3
Waldenström-Hagelin	2
Waldenström-Sten Nordström	1
Waldenström-Löfstedt	1
Brodin-Lindh	39
Brodin-Englund	1
Brodin-Sten Nordström	1

Waldenström's dedicated supporters appear to have voted for him, even when that meant a mixed ticket. This had resulted in the impossibility of a victory by a "pure" party list (that is, two names from the same party). Waldenström was considered neither "right" nor "left," having not been accepted by the various political and social organizations as their official candidate. The fact that Waldenström still won is remarkable and demonstrates a deep level of personal loyalty to him within the electorate. *Arbetarbladet* encouraged their readership to not make the same mistake of 1899, and instead stick to voting for "pure" party tickets.[238]

One of his main opponents was the editor of *Gefle Dagblad*, Karl M. Lindh, who presented Waldenström's claims to being a Liberal as false. A letter to the editor in 1902 made the claim that Waldenström was not enough of a "liberal-minded thinker" (*frisinnade*), primarily because of his view on suffrage. The paper that year endorsed A. Larson, and urged its readers to see through Waldenström's deception. It is evident in the language used by *Gefle Dagblad* that such a rejection of Waldenström was a risky position to take, as he enjoyed such a high level of support in Gävle, a fact that the columnists drew attention to in their articles. Such accusations often begin with the qualification that they did not aim to attack Waldenström personally, but instead simply critiqued his politics. The papers' editorial opinion in the days leading up to the election stated that Christians should not worry about a possible loss by Waldenström as hurting their cause (as had been claimed by the paper *Hemlandsvännen*). Conversely, a win for Waldenström would mean a setback for the agenda of the progressive wing of the Liberals (*frisinnade*).[239] The campaign editorials that appeared in both 1902 and 1905 demonstrate that Waldenström faced some fierce opposition from within the Liberal camp, not just from the Social Democrats. The Social Democrats hoped to play on this dissatisfaction within the Liberal fold, and urged Liberals to abandon their support of Waldenström, which would serve both parties' interests. It was often Waldenström's undependability as a party member, not his particular politics, which was blamed for defeating reform. His role on the constitution committee in 1902 was presented as an example, during which he was accused of being one of the members of parliament who had helped the First Chamber conservatives defeat voting reform proposals. The paper related that Waldenström had cast the one vote on the constitution committee that had decided against a proposal that had the support of the advocates of voting reform in the second chamber.[240]

However, some of the letters printed by *Gefle Dagblad* were sent by supporters of Waldenström, who made the case that he should not be replaced by A. Larson. In these responses it is clear that one of Waldenström's strongest groups of allies was in the temperance movement. *Gefle Nykterhetsförening* (Gävle Temperance Society) endorsed Waldenström with a long list of reasons, one of them being his consistent support of universal suffrage as the final goal of suffrage reform.[241] Various friends of temperance also defended his continued presence in the *Riksdag* as being more important than minor differences in the solution of the suffrage question, pointing to his contributions to the temperance movement, as well as praising his support of the "Own-Your-Own-Home Movement" (*egnahemrörelsen*), which was a movement to facilitate the ownership of homes among the working classes, and seen as a beneficial program to the cause of temperance. Furthermore, this endorsement also looked favorably on Waldenström's support of suffrage reform.[242] In the same paper, another letter confirmed the claim that Waldenström "should not be placed on the shelf, because he is the conscience of the *Riksdag*" (. . . *bör ej läggas på hyllan, ty han är riksdagens samvete*), saying further that he has often been the one to say what many had wished to say, but had not dared.[243]

This debate hinged on very slight differences of opinion regarding suffrage reform. In a letter to the editor in *Gefle Dagblad* by a certain "J. N.", the author pointed out that there was no practical difference between the voting reform of Waldenström and that of the Liberal party. Waldenström had also explained these matters himself in *Gefle Dagblad* on August 12, in which he distanced himself from the idea of using the municipal voting requirements as the basis for *Riksdag* voting requirements (once again, this would have likely still linked the weight of a person's vote to their income level, something that was objectionable to Waldenström). This had, according to the author, been the only hurdle to agreement with the Liberal party on that issue. The author also pointed out that *Gefle Dagblad* had endorsed A. Larson, despite the fact that staunch conservatives had been campaigning for him, which demonstrated a personal attack against Waldenström, rather than a genuine complaint against his policies.[244] The editor only gave a brief answer to this long letter, which pointed out that there were many ways of being a supporter of universal suffrage, and that not all of these were equal. He also pointed out that the Agrarian party (*Lantmannapartiet*) had elected Waldenström onto the constitution committee against the votes of the progressives (*frisinnade*).[245]

It was the practice of various social and political organizations to hold their own meetings in advance of the elections, in which they decided on the candidates they would endorse. The 1902 campaign for A. Larson claimed to have the support of many groups in society who were currently without voting privileges, ranging from moderate Liberals to Social Democrats. These endorsements for Larson also disputed Waldenström's claim to being a Liberal, claiming that Liberal voters should not be fooled into voting for him: "He is not the left's man and should not receive the left's votes" (*Vänsters man är han icke och vänsterns roster kan han icke få*).[246] Dissenting members of the Moderate party also voiced their disapproval that fellow party members had supported the "Waldenström party." They claimed that this support had ignored the fact that in the last election, some members of the Moderates (as the conservatives were beginning to be called) had tried to prevent the endorsement of Waldenström within their party organizations. These efforts had not been successful, as they had been outvoted by Waldenström's "well-disciplined and religious co-confessionalists" (*väldisciplinerade och religiösa trosfränder*), of which there was a strong presence in Gävle. These Moderates claimed that any further endorsement of Waldenström would be bad for business and would result in a loss of the party members with *frisinnade* leanings, who would exit the party in order to avoid supporting Waldenström.[247] This complicated debate about his worthiness in representing the values of Liberals as well as Moderates regarding suffrage reform resulted in a narrow victory for Waldenström. The results of the election were announced on September 20, as O.A. Brodin 2,244, P. Waldenström 1,219, and A. Larson 1,037.[248] Waldenström managed to stay alive by a margin of less than 200.

In the 1905 election, two of the most common options for the various liberally-oriented organizations in Gävle came down to two options, either O. A. Brodin and Waldenström, or O. A. Brodin and A. Larson. Among those who fervently supported Larson's exchange for Waldenström were Gävle's "Liberally-minded Voter Association" (*Gefle frisinnade valmansförening*) and the *Gefle Arbetarförening*, on which side the newspaper *Gefle Dagblad* threw its weight.[249] This demonstrated an apparent reversal of opinion on the part of *Gefle Arbetarförening*, as this organization was originally credited with aiding Waldenström's entry into politics in 1884.[250] Waldenström remained personally active in the organization through at least 1901.[251] Among those who supported him were Gävle's "Moderate Voters Association" (*Gefle moderata valmansförening*) and the *Gefle Nykterhetsförening*, further demonstrating his lasting appeal among temperance groups and the political moderates.[252]

The election of 1905 was a continuation and intensification of the debates of three years earlier. Lektor Karl Starbäck and Editor Karl M. Lindh based their campaigns on opposing proportional elections, of which Waldenström remained an avid supporter. Lindh's success was undoubtedly tied to his visibility as the editor of *Gefle Dagblad*. During the 1905 elections, *Gefle Dagblad* carried an endorsement for Starbäck and Lindh as the sound candidates due to their opposition to proportional elections.

> When such great and valuable interests are at stake, every conscientious voter must transcend all personal sympathies for this or that candidate and voice his support only for the one who has expressly explained that he will not under any circumstances contribute to botching voting reform through the introduction of proportional elections.[253]

The "personal sympathies" in question were for the incumbent, Waldenström, who remained a dominating presence in Gävle among his loyal free-church constituency. The article took the argument that proportional elections would actually hurt the second chamber, as it would prevent them from gaining a majority. A reprinted lecture from the previous day by Dr. David Bergström made the claim that proportional elections would guarantee the first chamber an "annex" in the second chamber if this were passed.[254] The article also described the elections as the most important since the last representation reform, and identified this as leading to two likely outcomes: if the conservative parties won, they could impose proportional elections on the second chamber, gain a larger corps of sympathetic conservatives in that chamber, and thereby block a takeover by Liberals and Social Democrats; if the *frisinnade* won, they could "confront these plans, make possible the solution of the suffrage question according to the wishes of the people, and proceed with the productive work of reform." He also pointed out the risk of voting for Waldenström in that he had been paired with Brodin on the ticket (who was an anti-proportionalist), which would make cooperation impossible and negate any outcome.[255] In an endorsement written by the *Gefle frisinnade valmansförening* and the *Gefle arbetarförening*, among other groups, the ad reminded voters that they needed to detach themselves from personal loyalties to Waldenström and vote according to the central issue. If Waldenström won, proportionalism could succeed, which would allow the First Chamber to dominate.[256] Two days later, after the elections and after Waldenström had lost his seat, *Gefle Dagblad* heralded this as the city of Gävle's decisive rejection of proportionalism, pointing out that this had been by a wide margin: Waldenström had dropped from 1,219 votes in 1902 to 880 votes in 1905.[257]

Waldenström's recommendations for expanding suffrage and reforming the voting system in Sweden demonstrated an openness to a variety of strategies for achieving that goal, but a staunch opinion that universal suffrage must be based on the national constitution (*grundlagar*), specifically paragraph 14,[258] as opposed to the municipal laws (*kommunal lagar*), and furthermore that there be no financial threshold as a qualification for suffrage provisions in the *grundlagar*. Because of his practice of non-affiliation and his firm stance on the above-mentioned principles, Waldenström was accused by his opponents of changing his position and of defending conservative attempts to prevent the expansion of suffrage. However, historian Ragnar Tomson saw far more consistency in Waldenström's stances on suffrage than was conceded by his Liberal and Social Democratic opponents. In reading through the minutes of the *Riksdag*, Tomson pointed out that Waldenström had remained consistent in his expectation of universal suffrage, beginning in earnest in 1890 and 1891, when Waldenström presented motions on that issue in the *Riksdag*.[259] The point of contention was that Waldenström had openly protested motions in 1899 presented by other

Liberals that would have merely lowered the income requirement from 800 crowns per year to 500. Waldenström's reasons for opposing this proposal were obscured, and instead he came to be portrayed as a conservative merely for opposing the Liberal party's program of that particular day.

The Liberal stance had changed by the next election year, 1902 when they abandoned the half-measure of lowering the income requirement and actually aligned themselves with Waldenström's original position. Ironically, this was presented by his opponents as being an example of Waldenström changing his mind. In 1902, the embattled Waldenström responded to his critics in an attempt to explain that he had been a consistent supporter of universal suffrage throughout his career.[260] In his defense, Waldenström laid out a detailed progression of the various motions that he had written and supported in his time in parliament. On the few exceptions where Waldenström had expressed support for reducing the minimum income requirement, such as one utterance in 1899, he claimed he had done so as a last resort. As a guiding principle, he supported the proposals that he thought would be the quickest and most practical means toward achieving universal suffrage.

> *I have always fought against the so-called municipal threshold as an altogether insecure and wavering basis for political voting rights. [. . .]*
>
> *The municipal threshold, after a very short lifespan, will be buried by the same people who introduced it to the world. Without a doubt people have also generally realized that it is unnatural and dangerous for the basis of the political voting rights of citizens to not be based in the constitution but instead on the municipal laws. And thus this one and only point of conflict between me and the Liberal party will forever disappear.*
>
> *This has been my stance within the Riksdag and my work in the suffrage question, and outside the Riksdag, I have repeatedly—especially in my patriotic speeches at the farmers' meeting in Gävle—expressed myself in favor of political voting rights for every honorable citizen. At the previously mentioned event, I also expressed my belief that the time was not far off when we shall reach this point.*
>
> *In the future one can certainly expect that there will not be any other talk of voting reform in the Riksdag other than on the basis of universal suffrage, independent of all [financial] threshold conditions. And you will have to forgive me if I take pride in the belief that it was precisely my struggle against the Liberal party's municipal threshold idea that contributed to bringing the situation to the point where we now seem to have a genuine point of agreement.*[261]

Furthermore, he accused one of his biggest opponents, editor Karl H. Lindh of *Gefle Dagblad*, as representing the epitome of partisanship and attacked his journalistic integrity.

> *One would think that the tiniest sense of justice, if even ever so little, would make it impossible for a newspaper that calls itself liberally-minded to make such a gross manipulation of generally known facts. But such is the nature of party tyranny.*[262]

"Party tyranny" was a way of expressing what Waldenström feared was the developing trend in politics and journalism. Commitment to party ideology would overrule open debate, political candidates would reduce their opponents' track records to one- or two-word slogans. However, by using the term tyranny, Waldenström himself played the same game, presenting the notion that an absolutist ideology, perhaps even with Marxist leanings, had worked its way into the Liberal party.

Waldenström's support of proportionalism was also picked up in the newspaper *Svenska Morgonbladet*. In advance of the elections in both 1902 and 1905, *Svenska Morgonbladet* defended Waldenström's candidacy with one of the main reasons being his support of proportionalism, which at the time was being abandoned from the Liberal agenda.[263] Responding to criticism from the papers *Dagen*, *Svenska Dagbladet*, and *Dagens Nyheter* that the free-church voting block blindly wanted to keep Waldenström in power at the expense of all else, including voting reform, *Svenska Morgonbladet* replied that it was not only Waldenström they were defending, but voting reform itself. Without proportionalism, there would be no acceptable voting reform.[264] In a long article explaining the benefits of proportionalism, the paper explained that it would greatly reduce the animosity between parties that results when minority groups are deprived of their voice. This would nip revolutions in the bud, as dissenting groups would find space to be able to argue for their reforms within the existing order, and not seek revolution.

> *In proportional elections, every party gets what they deserve—all groups of any significance retain their members of parliament to such a number that corresponds to the size of the group. The majority get more and thereby its natural reward, but the minority does not go without a share. The resulting atmosphere will reduce the intensity of the struggle, will place a damper on the suffering, will promote calm and presence of mind. Every party freely chooses their men, in whom it has complete trust, and these candidates in their turn are presented by their likeminded supporters; it is on their trust that they rest, they do not need to seek the favor from all sides, nor make promises to all the parties. Proportional elections*

> will administer justice between parties, promote character, and a
> sense of independence among both parties and candidates.²⁶⁵

The author made the claim that proportional elections should be an essential part of any just program of universal suffrage, in that otherwise minorities will feel that their votes do not count. As examples, the author pointed to problems that could be attributed to "majority rules" elections in the United States, Britain, and the local German elections in Saxony.

> Where majority elections will lead, one can see the clearest proof
> in the latest general elections in Saxony. The socialists made up
> 58 percent of the electorate and took 22 seats out of 23; all of the
> bourgeois [conservative] elements together—42 percent of the
> electorate!—received 1 seat to share!²⁶⁶

Making an analogy between political parties and children, the author pointed out that if something was going to be divided this way among siblings in a family, it would be called the worst of injustices for a winner to take all and the loser to receive nothing, even if he or she lost by only one vote. Furthermore, *Svenska Morgonbladet* also defended another of Waldenström's assertions, which was an accusation that the division among the Liberals would result in the party's impotence to accomplish its goals, as well as its eventual decline. The paper identified the attempts by Liberals to unseat Waldenström as shortsighted and self-defeating; "He is for us a unique representative. There is at present no one else who can take up his mantel."²⁶⁷

Even after leaving elective politics in 1905, Waldenström remained vocal in his support of proportionalism, especially in the months surrounding the suffrage proposal that passed in 1907. While Waldenström was en route to China in 1907 to inspect the mission stations of the Swedish Mission Covenant, he maintained correspondence with the Swedish newspapers.

> Both in Aden and Suez I received newspapers from Sweden and
> rejoiced greatly to see that the suffrage question had been solved,
> and that it was based on proportionalism. May God lead every-
> thing to the good of our country and people. The socialist tyranny
> is making a lamentable spectacle, which is becoming all the more
> brutal and violent. The liberal newspapers blame the socialistic
> press as the cause of the shocking deterioration of civilization that
> can now be seen. But they do not think much about the fact that
> it was their own, prolonged flirtations with socialism which not
> only prepared the socialist press with the opportunity to sow their
> dragon's teeth in peace and quiet, but even watered those seeds, so
> that they could grow with such rapid speed, as is now evident.²⁶⁸

Waldenström's concern about a Socialist takeover is evident here, and there is some validity to the claim that he advocated proportionalism as a means of creating a strong buffer against socialism. However, this was not for the reasons given by his opponents in the election of 1905. Waldenström explained his commitment to proportionalism as a matter of democratic principle, not an endorsement of First Chamber conservatism. He endorsed proportionalism first and foremost on a philosophical level, as a means of preventing minorities from being shut out of parliament, and as a precaution against sweeping political revolutions that might threaten the rights of dissenters.

> In the political arena it is relatively calm since the divisive, perennial suffrage struggle has led to the voting rights decision, which was approved by the previous Riksdag and which will come to last. This decision meant that the elections would be conducted proportionally, that is to say that each of the more significant parties can bring into the Riksdag as many representatives as corresponds to their strength in the electorate. By this it becomes impossible for the majority to completely shut out the minority. And that is fair. The so-called liberal party fought the proportional elections with a [??] energy. But now events have occurred which have made it so that the liberals should be rather pleased that the outcome is proportional elections. Namely, there have recently been some so-called by-elections, where the liberals lost seats, some to the right and some to the socialists, under the current election system. And this is an omen of what might have awaited them if proportional elections had not been passed at the same time that elections became universal. Now the liberals are of course not saying: "It is good for us that we have proportional elections." No, for them to do so would be more of an acknowledgement than one could expect from them. But they talk so patronizingly about how they will not attempt to overturn this recently passed decision at the next election. And that will be so gracious of them to kindly refrain from smashing the lifeboat while the ship is on the verge of capsizing.[269]

In addition to proportionalism, there were also other ideological differences at play, which set him at odds with the Social Democratic party, as well as the progressives within the Liberal party (*Frisinnade landsförening*). *Arbetarbladet* did much to identify Waldenström as both a fickle politician, as well as a right-wing candidate, drawing on similar pronouncements in *Dagens Nyheter* and *Upsala Nya Tidning*.[270] His stance on proportionalism was seen first and foremost as a scheme to thwart universal suffrage and to restrict the rights of workers to organize.[271] *Arbetarbladet*, like K. Starbäck and Karl Lindh,[272] took a firm stance against proportionalism, seeing it as giving rise to a new period of reactionary conservatism.[273] The paper even speculated that Waldenström had initially intended not to run in this election but had been persuaded to remain in politics by "the gentlemen in the first chamber" (*första kammarherrarne*).[274] *Arbetarbladet* predicted that Waldenström's supposed alliance with the first chamber conservatives was resulting in the extension of their dominance into the second chamber, an alliance which would defeat all reform movements.[275]

So great was the resentment against Waldenström within *Arbetarbladet* that the paper reported his defeat from parliament as the end of a "nightmare," describing the jubilation with which people streamed out onto the streets of Gävle, whooping their hurrahs and shaking each others' hands, and attending celebrations with choir music.[276]

> *Mister Waldenström has finally fallen for his deeds, and his fall represents the working and taxpaying people's vehement protest against the plans of the First Chamber regarding the suffrage question, against the politics of war, against class legislation, in short against the entire torrent of reactionary [politics] that was close to drowning the nation, but which everyone who is at all awake and aware of their strength, are now shaking off like a tortuous dream.*[277]

Waldenström had expressed his hope that proportionalism would help protect minorities from the potential abuses of majoritarian democracy. However, his opponents interpreted "minorities" to mean the privileged elites of society, who were attempting to buffer their status against the majority of the poor working class, much of which had no voting rights.

> *They claim to be protecting* the minority. *But it has* never occurred to P.W. to protect those without voting rights, *the majority who in terms of rights are to a great extent standing without a roof over their heads against the assault of the minority [. . .]. This is P.W.'s program! He is silent about the questions of class legislation. His position here is also sufficiently known.*[278]

While Waldenström on this issue was aligned with Conservatives in the support of proportionalism, this alliance was only as deep as any of his other alliances. Waldenström's commitment to his principles was greater than to party strategies. His fear of party tyranny has been related already. Waldenström seems to have had a vivid expectation that there was a real chance that the Socialists would dominate the *Riksdag* in the coming years. In his campaign, he made a famous and oft-cited remark that the rigid ideology of socialism, if left unchecked by principles like proportionalism, would result in a "rule of terror" (*skräckvälde*) that would make the Danish despotic ruler "Christian the Tyrant" look like an angel.[279] Ensuring that minorities always were guaranteed representation would be to the benefit of all parties.

It should be underscored that although the Liberals and Social Democrats opposed proportionalism in 1905, they later came to reverse this stance. Furthermore, proportionalism had been endorsed by A. Larson's candidacy in 1902, who together with O. A. Brodin had comprised the official ticket of the *frisinnade*.[280] This same pair was endorsed by the trade unions (*fackföreningar*), indicating at least an indirect support of proportionalism within the Social Democratic electorate in 1902 as well.[281] It is ironic that in 1905, Waldenström's support of proportionalism was one of the main arguments for voting him out of office, whereas posterity would later come to embrace proportionalism as integral to Swedish democracy. This is in stark contrast with the way in which Socialists and Liberals alike portrayed it in 1905, as merely a conservative plot to *prevent* democracy. As evidenced in Waldenström's explanations, proportionalism was not simply a measure to save the Conservatives and Liberals from total defeat, but was also valued as a means to safeguard pluralism in general.

The arguments that Waldenström made in defense of conscience in the religious sphere (discussed in chapter 6) also had application to the political arena, and he took several opportunities to explain what he understood as the rights of political dissenters. A prime moment for articulating these rights came during the numerous strikes organized by the labor movement, most notably the Great Strike of 1909. Other general strikes were called both before and afterward, but the strike in 1909 was significant both in its scale, as well as in the implications that were drawn from it. During these strikes, the chief point of concern for Waldenström was the protection of the rights of workers who dissented from participation in the strikes. His concerns were not well received by the strike organizers, however, as they held a very weak position against the employers' associations. Waldenström's dramatic warnings against the dangers of strike practices were assumed to be a statement in support of the employers' interests. The pressure for labor organizations to rally as much of the workforce as possible seemingly required a hard-line against strike breaking, evident in the language used by the columnists in the Socialist newspapers. In 1905, the Gävle paper *Arbetarbladet* defined strike breakers as follows (citing a definition published in *The New Yorker*):

> *A strike breaker is for his occupation, what a traitor is for his country, and even if he in time of war is a great help for the one party, he will become despised by both parties after the conclusion of peace. If help is needed, he will be the last one to assist, but if he*

can take part in something good, which he has not himself helped to achieve, then he will be the first to take part. In terms of his own affairs he is the greatest egoist and can betray family, friends, and country for a couple of "silver coins."

He is a traitor on a small scale, who first sells out his co-workers to later be sold himself by his employer after the peace is concluded. He is despised by both parties and by the entirety of humanity. He is an enemy to himself, in the present and in the future![282]

The religiously charged comparison between a strike breaker and Judas Iscariot (the disciple who betrayed Christ for silver coins) would certainly have been provocative for the many Waldenströmians and other religious people in the Gävle workforce. The purpose of this type of rhetoric can be seen as an effort to reduce and even eliminate what sociologists refer to as the "free rider" problem.[283] That is, in order for members of a social movement to achieve the desired goals, they need to be able to convince the minimum number of participants necessary in order to be able to overcome their opposition. The free riders are those members of the group who stand to benefit from the movement, but who do not contribute or who contribute minimally. When the situation appears to be an uphill battle or unwinnable, leaders of social movements can be expected to resort to shaming free riders into action. The problem that this creates for a pluralistic democracy is that the leadership of a movement can easily come to identify any and all dissenters as harmful to the cause, and thereby legitimize the elimination of all challenges to the dominant party ideology.

In order to understand the nature of the debate about strike breakers, it is important to describe the situation of the workers in Sweden at the time. It should be repeated that the position for workers was quite weak in comparison to that of the employers. The main goal for striking was to gain leverage in setting the terms of contracts. While the practice of using strikes had been going on for several decades, the resulting labor agreements (*avtal*) came hard and almost always on the terms of the employers. The employers maintained the upper hand by resorting to the threat of lockouts, in which striking workers would be prevented from returning to their jobs and those positions would be filled by temporary or permanent replacements. In 1902, one of the more significant employer organizations in Sweden had been founded, *Svenska Arbetsgivare Föreningen* (Swedish Employers Association—SAF), although it would take two more years for the SAF to develop into a functioning organization. By 1908, the SAF's participating members represented companies which employed 150,000 Swedish workers. Two other organizations with similar agendas, The Factory

Association (*Verkstadsföreningen*) and The Central Employers Association (*Centrala Arbetsgivareförbundet*) represented companies with a combined workforce of upwards to 100,000 more laborers. These organizations held a strong position, not only in that they worked together, but also in that they collected enough financial resources to be able to survive work stoppages and lockouts. Although in a weaker position, laborers had organized their own negotiating organization earlier than the employers, "The National Organization" (*Lantorganisationen*—LO) in 1898. Prior to 1909, LO reached a high point of membership of 186,000 members. One of LO's demands from the employers was that workers not be allowed to "break" a strike. SAF members instead maintained that employers had the right to hire and fire workers, including during a strike, without this constituting a "breach of contract." This policy was summed up by the SAF in the slogan "freedom to work" (*arbetets frihet*), and the SAF defended the rights of workers to break the strike in order to resume their jobs.[284]

As the industrial revolution came somewhat later to Sweden than other parts of Europe, there was an opportunity for Swedish employers and laborers alike to learn from the developments of their southern neighbors, and they were well aware of the labor situation in Germany and Denmark. Berndt Schiller describes the Swedish employers at the turn of the century as being in a position to choose between two pathways, the German and the Danish. In Germany, employers had been largely unwilling to negotiate with laborers, and when possible, had taken a firm stance against negotiations. In Denmark, however, employers had organized in associations, which operated jointly to negotiate labor settlements. The Swedish employers by and large followed the Danish approach, and resorted to coordinated lockouts in order to negotiate settlements that were favorable to the employers. In general, the Swedish employers demonstrated a greater openness to the concept of striking than existed in Germany, but nevertheless attempted to tightly control the bargaining.[285] Collective agreements were becoming standard practice. In addition, in some cases national agreements (*riksavtal*) were reached between employers and entire branches of labor. The SAF's strategy in these cases was to negotiate terms based on the average workers within a certain industry, rather than on the basis of those workers who held the most advanced contract principles. It was the failure of such national agreements within the clothing industry and paper pulp (*pappersmasse*) industry that became decisive in the months leading up to the Great Strike in 1909.[286]

As the years of 1906 and 1907 enjoyed a relatively good economy, there were some improvements in the situation for workers regarding wages and working conditions. This good economic situation allowed the SAF to stand by its principle of ensuring workers their "freedom to work."[287] However, in

1908, the economic situation worsened, and the membership decreased by 25,000. By the beginning of July 1909, it is estimated that there were about a dozen unresolved contract disputes, which contributed to the SAF's decision on July 14 to extend current lockouts to the end of the month. Mediators appointed by the Swedish state were called in to negotiate a settlement on July 24. However, these negotiations did not result in a satisfactory settlement for either side. LO called into effect a general work stoppage on August 4. In the first week of the strike, over 300,000 workers were estimated to have participated, with a little over half coming from LO's membership. Despite the impressive numbers, the financial resources collected by LO to support the striking workers were low, due in large part to the poor economy in the year and a half leading up to the strike. SAF ended the lockouts with some of the workers in the mining and iron industries, and the remaining workers were not allowed to return until December 1. The Great Strike had ended after almost four months without reaching any kind of decisive agreement. Though the immediate result of the strike signaled a defeat for LO in the short term, LO and the labor movement continued. Precedents were set on a number of levels. The government had intervened, albeit unsuccessfully, to play a role in brokering an agreement, thereby acknowledging the validity of the striking parties' claims. The employers had upheld the principle of "freedom of work." Although this served their own interests in maintaining production and defeating the demands of LO, the positive byproduct was that this also answered the concerns that individual workers be able to dissent from the majority of workers in their industry.

Waldenström feared the potential outcome that strikes would create a "rule of terror" if they progressed past the point of allowing dissent. The ambitions of LO to mandate all workers' compliance during strikes was a prime example for him that such a rule of terror had been reached during the Great Strike.

> A couple examples can be presented of how the leadership of the strike is brutal to no end. It should be conceded that they were gracious enough to allow doctors to be able to travel to the sick, and for the sick to be transported to the hospital, for milk to be driven to the hospitals, and for corpses to be carried out to the cemeteries. But all of this was only allowed on the condition that every driver performing these services obtained and carried with them special permission papers from the so-called landsorganisation, i.e. the leadership of the strike.[288]

Although the strike leadership intended to impose these strict rules only during the short term of the strike, Waldenström's fear was that if such a restriction of individual behavior were allowed, even in the short term, this could have long-term consequences on the rights of dissenters. This would be particularly true if the freedom of the press was restricted, which Waldenström accused the strike leadership of attempting to do.

> Yet the worst part of all of these dirty breaches of contracts has been the fact that the typographers have laid down their work almost everywhere across the country. The typographers' union is precisely the one that has worked most to achieve collective agreements between workers and employers. Such an agreement is in effect now and expressly forbids strikes or lock outs during the settlement period. But honor and faith mean nothing now. The newspapers were lacking their printing staff. Only one newspaper was able to be published, namely Social Demokraten, which has even for the time being changed its name and called itself "The Answer." Its openly expressed intent was to place thumb screws on the segment of the press that was in opposition to the great strike.[289]

Open debate is a prerequisite for a plural society. If in the short term of a strike, only one newspaper was allowed to be printed, the consequences for a pluralist debate are obvious.

As a result of his concerns about the preservation of democracy, as well as the potential threat that an atheistic socialism posed against Christianity, Waldenström drew sharp lines at times in his attack against socialism, urging and even shaming the members of the religious awakening into not participating in any strike activity that broke with democratic principles.

> No matter how much sympathy one might have for the welfare of workers—crimes still need to be considered crimes, even if they are committed by workers, including even when they are also taking place against employers.
>
> Our workers are deeply to blame for their lack of judgment and the ease with which they have entrusted themselves to swindlers. The position of believers has become particularly difficult. Crowds of them have allowed themselves, crippled by an inexplicable spirit of weakness, to be ushered along under the godless whips of the tyrants. May God save them! May God break in pieces the yoke of their burden and the whip on their shoulders and the staff of their tormentors (Isaiah 9).
>
> But "there is a silver lining." Now even the eyes of the blind have been opened to see what Social Democracy carried in its womb, and what a curse it is precisely for the workers, despite its deceitful boasting about its great benefits for them. Now all sensible workers and hopefully also the believers will gain the strength

> to pull themselves away from all "solidarity" with those, who hate and mock their God and savior. It is furthermore inexplicable how there could ever be talk of such solidarity—solidarity between Christ and Belial. Now we will also certainly get laws, which effectively protect those willing to work in spite of the persecutions of the strikers, as well as make it clear for everyone, that the freedom to work and provide for yourself prevails in Sweden, and everyone who tries to assault that freedom, assaults the state itself.[290]

Harsh as these words may be, they should be understood in light of Waldenström's arguments in favor of free speech and democratic process. The free-church members were being warned against making common cause with a political movement that seemed to him to endorse limitations on both freedom of speech and on the right to dissent. It is important to point out that Waldenström made a distinction between the labor movement and socialism. In his mind the two were not the same, evident in his comments to newspapers in the USA.

> Here the trade unions are forced to adhere to socialism, and the Swedish Worker Association, which tried to construct trade unions that were independent of socialism, has had to endure unbelievably bitter persecutions.[291]

In Waldenström's imagination, it was possible for a labor movement to be driven by more than one ideology and more than one political party.

What was objectionable for Waldenström about LO's attitude toward strike breakers was that it affected both members and non-members of union organizations. In other words, it is one thing for workers who consent to join in a strike, but for those who are economically unable to provide for their families for four months without income, the social and financial costs of strike-breaking were enormous. The practice of many of the unions (*fackföreningar*) was to expect complete compliance of all workers, members or not. Harsh treatment was the result of noncompliance. Strike breakers' names and addresses were published, and those who wished to be restored to the unions needed to first make public confessions and apologies. In addition to the formal punishment by the unions, informal abuses could take place between workers. When strike-breaking resulted in lost jobs for workers who had observed the strike, severe social ostracism could result. If strike breakers ended up taking jobs left by striking workers, and they continued in these positions after the end of the strike, the unions demanded that they be fired. This resulted in an unpleasant situation for the strike breakers, who were persecuted and barred (*utfryst*) from the workplace afterwards if they remained. These strike-breakers, furthermore, were not always co-workers, but were often unemployed before the strike, and thus worse off than those who had gone on strike.[292]

Waldenström's frequent travels to Germany offered him plenty of opportunities for international comparisons, which he related to newspapers at home through his travel letters. In a letter from Dresden, Waldenström related some of the political conflicts that were occurring in the Prussian parliament, the *Landtag*, as well as elsewhere in Germany.

> Here in Germany these days there has been much commotion due to two social democratic events, which are quite characteristic. A social democratic author in Solingen has been kicked out of the party because he criticized in one of his own published works some of the points of social democracy's program. Newspapers are commenting quite bitterly that, in effect, heresy trials have begun within social democracy, "altogether like those within the church." But, of course. One begins by breaking all the "bourgeois" restraints and finishes by imposing restraints that are sevenfold worse.[293]

Waldenström here resonated with the comparison made between the search for true political doctrine within the German Social Democratic movement and the heresy trials that had occurred during the various periods of Christian history. In making this comparison, there is an effort to explain that although an ascendant ideology such as socialism might begin as a radical movement of protest, it can be expected to behave in similar ways to other ideologies, secular or religious. Radical protest movements can also evolve into rigid orthodoxies once they achieve positions of power and dominance, and then seek to eliminate any dissent. Waldenström here and elsewhere expressed the fear that socialism was not automatically going to be compatible with democracy. Provisions to protect the rights of dissenters in Sweden would be essential in making sure that democracy could continue to thrive, regardless of which ideology was dominant at a given time. Although there is no way for Waldenström to have been able to predict the rise of National Socialism in Germany from his vantage point in 1912, his commentary comes as an eerie reminder to modern readers of the ways in which dissent was so drastically restricted and eliminated in German politics to the complete breakdown of democratic praxis.

Waldenström's pronouncements in favor of workers' rights, as well as his defense of the free speech of Socialists in 1889, seem to have never been widely acknowledged. Rather, the image of Waldenström's relationship to socialism that has endured has been the picture painted of him by *Gefle Dagblad* and *Arbetarbladet* during the campaigns of 1902 and 1905. At the forefront of this mudslinging campaign, these papers made the claim that

Waldenström was an ally of attempts to limit the free speech of striking groups. The foremost example of this in 1902 was the so-called "Åkarps Law" (*Åkarpslagen*) spearheaded by Robert Dickson in 1899, which would have made inciting strikes illegal. *Arbetarbladet* saw Waldenström as an ally of Åkarps Law and voiced this as one of its concerns in urging its readers not to vote for him in 1902.[294] Although Waldenström expressed his opposition to certain practices of strikes, such a law was not in line with his agenda. Quite the contrary, he had turned heads with his early defense of free speech for Socialist groups in 1889, when the famous "Muzzle Law" (*Munkorgslagen*) was debated in the *Riksdag*. During these debates, he spoke in opposition to this law, which would have introduced a provision in chapter 10 paragraph 14 of the penal code that would make it illegal to speak publicly or to disseminate in writing any utterance that might lead to violence against persons or property.[295] This law primarily targeted Socialists, who that same year had organized as a political party.

Waldenström and a corps of volunteer laborers putting the final touches on the grounds of the new Seminary at Lidingö, the inauguration of which fell right during the general strike of 1908. For Waldenström, the work party became a silent protest of the labor organizers, who had attempted to prevent any work being done during the strike, and had attempted to scare off the volunteers with ominous warnings of the consequences of their "strike breaking." For the labor organizers, however, this was confirmation of his lack of support for the labor movement. Photo from N.P. Ollén's *Paul Peter Waldenström: En Levnadsteckning*. 261

Defending the tradition of freedom of speech, which had been codified in Sweden beginning in 1766 (*trykfrihetsförordningen*), was a point of concern for Waldenström for obvious reasons. Waldenström knew from personal experience that although this right was long established in law, it had nevertheless often been severely restricted. Various groups of Pietists had faced extreme antagonism from the state in the form of the anticonventicle edicts formally in place from 1726 through 1858. It therefore became an all the more delicate issue when Socialist agitators faced similar sorts of oppression from the state, as well as threats of increased suppression voiced by members of the *Riksdag*. What is most interesting about Waldenström's complicated relationship to socialism is that his commitment to protect the rights of conscientious dissenters led him to, on the one hand, accuse the Socialists of threatening to weaken these rights for others, while on the other, occasionally coming to the defense of Socialists' own rights to freedom of speech and the rights of workers to organize and strike. In practice Waldenström accepted the reality of socialism's influence in Swedish society, as articulated in the *Riksdag* during the Muzzle Law debates of 1889.

> It should not be unknown to you gentlemen that we are already a good degree on the way toward a state socialism, in which the state takes care of certain classes of society, guarantees them certain advantages, helps them to keep the price of their goods up and so on, and it is among the foremost claims of social democracy that the state in the same way will take care of the working population, guarantee them certain maximum working hours, a certain minimum wage and so on, something which a great deal of the inhabitants of Sweden already possess due to the intervention of the state.[296]

As trade unions and the prominence of Social Democratic party ideology have become an integral part of social life in Sweden, it is easy to conflate all the historical opponents of the labor movement and thereby miss the nuance of their messages.[297] Waldenström was identified by the Socialist papers as part of a conservative defense of upper class privilege. It is important not to miss the valid concerns that were raised about the compatibility of socialism with democratic practices. Waldenström's opposition to strike practices was primarily driven by concern for workers who dissented, and the negative implications that an absolutist form of socialism might have for Swedish democracy. Although the labor movement was highly inspired by and infused with Socialist thinking, Waldenström attempted to distinguish between the labor movement and socialism, and claimed that the two were not the same.

CHAPTER 12

An Exchange of Words: A Re-Socialized Christian Vocabulary and a Democratized Socialist One

While the language of conflict dominates the exchange between Pietists and Socialists during the period in question, each movement was profoundly impacted by its confrontation with the other. One of the clearest examples of this is in the changes that took place in the vocabulary used by each group. These changes can in some ways be attributed to rhetorical strategies designed to preserve positions of power. A prime reason for incorporating the vocabulary of another group would be to retain members who feel drawn to the opposing party's ideology, as well as those who are disillusioned by their own party. These vocabulary changes can also be interpreted as genuine alterations of values and ideology, when critiques are internalized and noticeably adjust the goals of a movement. To the degree that this confrontation became an exchange rather than a stalemate is due to explicit efforts made toward that end by members on each side. The motivations for these strategies are complicated, but the net result seems to have been an exchange of vocabulary and the maintenance of civility in Swedish society. Tracing some of this exchange of vocabulary will be the task of this chapter.

During the elections in 1902, *Gefle Dagblad* made some efforts to blur the lines between the starkly conservative religious camps in Gävle and those sympathetic to the progressive element of the Liberal party. The paper identified the religious newspaper *Hemlandsposten* as a reactionary force, and accused its editors of making the campaign more ideologically charged than necessary. *Hemlandsposten* was quoted as saying that the opposition to Waldenström was due to hatred toward religious minorities and that, if candidate Larson won, this would demonstrate the Liberal party's animosity toward religion.[298] *Gefle Dagblad* refuted this, saying that the Pietist camp (*läseriet*) and the temperance movement would not be harmed by the loss of Waldenström, and furthermore, that they feared that his supporters were voting for him without consideration for his political leanings; "May we respect each other's religious views, but avoid mixing them into the political struggles of the day."[299] From the Socialist side, there were attempts to convince the sympathetic members of the free-church movement of the validity of the claims of socialism and its relevance to basic Christian principles. *Arbetarbladet* occasionally included articles presenting Socialist arguments in Christian terms, presumably in the hopes of winning over Christian voters in Gävle to the Socialist cause (reprinted from *Folkbladet*).

> *Christ was poor, a beggar, who did not know where to lay his tired head. He preached the rights of the poor unceasingly. He explained that it would be easier for a camel to go through the eye of a needle than for a rich man to enter the kingdom of heaven. But his followers, the priests, what do they do? They have enormous incomes [in footnote: for P.P.W., a mere 22,000 excluding additional income from stock], they live in luxury and abundance and the high shepherd of souls, Christ's ruler on earth, who is also called pope, has 500 million deposited safely in the Bank of England. A true follower of Christ! [. . .] Indeed, it should be otherwise! For we want to become Christians—not Christians for profit, not bastard Christians, but socialists, in other words true Christians. We want to preach love, equality, and justice for the oppressed and the enslaved.*[300]

In turn, it seems Waldenström's confrontation with socialism caused him to rediscover and re-emphasize the social and communal aspects of Christianity. In discussing his reservations about socialism, Waldenström latched on to several key words and reframed the discussion of those concepts. His difference of opinion on the definition and use of the term "moralism" has already been discussed. Solidarity and freethinking were other terms that were current in the Socialist press, and Waldenström had his own thoughts about what they should mean. Socialist columnists in *Arbetarbladet* invoked a "feeling of solidarity" (*solidaritetskänsla*) in their attempts to rally readers around the cause. Solidarity was even personified as an agent in the development of human civilization: "it is the *red thread* of evolution" (*den är utvecklingens* röda tråd). This notion of solidarity was at times reified as a power that could bind together individuals for common purpose.[301] The "Socialist priest," H. F. Spak, had proposed a Marxist understanding of human evolution in which human ethics could be viewed as being in a process of transitioning from a primitive "wild animal morality" (*vilddjursmoralen*) to a higher "morality of solidarity" (*solidaritetsmoralen*).[302] The former was a morality based on self interest, whereas the latter was based on equality, justice, and cooperation in the best interest of humanity. Spak identified this second morality as being the morality of Jesus, and even called on Social Democrats to become followers of Jesus. Spak was unusual in his unrestrained fusion of Christianity and socialism, but as evidenced by Branting's commentary, he had gained considerable attention in the mainstream within the party. In attributing this agency to solidarity, the members of the labor movement had reworked and redirected some of the strategies of the religious reform movements and applied them to their causes.

In rebuttal, Waldenström's political speeches often took up the task of defining, or redefining, what he thought solidarity ought to mean. He urged his listeners that they should look for a deeper solidarity, beyond conservative and liberal, left and right. This solidarity needed to be a "patriotic feeling of solidarity" (*fosterländsk solidaritetskänsla*). The solidarity that existed within various parties needed to be lifted up so that it could transcend party lines and encompass the entire nation (*behöver lyftas upp öfver partigränserna till fosterlandet*).[303] Waldenström was making the claim that solidarity should return to a broader, national meaning, and not just be limited to a single political movement or class. This was not simply a conservative defense of nationalism. He also qualified his notion of what healthy nationalism ought to be, and differentiated between "pure and impure love of country" (*ren och oren fosterlandskärlek*), pointing in one of his speeches to the difference between the positive and negative outcomes of patriotism.[304] While on a speaking tour in the United States in 1910, Waldenström gave a speech titled "The Nation" (*Landet*), in which he explained to his Swedish-American audience that there was a grave problem with class hatred back home in Sweden.[305] The solution to this problem was to cultivate positive expressions of solidarity. In a December 1909 issue of *Pietisten*, Waldenström explained his views in a short reflection titled "Solidarity."

> *Solidarity is a word that is used very often nowadays. It is a beautiful word, the name of a very beautiful virtue, namely a relationship and feeling of belonging within a certain circle and for a decided purpose.*
>
> *[. . .] When citizens in a country are pervaded by the feeling that they make up* one *people, in other words* one *body with*

> *many limbs, and also that each and every one within his influence does with joy what he is able to do to support the homeland and promote its well-being, then that is solidarity, and is a highly admirable virtue.*
>
> *Such a solidarity can also be found within different associations, different classes of people, different professional fields, and so on. It serves in this case to the highest degree to support, strengthen, and edify the individual members, as well as promote their best interest.*
>
> *There is, however, a line, over which solidarity may not go. Solidarity in such things that are unjust is a detestable crime, just as solidarity in the good sense is an admirable virtue that brings blessings.*[306]

As he draws on the image of "one body with many limbs," this is an allusion to scripture that his readers know well. The image is found in a passage Waldenström often preached on, and which would have been familiar to his listeners (1 Cor 12:12). The fact that he makes the connection between this word cherished by Socialists and a beloved analogy from scripture would have been a provocative notion, as it blends traditional lines of party and religious ideology. This in effect served the purpose of taking a word that was in the exclusive domain of Socialist agitators (often used against the Christian establishment) in order to make it available for Christians to use to describe their own social dynamic. It is also an opportunity for readers to see that they may have more in common with their political opponents than previously realized.

Waldenström saw congregations as filling a powerful role in creating solidarity across lines of class, profession, and affiliation, and thus healing what he saw were the negative effects of class hatred.

> *But there is another area, where solidarity ought to play a much greater role than it usually does and that is in the congregation. If anywhere it is there that the individual members ought to feel truly in solidarity, truly belonging, truly responsible for each other, according to the words of the apostle: when one member suffers, so all the members suffer, when one member is exalted, so all of them are exalted. To remain together in the congregation as one, supporting, serving, carrying one another's burdens and so on, that is one of the most marvelous virtues that can be conceived or named.*[307]

Much of Waldenström's message in his newspaper articles was focused on encouraging volunteerism among the free-church members. This voluntary spirit was, after all, an essential aspect of how the awakening functioned as a movement of people in joint mission enterprises. In some letters he applauded those church members who had demonstrated an extraordinary sense of "responsibility and solidarity" (*ansvar och solidaritet*), with selfless missionaries in far off places like the Congo usually topping the list. Through their group activity these people had generated an unparalleled sense of solidarity, which should be imitated everywhere. Through self-sacrifice (*offervillighet*), congregations and mission organizations could tackle large projects, such as the funding of buildings, as well as paying off these debts as quickly as possible.[308] It was also important for Waldenström to clarify that his audience should be wary about subscribing to notions of solidarity with people who wanted their votes, but who did not share their values. While solidarity could be praised in a Christian context, solidarity with the Social Democratic party ideology was sternly rebuked: "Now may all sensible workers, and in particular all believers, gain the strength to cut themselves loose from all 'solidarity' with those who hate and mock their God and savior."[309]

Frisinne ("open-mindedness," "liberal-mindedness," or even "free-thinking") was another term that Waldenström attempted to re-define. In the notes from an undated political speech called "What the Homeland Needs" (*Hvad fosterlandet behöfver*), Waldenström began by addressing the anxiety that existed in the political, social, and religious spheres. Part of the solution for Waldenström was to address a spiritual "sickness" that was clouding the national discussion about reform. Reforms were being applied like bandages on a superficial wound, instead of attending to the deeper, internal damage that lay below, he explained. The political debates were too starkly ideological and partisan, and the answer to this overemphasis on ideology was to return the focus to reforming the individual. The family was the basic unit of society, and it was here that the individual could be formed holistically. In order to address societal reforms, individual citizens needed to be spiritually mature, and part of that maturity rested in the ability of the citizen to engage in a healthy public dialogue where true *frisinne* could take place. *Frisinne*, he explained, was not just a particular set of political beliefs, but an ability to engage with a question in a non-partisan frame of mind. In contrast, the way that many columnists and politicians were using the term *frisinne* was precisely with certain ideologies in mind (specifically the progressive wing of the Liberal party, which Waldenström feared was listing toward the Socialists). Waldenström pointed out that there was often a lack of any *frisinne* among the dogmatic agitators who were using the term most.[310] Many radical Socialists would have found his speeches unpalatable. It is no surprise that critics would paint him as a highly conservative defender of traditional moral values, especially when he strayed into exhortations to mothers to rise up as agents in the creation of happy homes, or to reject the temptations to use birth control as a means to flee from their maternal calling. On these points he would have made few friends in Socialist circles. Nevertheless, it is striking that Branting was of a similar mind regarding *frisinne* and solidarity. While many other Socialist agitators were framing the strikes in terms of class warfare or portraying Christianity as the weapon of the upper classes, Branting resisted the trend of appealing to class-based vocabulary.[311] While upward mobility in Sweden at the time was extremely difficult, Branting and Waldenström both seem to have seen "class" as a fluid and unreliable concept, and thus both of them urged their audiences not to talk of class warfare. They each seemed to realize that their respective readerships drew from all classes, and therefore did not wish to restrict this audience.

The two movements also exchanged practices. Waldenström complained that the Socialists had taken a page out of the revival movement's book by copying techniques of disseminating information. Since the early 1800s, itinerant booksellers had been employed to travel the country roads and sell or give away books on devotional topics. These trips sometimes instigated small revivals, as the colporteurs, as they were called, would hold impromptu sermons along the roadside or in the marketplaces. Wittingly or unwittingly, Socialists and other political groups had developed similar means of disseminating information and sparking local revivals. Waldenström described these new political strategies with uneasiness.

> *Another new development in the ongoing election campaign has been that the various parties have sent out automobiles over the entire country with itinerant speakers, who on the roads and in the squares and other places have held campaign speeches. These automobiles have had different colors. The Moderates' have been blue, the Social Democrats' have been red, the Liberals' have been white. I have not seen more than one of these myself. That one was in Luleå. It was red and came like a blizzard one evening. It honked wherever it went. Then people were gathered, and speeches were held half the night out under the open sky.*[312]

Waldenström remained suspicious that these political meetings were intentionally planned to coincide with the religious revival meetings traditionally held during the summer months. A number of political and cultural groups had now started holding "folk meetings," which were sometimes planned for the same days as the meetings of the mission societies, such as the Värmland St. Ansgar Association (*Ansgariiföreningen*). Claiming to have been invited by some candidates to speak on their behalf, Waldenström explained that he had declined these requests, preferring to hold his own political speeches, even though he was not a candidate himself.[313] Such strategies for grassroots, community organizing that the Pietists had been doing since the 1830s and 40s were now becoming standard practice within Swedish politics. Waldenström's uneasiness is no doubt a result of his realization that political reform ideologies were competing with religious ones, and his choice to hold his own political speeches was an attempt to adapt to that reality and try to reverse the trend.

Whereas the means of socialism were objectionable to Waldenström, many of the ends were quite appealing. Survival in politics also required that he and other opponents to socialism offer alternative avenues toward the reforms demanded by Socialists. It was toward the family and the congregation as the basic building blocks of society that Waldenström directed his appeals for solidarity. This emphasis on social transformation through the religious transformation of the individual is a traditional Pietist approach. Such is expressed in the poem by Leipzig professor Joachim Feller in 1689; "What is a Pietist? He who on God's word in his study feeds / and then, accordingly, also a holy life leads."[314] This type of indirect transformation of society was objectionable to many Socialists, whose righteous indignation about social injustices did not have the patience for this type of "trickle-up" approach. Even Lutheran historian, Eric Gritsch, concludes that the German Pietist August Hermann Francke's (1663–1727) vision to "change the world by changing people" was a utopian dream that would be quickly overrun by other movements, notably the Enlightenment.[315] However, it is clear that Francke's utopian community at Halle and his ability to impact national institutions and politics set a precedent that would remain relevant and influential in Scandinavian Pietism throughout the nineteenth century. On several occasions, Waldenström traveled to Halle, Herrnhut, and Basel and found inspiration in these historic centers of socially-conscious Pietism. The international Deaconess movement had impressed Waldenström and he frequently took the opportunity to advocate such institutions in his newspaper articles.[316] The Deaconess movement had started in Germany as a Lutheran movement to train young women as voluntary nurses and had later spread to Sweden, notably finding early support in Rosenius's congregation at Bethlehem church.[317] Waldenström's travel literature is replete with praise for religious organizations that attempted to provide low or no cost medical help, education, and living accommodations, such as international sailors' homes, orphanages, and immigrant homes and assistance programs in North American ports of entry.[318]

Whether in reaction to the criticisms of his religious-ethical strategy for reform, or as an effort to compete with Socialist ideas, Waldenström also threw his weight behind state-sponsored strategies of addressing social inequalities. The foremost of these was his support of the temperance movement as a solution to the problems of poverty (which will be discussed in Part IV). As already mentioned, his advocacy of voting reform through proportionalism should be seen as a significant component of his alternative reform strategy. To a lesser degree, Waldenström also demonstrated a shift in emphasis away from "charity" and toward educational programs that gave practical skills to the poor that would assist in upward mobility. He preferred that members of the revival would funnel their efforts into religious programs that offered social services. To the modern, secular perspective this might seem to be a marginal venture. However, some of these institutions that once were religious have over the course of the last century evolved into a network of social services now supported by the Swedish state, including many former Deaconess hospitals, as well as schools and orphanages. Because of this there is great difficulty in drawing a line between religious and secular social services in the nineteenth century, and therefore these institutions cannot be simply dismissed as "charity." They were also transformative of society and foundational to the contemporary Swedish health care system and education system, even if they lacked the radical scope of the competing Socialist proposals.

There were also occasions when Waldenström showed criticism of philanthropic work that was too exclusively educational and lacked practical applications. In terms of poor relief, he demonstrated a strong interest in skill-based training programs, which is evident in his praise of programs he observed in Germany that were designed to provide occupational training between school and adult life.[319] At home, there were also occasions when he backed secular conservative efforts as a means of outmaneuvering Socialists. The "Own-Your-Own-Home" movement (*egnahemrörelsen*) was one of these alternate strategies. This movement was a response to the social upheaval that occurred during the great emigration, which politicians increasingly came to see as a national crisis. The old agricultural society was under stress, as unsuccessful farmers or landless servants and laborers moved to the cities and from there to North America and other destinations. *Egnahemrörelsen* was an attempt to buttress the agricultural model, by providing opportunities for people to own affordable houses, and thus to prevent the future workforce from leaving the country. According to Gustav Sundbärg of the Emigration Commission, the cause of this problem was not overpopulation, but lack of new cultivation of land and settlement. In particular, northern Sweden could be opened up to settlement and become like the frontier of the American West and counteract the emigration trend. "Unemployment" became a concept for the first time in politics in the 1880s, and was key to understanding and addressing the migration of people within and out of the country in search of work. Proposals in parliament in 1889–1891 began to see the establishment of new farms and settlements as the prerogative of the state, and by 1899–1901 a committee had been established to investigate the proposals. In 1904, state financed loans were made available for lower-income families to be able to purchase dwellings, with or without acreage. Some of the early designs for these homes resembled idyllic, Carl Larsson-inspired cottages, and there was a clear Romantic ideology behind this effort to strengthen the traditional, agrarian dimension of Swedish society. It was a backward-looking reform effort at first, but it came to serve as a precedent for later models of state-sponsored aid. By 1908, the loans for these homes ceased to be an exclusively rural project and could be applied to urban housing, a change which made the proposal potentially more interesting to its former Socialist critics.[320] Most important to note about this movement is that despite the fact that it came from Conservative and Liberal politicians, it set a precedent for the kind of state-sponsored aid that would become a quintessential aspect of the Welfare State ideology of the Social Democratic party. Socialist critiques had clearly inspired Conservative solutions, which in turn would later inform Socialist solutions.

An exchange of ideas is apparent in reading through Waldenström's discussion of "work cottages" (*arbetsstugor*) in the province of Norrbotten in 1910. Waldenström saw these programs as far more effective than simply throwing money at social problems.

> *Another lasting remnant of this enterprise was the so-called work cottages in Norbotten. Instead of gathering relief funds and casting alms here and there in the homes of the poor, which will quickly be eaten up by the inhabitants, they took care of the children in the work cottages, where they not only got room, board, and clothing, but—what was even greater—they received education, got to learn how to work and in the process, were taught how to earn an honest living in the future. Of the relief funds that I brought back from America, I used part of them to help in these work cottages, but since I received the complaints from the [Mission] Covenant already mentioned, then I had to stop. "The people were supposed to have the money as a gift and not as payment for work," is what they said, quite simply. And that is how it went.*[321]

One of the criticisms of the old poor relief system (*fattigvård*) was that it undermined the dignity of the people receiving the aid, as they were forced to appear before a board, hat in hand, and explain the reasons for their need, which could often be a humiliating experience. Some people opted not to ask for aid, simply to avoid this assault on their dignity. The attraction of the work cottages for Waldenström seems to have been that it connected aid to labor, thus allowing it to take on the sense of being a wage, rather than a handout. He expressed similar sentiments during the *Riksdag* discussions to implement a national pension system (*allmän folkpensionering*, introduced in 1913), arguing that it was time that Swedes abandon the stigma of accepting aid. Pointing to the historic shame attached to accepting poor relief, he expressed his support of proposals for national pensions and hoped that this would change the way that such aid was perceived. While this would mean that new annual taxes would be introduced, he explained that this should not be understood as a new burden, but as a rearrangement of the burdens that people were already carrying.[322] Here is a clear endorsement of a welfare program that accepts the notion that the state will redistribute funds through taxation. While he was warm to these ideas, he also qualified this endorsement with traditional clerical warnings against idleness, encouraging the Swedish people to be diligent in their work, take care of their family and neighbors first and foremost, demonstrate good financial saving habits, avoid living on credit, and "eat their own bread in peace."[323] This is sometimes referred to by Socialist critics as the "message of contentment" (*förnöjsamhetsbudskapet*),[324] in which they saw preachers as agents in undermining the labor movement by shifting the blame for poverty from employers to workers, and accusing the workers of being wasteful and not saving enough from their wages. Waldenström was indeed known to make exhortations to workers to be better stewards of their resources. However, it was not the only solution that he explored, and he seems to have been increasingly interested in systemic solutions to poverty.

At other times Waldenström's language sounded almost indistinguishable from Socialists when he discussed social problems. While traveling through Härjedalen in 1903, Waldenström described the difficult situation of the small land owners and timber industry workers.

> *But it is deplorable that the freeholding farmer class is in this way increasingly becoming a class of tenant farmers for the companies. How one should advise a cure for this is a great social problem, the solution to which has not yet been found. For that matter, it is a trend throughout the world that the big people swallow up the little people. Great kingdoms swallow up the small ones, great companies swallow up the small ones, and so on. The power of capital is growing with a terrifying strength.*[325]

At these points, there is clear evidence that Waldenström had been influenced by the language, if not also the ideals, of socialism, and was using it to craft his own Christianized response to counter the claims of the Socialists. Ragnar Tomson was apt to point out that this influence of the language and ideals of socialism had appeared very early in Waldenström's career, most notably in 1879 following the general strike in Sundsvall. The strike had arisen when the timber industry experienced a depression, which caused the price of timber to fall. The response of the "timber barons" (*träpatronerna*) was to lower the workers' wages. When the workers began to organize demonstrations, strike breakers were brought in, as well as military forces to quell potential unrest. Despite the fact that the workers had been forced from their housing to make room for the strike breakers, they were remarkably well disciplined and even held prayer meetings in the evenings. The strike lasted eight days and culminated in an ultimatum to the workers that they could choose between imprisonment or returning to work, and the workers chose the latter. Though preachers in the area, some being employed directly by the timber barons, had encouraged the workers to return to work, there seems to have also been expressions of sympathy for the workers' plight, as well as a direct connection of the religious awakening with a demand for justice. After the strike, Waldenström is reported to have traveled up to Sundsvall to interview the workers who had gone on strike, later explaining that the workers had no choice but to strike.[326] One aspect of the strike in Sundsvall that may have made it more palatable to a liberal-leaning person like Waldenström is that the workers do not seem to have been as inspired by radical socialist sentiments, but rather demonstrated a kind of traditional antagonism to modernization, vaguely conceived. In other words, the exploitation of the timber barons demonstrated first and foremost a threat to traditional agrarian parish life. This follows the sentiments expressed by workers in the early formation of the labor movement in England, although appearing much later in Sweden due to the delay of industrialization.[327] Waldenström's sympathy for these workers, whose wages suffered the brunt of the depression, can be seen as a sincere pastoral concern for "victims of modernization." That these workers found inspiration in prayer meetings and behaved peaceably no doubt also helped to inspire him to come to their defense.

Waldenström demonstrated a mix of traditional attitudes toward civil order, which held to the notion that socialism and the kind of striking practices that Socialists advocated were dangerous because they risked anarchy. His Lutheran worldview reinforced the idea that the present order of society was to greater or lesser degrees ordained by God, and that a flawed social order was better than chaos. However, he was in favor of reform and consistently expressed a sympathetic attitude to the vulnerable in society, even though he refrained from dividing society into "classes." He sometimes drifted into traditional admonitions to workers to be disciplined, frugal, and obedient to the law, which was part of a good Christian character. But these admonitions also applied to the employers. Seldom did Waldenström directly address the labor movement from the pulpit, but Ragnar Tomson notes one occasion when Waldenström did in fact give a provocative sermon in Immanuel Church in Stockholm in 1892. Here he drew from Malachi chapter 3 and the prophet's harsh judgment against those who "defraud laborers of their wages." The current situation between employers and employees in Sweden was "highly disquieting," he explained. Though Christian workers have an obligation to remain dutiful employees and law-abiding citizens, this does not excuse the employers from abusing their employees, for which they can expect to be judged by God. There was an inexcusable culture of greed among employers in Sweden, who attempted to make every increase of profit possible, which were "scraped out of the marrow and bone" of their workers (*skrapade ur arbetarnas märg och ben*).[328] Vocabulary like this not only draws straight from the social justice tradition of the Old Testament and the Hebrew prophets, but also is strikingly similar to the vocabulary used by Socialist agitators, indicating that Waldenström was not afraid to borrow from his opponents. Tomson may be his greatest champion in terms of emphasizing his radical pronouncements, but he is not the only historian who has pointed out this pattern of Waldenström's nuanced consideration of social issues. Other historians have also offered glimpses of Waldenström as a man sincerely troubled by the plight of the working class, critical of abusive employers, and perceptive of his political opponents' critiques.[329]

As Waldenström's vocabulary evolved and appropriated the critiques of socialism, this can be seen not only as political maneuvering, but also as a genuine exchange of ideas. It also represents a grey area within Swedish politics where there is potentially more overlap than has been admitted in the past. Swedish historiography has sometimes presented a starkly polarized view of the political camps, which has obscured this overlap. As Åsa Linderborg has pointed out, the Social Democratic party has often looked to the revolutionary and inflammatory characteristics of its founding members when writing its history. The glorification of this type of politician is partly a creation, however, and thwarts investigation into the origins of Social Democracy. The type of socialism that developed in the formative decades of Swedish politics was very much tempered by a preference for democratic discussion. The language of class warfare was used by some columnists and agitators, but these people were often sidelined in favor of the Hjalmar Brantings of the party. The "middle way" seems to have succeeded because the belligerent vocabulary of both conservatives and radicals was defused. In contrast, the vocabulary of reform appeared across party lines.

Commentators of the middle way have often puzzled over the fact that Sweden did not see the type of revolution that occurred in neighboring countries. Part of the reason for this outcome can be seen by understanding why certain leaders succeeded and not others. Hjalmar Branting emerged as a leader in this period, not because he was revolutionary or inflammatory, but because his message transcended class and party lines. It was not a given that such a politician would succeed. One must also look at the whole political landscape and identify other leaders who set the tone for this choice. At this crucial time in Sweden's political history, Waldenström was one of the most visible critics of the Social Democratic party. Understanding his criticism and its potential appeal in Swedish society is therefore important to understanding why Branting succeeded in rising to the leadership of the Social Democrats and not other, more extremist leaders. The critical exchanges between these Pietists and Socialists invariably informed the perspectives and rhetoric of each movement, and seem to have led to the net result of a general preference for democratic pluralism.

PART IV

Tempering the Politics of Temperance

> *Temperance legislation has, for a long time—despite occasional mistakes—been based in a desire for forward progress. The same is true regarding our opinions about it. But anything that is going to last must grow from the inside out, and that takes time.*
>
> *One spring, there was supposed to be an inspection of an agricultural school. The principal had the students cut down a great many birches and set them up as an avenue. It looked very good, and he was praised by the inspector, who had no way of knowing that the birches had not grown on that site. But in a short while they withered. They had no roots. The story is true and may serve as a useful analogy for a legislation, which goes too quickly, which progresses past the general conception of justice, even if it runs in the right direction.*[330]

—Waldenström, Letters to *Svenska Morgonbladet* and *Jönköpings Posten*, New Year's 1916

CHAPTER 13

Defining Moderate v. Absolutist Abstinence Politics

THE TEMPERANCE MOVEMENT OCCUPIES a prominent place in the history of the Swedish folk movements. Though its influence is unquestionable, its legacy is complex and contested. On the one hand, the breakthrough of democracy itself is often credited to the political lessons that the participants in the movement learned as they developed competencies in public speaking and debating, organizational procedures, and familiarity with mobilizing the electorate and influencing parliament. Among these competencies were how to organize protests, how to raise money, how to inform and rally public opinion by making use of scientific data and statistics, and how to elect representatives into office. Perhaps most important was the ability to articulate a message that would resonate with the concerns of the time. How could the temperance movement best address the concerns that people had about society, in particular as it might relate to alcohol? In order to do this, the leaders within the movement needed to hone their vocabulary in order to make the case for abstinence from alcohol seem relevant, timely, fashionable, urgent, inevitable, or morally necessary.

On the other hand, in terms of democratic pluralism, the legacy of the movement is complex in that it has demonstrated waves of extremism that sought to restrict the lifestyle and behaviors of all citizens regarding alcohol, even those who dissented. Abstinence from alcohol took on varying degrees, from total abstinence at one extreme, to moderate restrictions on the other. Leaders had choices in how they framed the argument, as well as choices in the degree to which they cooperated with factions within the movement as well as with their opposition. The paradox of the temperance movement is that it was able to emerge as a result of democratic freedoms and ideals, but had the potential to restrict those freedoms if it overstepped foundational principles of pluralism. This paradox was not unique to the temperance movement, but can be shared by any number of similar democratic movements, historical or modern, that have as part of their program the restriction of human behavior in any way. This section will present these types of movements as "abstinence movements," and offer some conclusions on the relationship between such movements and pluralist democracy.

P. P. Waldenström devoted a great deal of time in his preaching and his political career to the temperance cause. Of the eighty-eight motions that he introduced in parliament in the course of his career, thirty-six concerned the regulation of alcohol and related matters.[331] Despite his active involvement and his high visibility in the movement, he remained largely detached from temperance organizations and also demonstrated an independence of opinion, which makes assessment of his legacy complicated. While many preachers denounced drinking primarily in moral terms (as "sin" for example), Waldenström routinely chose other strategies for discussing and solving problems related to alcoholism. These strategies involved incorporating a variety of perspectives on the debate that he had observed in his international travels and his participation in parliamentary debates, such as questions of consumer protection, the role of the government in ensuring public health, and the rights of local organizations, counties, and towns in deciding their own laws. Temperance concerns found plenty of space in his travel accounts. These books became a prime opportunity for him to present his views on a number of social issues, and the temperance movement was one of the foremost of these causes. In city after city that Waldenström visited in the United States and Canada, he gathered facts on the local policies regarding alcohol, which varied greatly. Comparisons were drawn with events and trends at home in Sweden, and Waldenström urged his readers to take up the temperance cause in their area.

> A short while ago here in Sweden, the production and sale of phosphorus matches was forbidden, and this on the grounds that one or another worker employed in the industry, who was incautious, became ill, and partially because women used the poison from these matches to induce miscarriages. All of this is trivial in comparison with the devastation that alcohol causes. This everyone knows. But despite this, alcohol is loose, and if there are people someplace who want to protect themselves against it, then it requires an enormous struggle and agitation on the part of the friends of temperance.[332]

Although he grossly understates the seriousness of the campaign to regulate the phosphorus match industry, connections like this between the regulation of alcohol and the general health of the public were often made. As is clear from the literature of the movement, Waldenström and other agitators presented a case that the government should not have a *laissez faire* attitude regarding certain risks to the public that were deemed too great for people to be able to overcome on their own. It was not sufficient to simply tell people not to consume alcohol, as the extent to which alcohol was woven into the average Swede's daily life was obvious.

> *Drunkenness is not least among the enlightened and educated classes. People even think it is impossible to celebrate our churchly parties without "wine and strong drinks." When couples are married, there shall be drinking; when children are born, there shall be drinking; when a family member is buried, there shall be drinking; when a church is dedicated, and a parish priest installed, there shall be drinking. The oldest memory that I have from my boyhood years of a burial was overhearing the host chatting with the priest, saying: "This is the last time we will get drunk for old Stina." Everyone complains about it, but no one has the courage to change the culture.*[333]

Alcohol was such a widespread part of Swedish culture, that it was virtually impossible for people to completely remove themselves from its influence. For the working class, alcoholism and extreme poverty were often combined, and the inability to escape the negative effects of alcohol was an especially acute reality. Education alone would not suffice in providing citizens with the foothold needed to stabilize their condition. Some kind of government intervention and regulation was deemed necessary.

From the perspective of the early twenty-first century, this type of grassroots citizen action campaign has become a staple in most industrialized, democratic nations, so much so that the practices and vocabularies of these types of awareness-raising movements follow predictable patterns and can even become a bit cliché. Whether it is a campaign to eliminate asbestos, DDT, lead-based paint, carcinogens of all kinds, additive hormones in food, animal fur clothing, or second-hand smoke, the leaders of such movements rely on similar narrative strategies to catch attention, "raise awareness," and appeal to the reason and emotions of different audiences. However, a century and a half ago, this type of populist campaign was by and large a novel idea. Temperance movement leaders were among the pioneers of this type of social action. In the past, "the mob" had certainly expressed its dissatisfaction with governments, but the temperance movement represented a departure from revolutions and mob frustration. This new type of movement was prolonged, concentrated on single issues, worked through democratic channels, and largely did not involve a change of regime, but rather a change of practice geared toward improving the quality of life for part or all of the population.

Gaining inspiration from the earlier international movement to abolish slavery,[334] the Swedish temperance movement became a practical outlet for a variety of other ideologies that were current. Revival Christianity often called for concrete changes of lifestyle and the application of one's faith to life and society, and this was certainly also the case among the Swedish Pietists. For different reasons, Socialists also sometimes identified alcohol consumption and alcoholism among the cultural and financial hindrances that prevented the working class from progress. The temperance movement offered an outlet for both of these populations to express their critiques of the relationship of the Swedish public to alcohol, and these unlikely allies could find common ground within temperance organizations. Regardless of the ideological origins, what temperance called for was a restriction of behavior, and thus a restriction on individual freedom. Either the individual could learn to restrict his or her own behavior and preferences and choose to do this freely, or society could do it for them through legal restrictions, or a combination of both. Whether alcohol was presented as merely posing a health hazard, an economic drain, or as a morally defined "evil," opponents who wanted to maintain their recreational pastimes, or who did not want to lose the income they made from alcohol sales, would cast these efforts as moralism and intolerance. The card that these opponents often played in their defense was an appeal to individual liberty as a foundational concept for democracy. Temperance advocates and opponents thus pitted different aspects of democratic theory against one another.

One of the classic ways used to discuss the Swedish temperance movement is to divide it into two camps, between absolutists and moderates; absolutists being the people who wanted complete prohibition of alcohol, and the moderates being those who simply wanted restrictions.[335] This interplay between moderates and absolutists makes for interesting speculation about the overall outcome of the temperance movement in Sweden, namely the failure of prohibition proposals in 1922 and the success of the so-called Bratt System of government-run alcohol regulation. Historian Lennart Johansson took up the question of the origins of what he called *Systemet lagom*, which can be translated as "the moderate system" or the "middle system" (*lagom* meaning "just right"). Whereas previous scholarship had assumed that absolutism was a foreign, Anglo-American influence, which was outdone by the more indigenous moderate temperance perspective of Per

Wieselgren, Johansson demonstrates that absolutism had a much stronger hold in Sweden.[336] The internal debate between moderates and absolutists in the movement was intense and could be sharply divided at times.

On this question of the role of moderates in the Swedish temperance movement, there are still areas where more research can be beneficial, in particular in clarifying exactly what it means to be a "moderate." To be an absolutist, or perhaps even an extremist, in a political or social movement, is to have a fairly clearly defined position. But moderates are more difficult to place and most often it seems that moderates are seen as lacking a position, or lacking the enthusiasm and commitment to the position taken by the absolutists. However, moderate political actors can be defined by more than simply the level of their commitment and enthusiasm. They can be as equally driven by ideology as their absolutist counterparts. Both seek to generate consensus in the broader public regarding their concerns. As will be asserted here, Waldenström can be defined as a moderate because of how he sought to cultivate consensus, which was *to prioritize education over legislation*. Waldenström viewed the individual as possessing sufficient agency needed to change his or her own situation, as well as to sustain societal change over the long term. He differed with absolutists who transferred this agency to society or the state, and who therefore gravitated toward restrictive legislation as a means to force societal change from the top down. In practical terms, if moderates are defined by a preference for education and absolutists as having a preference for legislation, one may also concede that these groups can serve a complementary role to one another. An exchange between these two camps may be necessary for any change to come about at all.

In understanding this dynamic relationship, a comparison to a contemporary social movement may be beneficial, namely post-1960s environmentalism.[337] More specifically, it is the discourse of a sub-movement within environmentalism concerned with the elimination of fossil fuel consumption that bears comparison to the temperance movement here. Both of these movements are what can be called "abstinence movements," in that each represents a call to society to cease a certain activity. Both movements have identified a toxic liquid as the enemy—oil in the one case, alcohol in the other—and have developed narratives that claim that the consumption of these liquids will spell disaster for the human race. The distinction between preferences for education or legislation can help in understanding the line between absolutist and moderate political stances in general. This becomes apparent when comparing their discourse. Like temperance advocates, environmentalists often emphasize the "addiction" of human society to fossil fuels and the imminent need to cease consumption in order to mitigate global climate change.[338] Many environmentalists take an absolutist stance on eliminating fossil fuels and advocate drastic restrictions on emissions. Within the context of a pluralist democracy, this can become a problematic tension between restricting negative behavior and restricting human freedoms. While people are encouraged to strive for a "carbon footprint of zero," in practice regulating this can become difficult to achieve without significantly restricting human liberties.

The second similarity between the temperance movement and environmentalism is the apocalyptic or millennial imagery that is used. This language invokes the prospect of the end of the world as a means of communicating the disaster that will come about as a result of current human behavior. "Millennialism" generally describes how religious groups discuss the end of the world. It is also understood as a form of fanaticism, and furthermore, as a fanaticism that poses a threat to free and democratic society. However, there are two aspects of millennialism that are not typically acknowledged. First, this language is employed by many types of movements, even those who present themselves as wholly secular. Second, this language can have the practical effect of mobilizing people for collective action. Folklorist Ted Daniels describes a vast array of religious and social movements which use millennialist discourse as a means of bringing about change.[339] Whether leaders in a movement believe that the catastrophe is destined or can be avoided, and whether this catastrophe is real or figurative, the vocabulary they use is designed to create the sense of urgency, the type of urgency that is often required to prompt and sustain collective action. Daniels does not hesitate to include environmentalism in his survey of the movements that employ this language, and even suggests that environmentalists' use of millennialist language may at times be an essential strategy in motivating the broader public to embrace the values of a minority movement.

In terms of the temperance movement, Waldenström has most often been identified as having been a moderate, although this identification is not clear-cut. Although he remained aloof to both temperance organizations and political parties, Waldenström was nevertheless an influential figure in the temperance movement as a whole, even among absolutists. Waldemar Skarstedt's commemorative book from 1903, called "Standard Bearers of the Temperance Movement," contains short biographies of 119 so-called "contemporary temperance warriors."[340] In the listings, Waldenström scores rather highly. In this "who's who" of temperance warriors, he receives eight pages of space, being outdone by only five other people.[341] Skarstedt is an absolutist, and in his foreword explains that he mainly included absolutists in his book. Even Waldenström is identified as an absolutist, although with the qualification that he technically operated independently. Lennart Johansson's work more convincingly places Waldenström in the moderate camp, however.³⁴² Skarstedt was not entirely incorrect by including Waldenström in his book of absolutists. Waldenström was indeed passionately of the mindset that alcohol was a cause of many social problems, and was best removed from society, and furthermore he thought that the state should take an active role in removing it. Had Swedes in fact voted to embrace prohibition in 1922, it is unlikely that Waldenström would have been disappointed. However, where he differed from absolutists was not in passion, but in priorities for building consensus. Waldenström preferred education over legislation, and when he did make motions for legislative measures in the *Riksdag*, he preferred incremental policies and programs to mitigate the effects of alcohol, rather than complete restrictions. These included medical treatment for alcoholics, restrictions on the placement of pubs near jobsites of industrial workers, and transportation safety laws that would prohibit train conductors from drinking while on the job (which in the 1890s was apparently commonplace and legal).³⁴³

An alarmist Waldenström says "Look, Mr. General Director, where all this terrible drunkenness will lead!" "Waldenström i farten" Edvard Forsström. *Söndags-Nisse*. Jan. 1899. Reproduction: Kungliga biblioteket.

However, although absolutism may not inherently be fanaticism, it can easily become fanaticism. Fanaticism is defined here as the point when discussion and dissent are no longer possible. Waldenström demonstrated his own awareness of the fine line between absolutism and fanaticism in his writing. One example is a political speech that he gave in July of 1902 at the

Nordic Temperance Meeting in Stockholm,[344] the title of which was "The Struggle for Temperance" (*Kampen för nykterhet*). In several instances, the language he used is rather indistinguishable from absolutists, and he echoed the sentiments of absolutists who argued that alcohol needed to be removed from society, and that solving the alcohol question should be the nation's top priority.[345] However, in other passages, he spoke with a more detached voice, making arguments that alcohol was more of a symptom of social ills, rather than a main problem. While he still held to the idea that alcohol was a substance best restricted, he indicated that the source of the problems of alcohol abuse lay deeper. His ultimate solution was the improvement of the overall moral character of Swedish citizens. Steeped in the theology of revival Christianity, Waldenström presents the struggle for temperance as a broader struggle for spiritual maturity, which prohibition alone would not be able to achieve.

> *Morality is a system of virtues, and immorality is, in its own way, a system of vices. Nevertheless, the Holy Scriptures do not identify our deliverance as being dependent upon a human being's ability to set aside this or that particular sinful practice, but instead identifies our deliverance as being based in the* complete moral restoration of humankind.[346]

On this point he resembles one of his contemporaries, the author Selma Lagerlöf (1858–1940), who explored the question of alcoholism in several of her novels, perhaps most directly in "The Phantom Carriage" (*Körkarlen*, 1912). After Lagerlöf's main character David Holm undergoes a transformative experience dealing with the effects of alcoholism on his family, he utters the pious wish: "*Gud låt min själ få komma till mognad innan den skall skördas*" ("God let my soul mature before it is harvested").[347] Her preference was for societal change to be based in the sound moral upbringing of individual citizens. Though Lagerlöf's spirituality was vague and nonconventional, she is emblematic of the moderate perspective, which saw this social issue as a symptom rather than the main problem; here there is common ground with Waldenström. What differentiates him from Lagerlöf is his sincere optimism that the form of Christianity presented in the revivals could indeed cultivate mature individuals who would in turn transform society. This maturity would depend on the degree to which the temperance movement was successful in education programs.

Another of Waldenström's speeches was given at Uppsala University in 1897 to the student temperance association, with the title "Leave the glass be!" (*Låt glaset stå!*). Here he made interesting comments on the interdependence of absolutists and moderates. Contrasting the Reformation leaders Martin Luther and Philip Melancthon, he stated that in this partnership, Luther was the extremist, who overstated his cause in order to be heard. Had he not made overstatements, he would not have been heard at all. Melancthon, on the other hand, was the moderate, who had the luxury of riding in Luther's wake, and would not have been heard either, if it had not been for Luther's prophetic voice. When one praises Melancthon's moderation, one misses the necessity of Luther's prophetic role, according to Waldenström.[348] He also reflected on this conflict (or synergy) between absolutism and moderatism in his 1901 visit to the United States. In his travel account, he devotes several pages to the story of Carrie Nation (1846–1911). Armed with axe in hand, Carrie Nation had led other women on vigilante charges into illegal bars in Kansas the year before, smashing kegs and furniture as a dramatic public statement against the inability or unwillingness of the police to enforce liquor laws. Waldenström was fascinated with Carrie Nation in that she represented a form of prophetic protest, and he echoed her own comments that she was fulfilling a similar function as Jesus Christ had done, when he used a whip to drive the money changers out of the temple in Jerusalem.[349] Carrie Nation's fanaticism may have been disturbing and problematic to Waldenström, but he seems to have seen this absolutism as a sort of necessary prophetic action that served to raise awareness for a cause that could not have been communicated through education alone.[350]

However, he ultimately concluded that, since Carrie Nation's sensational actions had a limited effect, they were perhaps no more effective than other measures of raising public awareness.

> *This highly remarkable movement, however, soon died down, and in a short while, no one was speaking any more about Mrs. Nation. The Lord was not in the tempest. The smashed glasses were replaced with new ones, the mirrors and other objects destroyed by her axe were repaired, and the flood of liquor flowed once again in its old furrow, oppressing, drowning, and overwhelming young and old, rich and poor, men, women, and children, domestic happiness, the health of youth, and the security of old age.*[351]

Waldenström's perspective on social movements was one that understood long, sustained reform movements to be more effective than dramatic, emotional ones. Carrie Nation's fanaticism continued to be inspiring to him on some level,[352] but ultimately problematic for his own philosophy of social action. The key to success in a movement was to educate people over a long period of time so that these values truly saturated the culture, rather than coming as a reactionary fad that would quickly wear off. He found occasion to express this concern while discussing the temperance politics in Iowa.

At the time of his visit in 1901, Iowa was a prohibition state, but there was a strong lobby attempting to overturn that status. Waldenström repeated the words of the newspaper *Minneapolis Veckobladet*, which identified the challenge faced by the friends of temperance as requiring the development of endurance and maturity among their numbers.

> . . . *the opinions on temperance are not mature enough for the majority of people to be able to persevere against the liquor mob's unbelievable endurance and power. It is not difficult to work oneself up into a momentary enthusiasm for a certain cause. But it is markedly more difficult to maintain this enthusiasm in the long run.*[353]

Perhaps the clearest way to understand how Waldenström diverged from the absolutists in the temperance movement is to contrast his speeches and pronouncements on the matter with those made by another temperance leader, Johan Bergman. Bergman had credited Waldenström with having been the "captain of the temperance movement in the *Riksdag*," but added that outside of the *Riksdag* he was far from it.[354] That place was apparently reserved for Bergman himself. Bergman was also an absolutist, and coincidentally enjoyed by far the most treatment in Waldemar Skarstedt's book, mentioned already. His zeal for the complete prohibition of alcohol is evident in his speeches, including one held in Lund in 1899, which began with a refutation of what he deemed were ineffective and harmful trends within the temperance movement.

> *I hate all obscurantism, all narrow-mindedness, and all fanaticism with a hatred that is so intense, that the strongest words of the language are too weak to give any real approximate expression to its passion. But just as intensively, I hate the culture surrounding drinking.*[355]

Earlier, Bergman had made an attempt to distinguish his "modern" version of temperance from obscurantism, narrow-mindedness, and fanaticism, and he had also included "Pietism" in that first list. The fact that he stopped short of expressing his hatred for Pietism in this second list is not surprising, for as much as he may have harbored a hatred for that movement, for him to go so far as to express this would have meant alienating a great deal of the most active participants in the temperance movement. An indirect allusion would suffice in communicating his critique of Pietism's approach to temperance. As he explained later, unlike the ethical-religious temperance movement of previous generations, which he claimed had emphasized a moral condemnation of the evils of alcohol and articulated them in spiritual terms, he instead argued in favor of a "modern" strategy, which was enlightened and based on scientific findings.[356] These findings, for him, pointed to the conclusion that the prohibition of all alcohol was not only in the best interest of society, but was urgently required. Anything short of full prohibition would be futile, and just as the Swedish government had dealt with the health dangers of the phosphorus match industry through legislation (not merely by issuing optional advisory warnings), so too ought the government to react against the undeniably negative influence of alcohol.[357]

Furthermore, Bergman challenged the notion that the traditional focus of the temperance movement in Sweden had been a moderate approach. Absolutism, as has been noted, has typically been seen as a latecomer to Sweden, inspired by developments in Great Britain and the United States, whereas "moderatism" was seen as the more homegrown, uniquely Swedish movement. Even in 1900 it was necessary for Bergman to try to dispel this assumption in order to make his case for absolutism. In his biography of the great temperance leader Per Wieselgren (1800–1877), for example, Bergman challenged the notion that this patron saint of the movement had truly been a moderate, and instead painted him as an absolutist (even though Wieselgren had primarily focused on the liquor known as *brännvin*, rather than beer and wine).[358] Such revisions to the historical narrative demonstrate Bergman's effort to make the case to his audience for a legally instituted prohibition, firmly based in scientific findings, rather than in religious ideology. As in response to any other poison or pollutant, the government had an obligation to draw conclusions from scientific research and act to protect its citizens from the toxic liquid of alcohol.[359] Although Bergman's passionate rhetoric of hatred cooled down as he explained the history of alcohol and its regulation throughout Europe, his absolutist posture remained throughout the rest of the speech. Bergman made the assertion that the legislative activity of the temperance movement was *equal* in importance to its educational activity. The educational agenda of the movement had a powerful role to play in changing the cultural norms regarding alcohol, but restrictive legislation was equally necessary if the movement was to be successful at all.[360] Only a society completely free from the temptation of alcohol would be able to free itself from its vices, he reasoned. He thereby rejected the dominant sentiment of the earlier temperance movement in Sweden, which had emphasized the use of legislation to promote moderation in the culture surrounding the consumption of alcohol.[361] Even as late as 1932, Bergman maintained that the government could not promote the cause of temperance and the health of the nation while simultaneously preserving a space for alcohol.[362]

That Waldenström would distance himself from full participation in the temperance movement is not surprising given Bergman's refutation of the ethical-religious basis for the movement. But it was not just this rejection of religion that bothered Waldenström. It was also the method. Waldenström agreed with Bergman that legislation was needed to facilitate the educational work of the movement, but he stopped short of giving legislation the same pride of place as recommended by Bergman. For Waldenström, cultural change through education was the primary function of the temperance movement; legislation was simply a means to facilitate that educational work, not the goal of it.[363] Waldenström, too, had his moments playing the role of a temperance prophet, but he proved himself to be a moderate by his preference for cultivating consensus through education, rather than through prophetic fanaticism or legislation. Waldenström appears to have seen absolutism as a useful and even necessary tool in raising awareness of the problems of alcohol in society, but saw his own role to be that of a moderate and to help society avoid the pitfall of extremism. It is important to repeat that he saw the relationship between moderates and absolutists as one of mutual dependence. Without the presence of a certain amount of prophetic voice, it becomes difficult for a social movement to articulate the urgency of social change. On the other hand, absolutism can devolve into fanaticism when it is not reinforced by moderates who pursue consensus with the greater public through education. Moderate positions are not simply the half-hearted or lukewarm versions of the positions taken by absolutists. Waldenström attempted to articulate that there was a dynamic role for moderates to play in crafting enduring cultural reforms through education. Finally, it is of course important to point out that within the debate on temperance, there was a diversity of opinions regarding the effectiveness and necessity of various strategies in legislative debates. Waldenström and Bergman are presented here due to the high level of their visibility and influence, and not at all to imply that Swedes had only two options in this question.

CHAPTER 14

Pragmatism and Experimentation with Best Practices

THE TEMPERANCE MOVEMENT, IN choosing the name "temperance," drew on the general concept of the virtue of moderation. In Swedish, *nykterhet* can be translated as temperance, and more specifically means sobriety. The goal of the movement was to instill positive virtues, the ability to manage or completely abstain from a potentially harmful relationship to alcohol. Historically in Sweden, efforts to instill temperance and sobriety had long been the goal of rulers and legislators, though this had typically been done through negative reinforcement. The individual who suffered from alcoholism was punished by threat of prison sentences, or through the general shame of public condemnation, or the humiliation of losing one's livelihood and not being able to provide for one's family. One of the lasting contributions of the temperance movement was the increased prevalence of the notion that the private suffering of individual alcoholics and their family members was not a private concern at all, but demanded a public response from the community, which could not simply be limited to negative reinforcement.

The strategy of using negative reinforcement (penalties) to combat the vices associated with alcohol was based on the assumption that the individual is primarily or completely in control of one's decisions, and will logically weigh the incentives of a given behavior against the consequences and arrive at the socially preferred conclusion. It became increasingly apparent for Waldenström and other temperance advocates, however, that for the great number of working class people who suffered from the effects of alcoholism, these traditional consequences were not sufficient and could in fact be harmful. Alcoholics and their families should not just be punished, but should be safeguarded with protective legislation to limit the distribution of alcohol. According to Waldenström, the very nature of alcoholism ought to be re-evaluated and focus on mitigating the effects of alcohol rather than simply moralizing against it. A progressive notion at the time was that alcoholism for some was the result of a disease, and could not be overcome through individual will power alone. Waldenström picked up on such medical findings and incorporated them into his temperance speeches. During debates on a temperance motion in the *Riksdag* in 1896, he argued that alcoholism should be considered a sickness and not treated with imprisonment, but with state-sponsored treatment.[364] While on tour in North America, Waldenström repeated these convictions, and relayed the claims of an unnamed French politician that alcoholism could be passed down through generations in the same family, and that it can affect the brain leading to loss of intelligence, insanity, and death.[365] These were not private concerns, but required public attention. Anticipating the argument of critics who would say that there was no funding for such progressive programs, Waldenström pointed out that society was already paying much higher costs by ignoring these problems. Pointing again to statistics circulating among the temperance societies, he explained that an enormous amount of resources were already being spent on medical treatment and mental hospitals, not to mention the great loss of productivity in the workforce and the crippling effects of poverty in the urban slums.[366]

Part of Waldenström's specific understanding about alcohol can be related to his general view about the function of the law in society, which he derived from his theology. Within Lutheranism, there had traditionally been a division of scripture into "law" and "gospel," the former end of the spectrum being associated with the Old Testament texts including Mosaic law, and the latter being associated with the New Testament and Christ's message of grace, forgiveness, and love. These two poles could be viewed as standing in tension with one another, the challenge for the person of faith being to navigate between legalism on the one hand and lawlessness on the other. Part of this dilemma has been discussed in the chapter on *Squire Adamsson,* in which Waldenström explained his strategy for maintaining unity among the faithful as they sought out the narrow way between these two extremes. Here in relation to the temperance movement, one can see a direct extrapolation of this strategy to a social and political issue. What was the function of religiously derived norms concerning alcohol consumption? Furthermore, what function should national alcohol laws and policies have in improving the well-being of citizens? Do the laws and the justice system exist to frighten them into correct behavior, or to shame them into improvement? Is imprisonment nothing more than a humanly instituted version of hell? The answer to such questions for Waldenström was based in the Rosenian ("new evangelical") tradition of interpreting the three functions of the law in Lutheran theology. The first function of the law was to view the commandments of Scripture as a means to uphold order in society. Since the Reformation, Swedish secular law had been an application of this religious worldview, as the laws of the land and societal norms could function alternately as a deterrent for negative behavior or as an inspiration for ideal moral behavior. The second and third functions of the law are more exclusively spiritual. The second function of the law was an instructive one, in which the realization of the impossibility of completely upholding the law served to awaken the individual to concede his or her utter sinfulness, and acknowledge the debilitating fact that human beings are incapable of living up to these standards on their own. God alone is righteous, and it is only through God's grace that humans can be made righteous. This realization was a spiritual crisis, which the Rosenians sometimes referred to as an experience of *anfäktelse*, in which the individual is tempted between, on the one hand, the will to have faith in God's promises of forgiveness and the hope of improvement in this life and salvation in the next, and on the other hand is tempted to doubt these promises. At this pivotal moment, there is the possibility that the individual will give in to the temptation of doubt and abandon faith altogether. However, if the second function of the law can successfully serve as a catalyst for spiritual growth, then this opens the possibility of the third function of the law, which is to facilitate the realization of God's promises once the individual has navigated through this crisis. Having been objectively instructed by the law in the first function, then brought to the subjective experience of crisis in the second, the third function facilitates a phenomenon more often referred to as sanctification, or the process of being made holy. In classic Lutheran vocabulary, this can only be through faith alone in God's grace alone.

In the 1850s and 60s, new evangelicals like Rosenius and Waldenström faced harsh criticism from the Church of Sweden for over-emphasizing the third function and under-emphasizing the first and second, a choice which prompted accusations of heresy and antinomianism (lawlessness).[367] Indeed spiritual crises of temptation (*anfäktelse*) remained an ingredient of Rosenius's and Waldenström's theologies. However, descriptions of these crises were usually quickly followed up with proclamations of assurance (*tröst*) that the individual can depend on God's promises and have faith in the potential to be transformed as righteous. The fact that Waldenström came from a Christian tradition that emphasized the third function of the law would come to be decisive in his political attitudes about temperance legislation. It was more important for him that laws and policies be outcome-based (producing thriving, spiritually mature citizens), and less important that these laws function as deterrents or punishment. His moderate stance on temperance legislation often came down to a pragmatic evaluation of the effectiveness of these policies to bring about the desired outcome.

Alcoholism was a primary cause of poverty, in Waldenström's mind. In the perennial, chicken-and-egg argument between the temperance movement and the labor movement on the origins of poverty, much of the temperance movement took the stance that if alcohol was removed from the lives of the working class, poverty would automatically be alleviated. Socialists, who were also often engaged in the temperance movement, usually disagreed. In Gävle, the newspaper *Arbetarbladet* refuted Waldenström's notion that alcoholism was the primary factor preventing the success of the working class, and called his theory a misplaced analogy.[368] Undeterred, Waldenström continued to defend the argument that alcoholism had far-reaching economic consequences, and furthermore, that these problems were cyclical and systemic. In one of his speeches, he declared that "drunkenness is a hindrance for the economy,"[369] making the case here as elsewhere that it is the culture of excessive indulgence in luxury items like alcohol and tobacco that are a prime cause of poverty.[370] Wherever he traveled in the world, he was quick to comment on the relationship of alcohol to poverty in the communities he visited. While in the United Kingdom, he pointed out that in many run-down areas of the towns he visited, the only attractive building was the bar, drawing the conclusion that economic vitality was visibly being siphoned out of the community through the conduit of establishments that placed alcohol at the center of social life.[371] The direct connection between alcohol and the plight of the working class was visible in the trend of bars being allowed to locate right in the heart of industrial areas, and in so doing, make it all too easy for workers to take a detour into the bars after work and spend their earnings on alcohol before that money ever had a chance to make it home. This was central in his argument that the local community needed the right to be able to create small prohibition zones, as deemed necessary.[372]

In terms of democratic values, Waldenström's economic argument regarding the temperance movement was at its core a statement about the interdependence of the individual citizen's well-being and the well-being of the society as a whole. While individual freedom of conscience and freedom of lifestyle are values that are prominent themes in the preceding chapters, the issue of temperance offers a prime opportunity for discussing where the boundary lay for Waldenström between individual freedom and societal obligation. Critics of the temperance movement argued that temperance legislation was an affront to personal liberties and an infringement on the lifestyles of those who dissented from the opinion that alcohol was a cause of societal ills, such as the economic argument. Waldenström countered these criticisms by questioning whether or not it was a matter of personal choice at all. He complained that people ". . . always speak so beautifully about the individual's right of self determination, to which one should not tread too closely," but in actuality, he explained that their chief concern was over the loss of income to the state and businesses that would result from these laws.[373] The right of self-determination, as he put it, was being used as a convenient distraction, designed to protect the financial interests of the parties who benefited from alcohol sales.

Among the opponents of temperance was an influential lobby that included the "Brandy Kings" (*brännvin kungar*), such as Lars Olsson Smith, the producers and distributors of alcohol, and numerous bar and restaurant owners.[374] In order to overcome this lobby, Waldenström sought to incorporate an economic element in his own argument that could convince those with vested interests that they too could profit under a temperance program. This explains his many attempts to include temperance statistics in his travel literature, for instance. In discussing the prohibition policies of the state of Iowa, he repeated the report of Governor William Larrabee, who had presented the case that prohibition had not only contributed to a decrease in crime, but that distilleries had been transitioned into mills and jam factories, deposits to banks had increased, and that living conditions had improved for the poorer classes.[375] Temperance legislation could apparently lead to a more efficient economy, if people were willing to reinvent their business models. With the outbreak of World War I, Waldenström's economic argument took on an even stronger prophetic condemnation of corporate interests in the alcohol trade. During a time of rations, grain needed to be saved for food, not wasted on harmful luxuries like alcohol.[376] He even went so far as to blame the war itself on the fact that European society, Swedes included, had lived beyond their means on credit, indulging in excesses like alcohol, which only had negative ramifications in creating a culture of greed that had erupted into military aggressions.[377]

Waldenström's theorizing about the general obligations of society to the individual found direct application in his participation on a special *Riksdag* committee charged with drafting proposals to revise national alcohol policies, the "Malt Liquor Committee" (*Maltdryckskommité*), beginning in 1898. As mentioned before, these committees played an important role in the *Riksdag* during the Boström governments in shaping the proposals that would be voted on in the *Riksdag* and become law. Waldenström's selection in this case is indicative of a perception within government circles that he represented the interests of the movement. The Malt Liquor Committee had been given the task to propose extensive revisions to the royal ordinance (*Kongl. Förordningen*) of 1885 regarding alcohol. There were eight members with Landshöfvdingen Boström as chairman, an Assessor Sundberg as secretary, Landsekreteraren Falk, Professor P. Klason, and the following four members of parliament, Hemmansägaren Gustaf Jansson, Konsul Meijer, Lektor Waldenström, and Direktören Östberg. After producing a proposal to be voted on by the parliament, the committee produced a report, which Waldenström had the task of writing and which was published 31 May 1900, called "The Malt Liquor Committee's Proposal with Introduction and Reservations" (*Maltdryckskommiténs förslag med inledning och reservationer*). This report was intended to generate support for the proposal, which was to be voted on in the coming *Riksdag* of 1901.[378]

The version that Waldenström published included a lengthy reservation written by him and seconded by Gustaf Jansson, which made the claim that the proposal would not satisfy the friends of temperance in that it did not go far enough in its reforms. Much of the committee's proposal had focused on the technicalities of how permission was to be obtained by establishments that wished to serve wine and malt liquor (*maltdrycker*), the occasions in which these establishments could lose their privileges, and the times of day in which sale was limited or forbidden. Following the proposal came Waldenström's reservation, in which he urged that more extensive measures be taken than those proposed by the committee. Most of all, Waldenström was opposed to the lumping together of all *maltdrycker* in the same category, as he thought that this would lead to certain defeat by the alcohol lobby, who would have an easier time rallying opposition if more beverages were classified as *maltdrycker*. It would be a more effective strategy, in his opinion, to focus on the distinction between "weaker" and "stronger" degrees of the alcohol content of all beverages, as this would be less objectionable to restaurateurs, for example, as it would reduce the number of beverages that would need to be regulated. Waldenström proposed that the focus should be purely on alcohol content; he thought an appropriate border would be 2.5 percent.[379] Those beverages that fell under this line should qualify as *svagdrycka* ("weak drinks"), as they would have such a low alcohol content that those who drank them were at little risk of becoming intoxicated.[380] As *svagdrycka*, they would be regulated as other drinks in that legal category, such as coffee.

This practice of lumping together all alcohol was, furthermore, a recent practice and a strategy introduced by the alcohol lobby. Waldenström pointed out that the Malt Liquor Ordinance (*maltdrycksförordning*) of 1866 had in fact made a similar distinction as he had between *öl*, *dricka*, and *porter*, (beer, beverages, and porters) presumably based on alcohol content. It was those people with economic interests who had defeated this idea in a law of 1874, in which this differentiation was removed. The argument given for removing this distinction was based on the needs of travelers. At the time, clean drinking water was not always available, and lack of refrigeration made it difficult to keep milk and other non-alcoholic beverages. It was in taverns, on train cars, and steam ships, therefore, that alcohol was presented as an "essential service," something that a tavern owner (*gästgifvare*) was obliged to provide. It was provided for by law that the proprietors of such establishments be prepared to offer travelers the refreshment they needed. If the temperance advocates were successful in distinguishing *svagdricka* from stronger *rusdrycker* (intoxicating drinks), then it would mean that this service could be done with *svagdricka* alone, and thus entail serious economic losses. The practice had become such that permission to serve alcohol was either granted for *maltdrycker* or no beverages at all. By combining the classes of beverages, this also meant that the minimum allotment (twenty liters) also applied to these *svagdricka*.[381]

What for Waldenström was so intolerable about the existing laws, as well as the Malt Liquor Committee's proposal, was that they seemed primarily designed to protect the economic interests of the sellers of alcohol, and not at all designed for the protection of consumers. The lumping together of these beverages made for a potentially ridiculous situation if a judge were to be faced with a case where someone overstepped their privileges regarding *svagdricka*. Waldenström made the argument that a judge would not treat violations with these beverages the same as he would with stronger *maltdrycker*. It served no practical purpose to combine them in the same law.[382] The argument raised in response to Waldenström's proposal was that the industry was not standardized enough to be able to monitor the fluctuations in alcohol content over time, according to the Royal Finance Departments Supervising and Regulation Bureau (*Kongl. Finansdepartmentets kontroll- och justeringsbyrå*). What Waldenström had argued in the course of the committee's discussions was that even allowing for fluctuations in alcohol content, if the boundary was set at 2.5 percent, even wide fluctuations would not make a practical difference: " . . . the alcohol content may just as well change one hundred times per minute, as long as it does not climb over a certain limit." It was the level of alcohol content that was the only question of interest to him. Waldenström's additional argument that the sale of beer be separated from other sales was an attempt to provide an economic incentive for the strategy. He pointed out that the limitations on the hours that beer could be sold would make it advantageous for merchants, since if they did not sell beer, they could stay open longer. He was thus attempting to turn the economic argument around in favor of temperance practices.[383]

A final element to Waldenström's objection to the proposal was that it would result in a centralization of the policies governing alcohol in Sweden, shifting authority away from the local municipality (*kommun*) and placing it at a higher regional level (*Kongl. Befallningshafvande*).[384] Waldenström made the argument that it was best for local areas to be able to assess their problems with alcohol and make decisions based on the actual needs of their constituents, as well as have the ability to experiment with the policies that worked best in their area. Conversely, a one-size-fits-all policy for the nation could do great harm. Waldenström based this claim on a large number of reports that had been sent to him from local temperance organizations and individual citizens. When he had been first named to the committee he had sent out a newspaper announcement in several papers for people to send in their observations regarding the state of alcohol policies; these responses numbered over five hundred letters from all parts of the country.[385] Waldenström then based his views on these reports, which included descriptions of the ways that people had circumvented the ten liter maximum, how accidents had occurred on job sites, how workers had spent hard earned money on alcohol instead of clothes, and how alcohol was often offered on credit by aggressive salesmen in traveling beer wagons (*ölvagnar*) throughout the countryside and at the harbors, selling to incoming sailors. These suggestions from the public were listed in twenty-three points.[386]

Since Waldenström had been criticized for moralizing politics and proposing legislation that would restrict individual rights, he took the opportunity here to address his critics.

> *The temperance work, which is carried out by the temperance societies in our country and which Your Royal Majesty's Regional Authority have so well testified to repeatedly in their five year report, naturally must, as its foremost task, counteract drunkenness by way of persuasion. They also realize and practice this. When people now and then have accused them of having abandoned this method and wanting to replace the moral work of temperance with legal measures, this is an unjust accusation. But whenever legislation—based on whether it is good or unsatisfactory—can profoundly support or counteract the moral work of temperance, then the movement needs to also direct itself toward the achievement of legislation, which as much as possible, can remove or decrease the hindrances, with which she has to contend. This is not anything new. The work of temperance has from the very beginning characterized itself this way. Her first victory in the way of*

legislation was also the greatest she has ever won, when distilling for household needs was abolished.[387]

As stated here, while he concedes that morality and politics have distinct and separate aims, there is a place and time when the educational work of temperance societies in raising awareness about the dangers of alcohol and changing the abusive culture surrounding its consumption needs to be supported by legislation. Moral practices could also be undermined by legislation. The solution that he offered to this dilemma was for these moral questions to exchange the language of the prayerhouse for the language of the *Riksdag*; in other words, to engage in the debate using the rationalistic, scientific vocabulary of politics instead of the language of religion and morality. The proponents of temperance legislation needed to articulate their arguments in a way that would acknowledge the tension between individual rights and the good of society. When these two sides of the issue were perceived to be in conflict, the determining factor would need to be scientifically-gathered health statistics and economic arguments. Waldenström's discussion of the nitty gritty of legislation proposals reveals a strong preference for experimentation and pragmatic flexibility.

Unlike the discussion of voting reform, which Waldenström thought should take place at the national level, when it came to temperance legislation he had a different opinion. Here it would be best if the local community experimented with proposals in order to address issues related to alcohol in a manner which worked best for their situation. This also became a moment for Waldenström to maintain a space for local dissent, whenever national laws conflicted with the interests of the local community. On the issue of temperance legislation, he appeared to be more of a proponent for decentralization than he was in the debate of voting reform. With voting reform, he had maintained that the best site for reform was the national constitution (*grundlagar*), in other words a centralized reform of the voting process. With temperance legislation, he maintained a preference for a policy known as the "local veto," and thus was in favor of a decentralized process for reform. While there were several versions of the concept of local veto, the basic premise was that a town (*stad*) or municipality (*kommun*) would be able to set its own policies regarding alcohol, which could be independent of the national laws. This strategy could be seen as serving two purposes; one being to create a policy that more adequately reflected the needs and desires of the local population, and the other was that this could be an incremental way of introducing restrictive laws and the ultimate goal of prohibition to the entire country. Waldenström's interest in the local veto was based on an assumption that the people in a local area knew best how alcohol affected their communities. He also assumed that most working class people would naturally vote for restrictions on alcohol if presented with all the facts. Popular support at the local level could in this way find the leverage needed to beat the alcohol lobby. The task of the temperance agitators was to inform the public and gain the support of public opinion, in order to gain the upper hand against the "Brandy Kings" and the restaurateurs. The local population should have the ability to "opt out" of national political laws, if it became clear that a minority of people with vested interests in the alcohol trade were preventing the introduction of stricter legislation that was desired by the majority. Perhaps the reason for his conflicting strategies for how to implement voting reform as opposed to temperance legislation has to do with an assumption that a different method is necessary in order to *grant rights* (i.e., suffrage) versus *restrict rights* (i.e., alcohol sales and consumption). In the former case, he seems to have thought it safest to start at the national level, whereas in the latter case, it was safest to begin at the local level.

Waldenström seems to have also based his convictions in this matter on the observations that he had made while on tour in the United States and Canada. The diversity of locations that he visited was remarkable. These included not only the expected visits to Swedish-American churches, but also to sites of general interest such as the factory town of Pullman in Illinois. Waldenström took on the persona of a journalist in his travelogues, and it is clear that he approached the process of travel writing with a mind to inform the Swedish and Swedish-American publics on "best practices" regarding social policy. During his first visit in 1889, Waldenström was interested in the decentralized character of the temperance movement. This was influenced by the fact that in America, temperance legislation was being decided state by state. The Midwestern states were a particularly interesting testing ground for local option strategies, as several states had decided to implement prohibition immediately upon the achievement of statehood, such as North and South Dakota. What is more, Waldenström was delighted to find out that it was Norwegians and Swedes who were credited with a great deal of this accomplishment, and he related that five out of six Swedes were estimated to have voted for the measure. Waldenström hoped that Minnesota and Illinois would be next—states where Swedes were present in large numbers—and thus he urged immigrants everywhere to participate in the movement. His comments were also meant as an inspiration to Swedes at home: "O, when will we see the like here in Sweden!" (*Ack, när skola vi få se något liknande här i Sverige!*).[388] Waldenström explained the profound significance for the international temperance movement if the plains states could create a temperance bloc and lead the way in introducing temperance to the rest of the country, one state at a time. This thought was so important to him that even after completion of the manuscript for the book, before publication, he sent a short update to be added as an epilogue, announcing that the temperance movement had suffered a defeat in Nebraska, but that there was still hope that this could be overturned as there was suspicion of voting mistakes or fraud.[389] Particularly, he thought Swedish Americans needed to see themselves as capable of such an accomplishment.

It was also on his first visit to the United States that he encountered the phenomenon of local communities and towns lobbying for temperance ordinances. For instance, the independent temperance colony of Greeley, Colorado was praised as a model of a countercultural movement that produced an experiment that the rest of society could learn from.[390] His interest in workers' towns only increased during his second visit in 1901. While on a visit to the town of Brockton, Massachusetts and its shoe factory, Waldenström took the opportunity to applaud the Swedish workers there, who had organized against the introduction of bars to their town. Swedish workers had related to him that they had fought to prevent the introduction of bars by defeating a referendum introduced by the bar owners—"But they did their duty and prayed to God and conquered."[391] On his way to Canada in 1904, he stopped in another worker's town in Proctor, Vermont, and was so impressed by the fact that alcohol was not allowed to be sold in this well-run worker's town that he called it "a paradise on a small scale."[392] Local control of alcohol policies was common in American cities, where public parks were often legally mandated as "dry." Waldenström was impressed by the fact that it was common that alcohol could not be served in public parks, such as in Boston's Franklin Park. He contrasted this with the situation back home, where it would be "unthinkable" for anyone to even attempt to protest the serving of alcohol in parks, as drinking was such a part of the culture of visiting parks like Djurgården in Stockholm and Stadsparken in Jönköping. In reflecting on the park in Jönköping, Waldenström related that,

> ... before the facilities were finished, the city council decided that a bar should be placed there, and in that way the park would be made into a pitfall for the people. That is so Swedish, so Swedish. What a shame for our wonderful country![393]

Waldenström did not have any illusions that local politics in the United States were idyllic or easy to influence, and in fact he included much critical commentary on the corruption of American politicians. One of the easiest targets at the time was New York's Tammany Hall, which he blamed for blocking the enforcement of existing laws that restricted alcohol sales. One such law required bars to be closed on Sundays, and attempts to enforce this law were repeatedly defeated, despite the fact that would-be reformers had been elected to office on this specific issue. Waldenström complained that the establishment was not brave enough to hold the government accountable to enforce these laws. Even church leaders had avoided confronting this corruption, including one Bishop Potter who had gone on record defending bars as a "club of the workers," which could be a beneficial social institution for workers, if not abused. The scene of corruption in New York prompted Waldenström to reflect that the excesses of this oligarchy, which ignored the plight of the lower classes, reminded him of "Rome in its last days of decadence." Chicago was another easy target for accusations of corruption, particularly as that city had recently been the subject of an exposé book, *If Christ came to Chicago* by William T. Stead (1894). Waldenström repeated Stead's criticism of the law enforcement of that city, who were accused of being sold to the highest bidder and protecting the interests of the proprietors of bars, gambling establishments, and whorehouses. This also extended to the sale of elections, which favored these types of establishments. Nevertheless, Waldenström also found occasion to praise some American politicians for their loyalty to the temperance cause, including President William McKinley, who among other things, demonstrated his Christianity by not serving "a single drop" of wine at his inauguration.[394]

Waldenström thus encouraged Swedish Americans to enter politics in order to take on all of this corruption. While he had already praised immigrants for their participation in the temperance politics in several states, he pointed out that they were mostly being represented by politicians from other ethnic groups. According to him, Swedish Americans themselves did not occupy nearly enough political seats, and seemed to be satisfied with letting their interests be represented by American politicians who courted the Swedish vote, just like they courted other ethnic groups as blocs.[395] Waldenström was confident that if Swedes would organize in the interest of temperance in their area, they would become a formidable force. In Chicago, there were already precedents for how local communities could organize to stand up for their interests. As a remedy for the corruption in city government, he encouraged his readers to consider using an alternative channel of protest, which was through community organizations, such as the then forty-year-old organization called the Hyde Park Protective Association. The association had managed, despite an uphill battle, to use a local option measure to implement a twelve-square-mile area of the city as free from bars. In all, thirty-four square miles of the city were such "oases," as Waldenström called them, in which bars would not be able to open without special permission.[396] This may well have galvanized the convictions among some within the Mission Covenant Churches of Chicago to push to make the neighborhood around their school, North Park College, a similar alcohol-free area.[397]

With clear inspiration from his travels in North America, Waldenström returned to Sweden each time with renewed enthusiasm for introducing some of these local political strategies at home. How to implement the local veto in the Swedish context was not straightforward, however. There are also mixed reports about the stance he took in relation to the local veto as it was expressed by temperance advocates in Sweden. Even Ragnar Tomson, whose accounts of Waldenström usually heralded the radical aspects of his politics, saw his stance on the local veto as an example of conservatism. Tomson even suggests that Waldenström was opposed to the local veto, and quotes an occasion when he spoke out against such an extreme version of democracy, even as late as 1908.

> *To refer the resolution of these questions to referendum by the masses must as a rule become the same as depriving them of a calm, insightful investigation and handing them over to the whirlwind of the passions. And that is what I am afraid of, even if it sometimes can go well. I do not believe that a general referendum in the alcohol question would substantially change the situation in our country for the most part. In most cases it would remain as it is, in some places the change would occur for the better, in some places for the worse.*[398]

However, interpreting this statement as opposition to the local veto is not supported by the great number of other statements that Waldenström made in favor of local veto, which continued to appear in his letters well past 1908.[399] The statement above is not a rejection of local veto, but instead demonstrates Waldenström's negative opinion of the practice of using a popular referendum to solve these types of questions, which is not the same issue. Waldenström, in step with the dominant trend in Swedish politics throughout the twentieth century, preferred that decisions be made by elected representatives and not be subject to swings in popular emotions that would make politics more unstable. The referendum has seldom been used in Swedish history, in contrast with its popularity in the United States, for instance. Swedish politicians, as explained in the preceding chapter, have largely preferred that legislation begin in the legislative committee, which Torkel Nyman sees as having been heavily influenced by Boström's reliance on committees during his terms as prime minister. Waldenström's hesitancy to rely on a referendum to decide local alcohol policies reflects this type of preference for a more indirect form of democracy, where the elected representatives at the municipal level decide policy based on consensus.

Waldenström's version of the local veto was not a referendum by the voters, but was a decision to be made by local elected officials.

With this in mind, it becomes easier to navigate Waldenström's pronouncements on the local veto. Responding to criticism that he had abandoned the local veto program, he explained in 1911, that it was not he who changed, but the definition of local veto that had changed.

> *But now people have inserted another meaning in the term "local veto"—a meaning, which it does not have—namely the right for all of the municipality's members who are of age to vote per capita on the extent to which the sale of liquor and wine shall be permitted or not. At present, it is the municipal authorities who decide this matter. And they have taken care of this matter so well on this point, that most of the municipalities in the country already have and have long had prohibition. From now on it will likely also continue in this direction, since the municipal voting scale has been so substantially reformed in a democratic direction.*[400]

As part of the voting reforms that had occurred several years earlier, the municipal (*kommun*) elections were made more democratic, which implied that the representatives would come to reflect their constituents more now than they had previously. Here again, Waldenström maintained his faith that the interests of democracy would be advanced more through a democratically-elected municipal government than they would through the use of the referendum method of having all the citizens vote on every single issue. Waldenström explained that the conflict between the Moderates (Conservatives) and the Liberals on this issue in 1911 was that the Liberals were in favor of a form of local option that would involve a referendum. Waldenström preferred the line of thinking of the political Moderates, which strayed from the referendum model, and instead sought to make the municipal governments more independent from the regional authority (*Kungliga Befallningshafvande*).

> *For the time being, the greatest number of municipalities have local veto, that is to say prohibition. If now the Kungliga Befallningshafvande's right to regulate the serving [of alcohol] is overturned, then this number will increase even more, most of all through the new municipal voting scale. Let us count ourselves fortunate, if we, in one blow, win so much as this. It is better to take one step at a time and succeed than to lose time and energy by taking two steps in one thrust and fail.*[401]

On the one hand, this reflects a form of decentralization in that it maintains independence from the national authority, while at the same time it represents maintenance of an indirect form of democracy by rejecting the referendum model.

It seems apparent from much of Waldenström's commentary that he viewed the local veto as a means of eventually achieving national prohibition.[402] Local victories would be easier to achieve, and could slowly build up support for temperance when a local ordinance proved successful and could be used as an example for the rest of the country. The diversity of local policies in the United States demonstrated precedents of best practices, which could be imported to Sweden. While in favor of national prohibition, he does not seem to have been dead set on the national prohibition of all alcohol as an essential victory of the temperance movement. As is evident in his minority report following the Malt Liquor Committee's proposal, he wanted to separate weaker from stronger alcoholic beverages. He did not have an "all-or-nothing" approach to the temperance movement. For example, in his commentary on the Swedish-language newspaper debates on temperance in North America, he had specifically criticized the paper *Missions-Wännen* for taking an all-or-nothing approach and shooting down proposals from other newspapers which argued that high taxes could be part of the solution or at least an intermediate goal to help curb the ill effects of alcohol: "Well, well, who knows! I have often thought that *Missions-Wännen* made a big mistake, when it thus made 'all or nothing' its goal."[403] In general, Waldenström's pronouncements in the debate on temperance legislation demonstrate a pragmatic willingness to experiment with best practices, and a localization of these experiments as a means to preserve space for dissenting local communities and thus allow the possibility for innovation.

CHAPTER 15

A Preference for Education over Legislation

WHILE NEITHER A FRIEND of alcohol nor of the culture that surrounded it, Waldenström himself nevertheless was not a teetotaler. From the discussion in the previous two chapters, it has been asserted that this moderate stance was not due to a lack of conviction, but had more to do with his preference for a decentralized process in instituting temperance reforms. This section will focus on another preference that Waldenström had, which was a preference for using educational means, as opposed to legislative means, to achieve the goals of a social movement. Historian Lennart Johansson's very brief evaluation of the circle around Waldenström gives some hints in this direction. Johansson repeated Lydia Svärd's analysis, which identified that in 1908, it was Waldenström who was the leader of the moderate temperance advocates, which accounted for thirty-one out of 109 members of parliament.[404] Furthermore, Johansson's summary states that educational means were a priority for the moderates.

> In the General Voters' Association election program in 1908, the temperance question was dealt with, symptomatically enough, under the title "Education and National Health," not "Social Legislation." This designation indicates that people on the side of the Voters' Association chose to view the temperance question as a question of national health with emphasis on education and morality, rather than a question that could be solved within the parameters of a more active social legislation.[405]

Regardless of the practical benefits that would come when legislation undergirded and encouraged healthy lifestyle choices, Waldenström and likeminded temperance advocates seem to have seen legislation as a secondary measure.

The vices associated with alcohol were not something that ultimately could be solved by legislation, but were instead the result of illness or a breach of moral character, which only medical knowledge or spiritual edification would truly cure. In this instance as in earlier pronouncements, Waldenström made a clear case for a preference for education over legislation.

This preference is evident in the charitable organizations that he chose to feature in his travel literature, which were often educational in nature, and only secondarily were involved with legislation or government regulation. Waldenström's journalistic conventions were such that he often included anecdotes or citations from newspapers and let these citations "speak for themselves," without adding his own explicit opinion. The result is that the reader most often encounters a broad spectrum of strategies and can get a sense of best practices without too much overt persuasion about which strategies are the best. When Waldenström did express his opinions about charities connected to the temperance movement, they were usually sentiments that were macro-level philosophical or theological in nature. Thus there were many "right" options that friends of temperance could engage in, not just one or two. For instance, Waldenström had a positive opinion of independent volunteer organizations like the YMCA (KFUM), which often had programs in Scandinavia and among Scandinavians in North America. While in London, he spoke highly of the sailor's home that he found there, a Scandinavian operation run by Axel Welin and his wife. Waldenström was particularly fascinated with the work of this and other Scandinavian sailors' homes, perhaps because they emphasized a transformation of the lifestyles of sailors by providing alternatives to the "loose living" that typified their visits to foreign ports.[406] Although these ministries were educational in nature, they were not simply about providing facts, but also encouraging alternative lifestyles. Coming from the perspective that the success of the temperance movement was dependent on changing the centuries-old centrality of alcohol in Scandinavian culture, providing alternatives that could replace the social role of alcohol would be essential. In his travel literature, he too tried to play this type of a role as an educator, including plenty of statistics and citing authorities in the United States to back up his assertions, as was the case with his description of the successes of the temperance movement in Iowa.[407] For instance, he was impressed to learn that schools in Chicago provided students with education on the negative effects of alcohol and tobacco, and even included a textbook on the matter in their curriculum.[408] He even includes his own anecdotal experiences, such as his evident excitement over having tasted a delicious lemonade soda drink (*läskedryck*) in the United States, which he thought would make an "excellent substitute for alcohol."[409]

The ultimate alternative lifestyle change, however, was much more profound than finding new beverages. As a preacher, the best solution to alcoholism in his mind was for people to become heavily involved in their congregations, which would have the indirect effect of removing them from negative lifestyles built around harmful social customs and providing them with a constructive social model built around biblical living. Although the temperance movement and the religious awakening oftentimes worked toward common purposes and included many of the same people, it is also clear that there was a certain amount of competition between the two groups, perhaps especially because there was so much overlap. Waldenström was famous for making the assertion that "the best temperance society was the congregation," and actually encouraged Christians who were passionate about the temperance cause to use their congregations as the vehicle for social action, rather than dividing their time between the congregation *and* a secular temperance organization. At times he became quite adamant that the temperance cause should not be allowed to drain members away from the congregations. One such moment came after a general conference of the Mission Covenant of Sweden had passed a motion that all the congregations should arrange a "Temperance Sunday" in their schedule. Waldenström made a quip that this would be more appropriate if the temperance societies were also willing to arrange a corresponding "Christianity Sunday" in their calendar of events. This was indicative of Waldenström's realization that many temperance organizations had distanced themselves from their Christian origins, such as the Good Templars, who had removed faith in God from their organizational charter.[410] This tension between the temperance movement and the awakening underscored the reality that each of these movements was restricted by the economy of time that governs human activity; people only had so much free time to engage in voluntary societies, and if they had to choose, Waldenström hoped they would prioritize congregational participation. He thus presented the congregation's temperance activities as a means to kill two birds with one stone, serving as a place for both spiritual community and social action.

Waldenström, like many preachers, resonated more with some aspects of scripture than others. As mentioned earlier, the aspects that he emphasized in his devotional books, prominent among these being *Squire Adamsson*, was a balance between legalism and lawlessness, or in more theological terms, between a legalistic view of salvation on the one hand and a picture of free, unmerited grace on the other. Both extremes could be pitfalls in the human journey of faith. The perspective on biblical interpretation that he presented to members of his church was framed as a middle way between these extremes. Truth had a nuanced nature, and the believer could only come to a workable understanding of the truth by accepting this nuanced nature, and studying all aspects of truth presented in scripture. Waldenström maintained a firm, perhaps naïve, belief that education would make this truth self-evident. If the Bible was translated correctly and made available for laypeople to study and interpret, they would come to the right interpretation themselves (i.e., his interpretation). This same assumption about education also extended to solving social questions, such as how to regulate alcohol. If, through extensive education, people could come to understand all aspects of the social context regarding alcohol, the natural result would be a change in the culture and in the laws of the land. Waldenström expected that by educating the public about alcohol, they would naturally gravitate toward prohibition. They would choose prohibition because they would realize it was in their best interests. Legislation could aid this process, but could backfire if society became legalistic as a result. Laws would follow as a result of changed hearts, but changed hearts would not follow as a result of restrictive behavior.

This was expressed in a draft of an article in which Waldenström called for "true free thinking" (or independence from rigid political ideology) in regard to the temperance movement. The article came in response to the rise of a new political organization called "Freedom Association" (*Frihetsförbundet*), of which Waldenström did not approve, but which he identified as symptomatic of the temperance movement overstepping its bounds.

> *Temperance legislation has, for a long time—despite occasional mistakes—been based in a desire for forward progress. The same is true regarding our opinions about it. But anything that is going to last must grow from the inside out, and that takes time.*
>
> *One spring, there was supposed to be an inspection of an agricultural school. The principal had the students cut down a great many birches and set them up as an avenue. It looked very good, and he was praised by the inspector, who had no way of knowing that the birches had not grown on that site. But in a short while they withered. They had no roots. The story is true and may serve as a useful analogy for a legislation, which goes too quickly, which progresses past the general conception of justice, even if it runs in the right direction.*
>
> *People might complain about the emergence of the so-called Freedom Association as much as they want. But according to my belief it is an expression of a reaction, which can be dangerous enough for the political work of temperance. This reaction has namely brought to the forefront the relevant and highly important question of the boundary for the right of society to intrude in the*

> *sphere of private life. For as much as such a right exists, there must also be boundaries for it—to the extent that might is not the same as right.*
>
> *Even I complain about the coming of the Freedom Association. But I find it understandable at any rate, and I have expected something like this, ever since the friends of temperance in the Second Chamber, according to my belief, allowed themselves to take the unwise step of throwing away what could have been won, based on their stubborn faith in the local veto. Now what remains is to take up the political work of temperance as it now stands in the current context, as well as thank God for what can be won, as long as something still can be won. What we need on this point is genuine liberal-mindedness, which not only desires but also believes in the possibility of a mutual understanding and works therefore . . .*[411]

The draft of the article trails off and is lacking a conclusion, but even from this fragment, it is possible to see what he was trying to communicate on the debate of freedom versus legalism. His criticism of some of the other temperance advocates in the *Riksdag* was that they were too committed to specific political strategies, which were divisive and risked losing everything because of partisan inflexibility. *Frihetsförbundet* was a reaction to this dogmatism, and as their name suggests, appears to have been inspired by a type of small-government libertarianism as expressed by international champions of freedom during the age of Enlightenment such as Thomas Paine and other American influences.[412] The imagery of the withering birch trees underscores once again Waldenström's preference for education and building sustainable moral character in the members of the temperance movement, instead of more drastic, superficial measures that would not last in the long run.

As indicated in the last quote, Waldenström also feared that the temperance movement could become legalistic by adopting a strict party ideology that did not accommodate dissent, or which became divisive. He claimed on more than one occasion that the very issue of local veto had become contentious, in that proponents of local veto in 1916 had undermined other temperance legislation that he felt had a good chance of passing.[413] Waldenström's general independence from political parties also manifested itself sometimes in a hesitancy to commit to individual policies, which is clear here. It is not surprising the Ragnar Tomson would conclude that he had been opposed to the local veto, due to Waldenström's statements criticizing the proponents of the policy here. But as stated before, there was a difference of opinion as to what local veto meant, or ought to mean, and Waldenström took the stance that what was being presented as local veto in 1916, was not what he had advocated (i.e., local veto by vote of elected officials, rather than by referendum). Most importantly, he predicted that the dogmatic adherence to specific policies would defeat the general cause of temperance, in that factions within the movement were focusing their energy on defeating one another, instead of cooperating and taking victories where they could be won. Countless times he warned audiences not to conform too completely to appeals to party solidarity, but instead to look critically at the implications of the policies in question on their long term goals.[414] What might be appropriate in one context might not be in another, especially in the ever-changing political landscape.[415]

"Thus far hath the Lord helped." Waldenström is leaving parliament after losing the election. On the door: "Parliament of Sweden—Admittance forbidden for unauthorized P.V." Bottles read: "Greek country wine," which was a brand of low alcohol wine that Waldenström had once endorsed, which his critics in the tabloids found comical for years afterward. "Allt hittills hafver Herran hulpit." Oskar Andersson. *Söndags-Nisse*. 17 Sept. 1905. Reproduction: Kungliga biblioteket.

Waldenström's moderate stance on the temperance issue, like his moderate stance in other political issues, made it difficult to gather a coherent political movement around him. As a result, the values of the "Waldenström party" did not become institutionalized in any one lasting political party in Swedish politics. But this is not to say that he had no lasting influence, and for the reasons outlined in this and the preceding sections, his ideology can be seen as surviving in a number of cultural assumptions that have become bedrock to modern Swedish politics. Furthermore, Waldenström resonated with a significant enough portion of the Swedish electorate to keep him in office for over twenty years, and the high frequency with which cartoonists and critical columnists invoked his name, as well as the sympathetic newspapers who were eager to print his articles and letters to the editor, suggests that his success as a political force has to be measured in other ways than an institutionalized party ideology. The case that has been made here is that Waldenström's political legacy can be seen in the degree to which his moderate political strategy became part of the fabric of democratic assumptions in Sweden in the century since his death. His "middle way" in attempting to navigate the pitfalls of legalism and lawlessness corresponds rather well with the middle way charted by Swedish politics in general. Perhaps the reason why this has rarely been acknowledged in past histories of the movement is that his complicated political allegiances were explained with theological language. While fellow Christians might easily recognize his political philosophy as an application of theology, secular minds may find this language foreign and off-putting. As he was first and foremost a preacher, it should not be surprising that his theology found expression in his political views.

Conclusion

THE THREE-FOLD CHARACTER OF this study has been inspired by the three interrelated social movements of nineteenth century Sweden: the religious awakening, the labor movement, and the temperance movement. As a prime example of the interconnectedness of these movements, this study has located one person, Paul Peter Waldenström, in the context of all three with the aim of clarifying this complex relationship. Each chapter has presented a different arena in which Waldenström applied his religious and political philosophy. While these spheres have often been kept separate in past historical accounts, there is much evidence that points to a direct connection between the religious awakening and the overall breakthrough of democracy. In crafting his own philosophy of pluralism, Waldenström exported ideas from the theological tradition that he represented, Lutheran Pietism, and applied them directly to the political questions of the day. What is more, as a member of parliament he represented a tangible link between the religious awakening and the legislative process. The type of religious pluralism that was valued as an ethical good by Waldenström and certain other Pietists proved to be highly applicable and even advantageous to the contemporary political situation and the creation of the emerging pluralistic public sphere.

While this study is not the first to point out a connection between the religious awakening and the breakthrough of democracy in Sweden, it goes further than previous studies in asserting two things in particular; 1) that Lutheran Pietism as it existed in Sweden at the time bore a profound democratic and pluralistic character, and 2) that Waldenström functioned as an agent in making the values of this tradition heard in the overall debates that charted the course of Swedish democracy in the twentieth century. In order to establish evidence that Waldenström's critiques were heard, the commentary of several of his political opponents has been laid side by side with his own in an attempt to reconstruct key parts of this debate. The resulting evidence is sufficient enough to conclude that an exchange of ideas occurred between these members of the debate: the most prominent of these opponents were Hjalmar Branting, Kata Dahlström, Viktor Lennstrand, and Johan Bergman. The two most important findings of this analysis are that the Social Democratic party appears to have been forced to cater to the interests of free-church voters as a result of Waldenström's prominence within the political sphere, and that Waldenström himself was forced to adopt language and concepts from socialism at the same time that he protested its entry into Swedish politics. The sheer number of contemporary references to Waldenström, particularly the political cartoons, that appeared between the 1880s and 1910s make it clear that his political opponents heard him and responded to his criticism. Waldenström was a household name, and cartoon caricatures of him were instantly recognizable.

A major obstacle in presenting a case like this one is a perennial assumption that has been common in Western thought since the Enlightenment, which is that religion is antithetical to liberty and democracy. A sweeping statement in contradiction of that assumption is beyond the intent and scope of this study, but it is appropriate to conclude here that Pietism of the Waldenströmian variety fits that stereotype poorly. It is also apparent from this study that his brand of Pietism and the liberalism that characterized his politics both share common roots in the Enlightenment, which further complicates a binary understanding of religion versus democracy. The connection between these ideologies was evident in reviewing Waldenström's educational background and philosophy, covered in Part I, but also in his classical liberal orientation in politics in general, outlined in Part III. The distinction between "absolutists" and "moderates" that arose in all the chapters was important in identifying a firm basis from which to argue that religion, despite being based on dogmas, can at times produce pluralism, and as such is not inherently "dogmatic," as it were. This point was also crucial in underscoring Waldenström's own argument that secular ideologies, socialism included, can also develop in decidedly dogmatic directions, and that these secular ideologies are not necessarily more compatible with democracy than are religious ideologies.

To recap the main conclusions of each of the sections of this study, the Introduction began by laying out a brief outline of Waldenström's career, presenting him as an overdue subject for study within the history of Swedish politics. While his influence in the religious sphere had been well documented, his political activity has enjoyed much less treatment, perhaps due to some of the assumptions above. It was in an attempt to remedy that imbalance in the historical record that this study has intentionally focused less on Waldenström's theology (such as his atonement theory) and more on his political engagement and social commentary. When theology was addressed, it was primarily done as it related to the concept of pluralism.

Part I set out to provide a working definition of pluralism that could be used in the rest of the study. A logical starting point was political scientist Arend Lijphart's articulation of pluralism as an active strategy for overcoming partisan conflict by including minorities and dissenting groups at the highest levels of governmental decision making. This notion of pluralism as a strategy for conflict resolution was then connected to Waldenström's own use of pluralism as a strategy for truth-seeking, which was demonstrated by analysis of his popular religious allegory *Squire Adamsson*. Since this study makes claims about the origins of Swedish democracy, it was also necessary to acknowledge one of the primary labels that this form of government came to bear in the twentieth century conflicts between Liberal and Socialist politics, namely the "middle way." In referencing Sheri Berman's and Åsa Linderborg's studies regarding the origins of Social Democracy, it became apparent that each scholar had concluded that this was a hybrid form of government that represented a merging of Liberal and Socialist ideologies. These findings were then used to make a case that Waldenström's criticism of socialism had the potential to play a role in the making of this hybrid form of government, due to his prominence among free-church voters.

Part II explained Waldenström's religious heritage in the context of Swedish history. Pietism in Sweden was a dissenting form of religious expression and appeared in protest of the religious monopoly of the centuries-old Lutheran state church, which had helped to manufacture a culture of national religious and civic unity. In this protest, it was advantageous for the dissenting groups to argue for religious pluralism, since allowances for diversity made their very existence possible by relaxing the laws and social stigmas that prevented their free expression. Though dogmatism also appeared among Pietists, the general strategy of these groups was to argue in favor of freedom of religious expression. Moravian Pietism, however, had also left a legacy of pluralism within Swedish Pietist theology itself, something that appeared in heavy doses in Waldenström's writings, not least in *Squire Adamsson*. In the long view of the history of Christianity in Scandinavia and elsewhere in Europe, Waldenström represented a transitional type of clergyman that facilitated the transformation of Christianity from a "Constantinian" model (the state-church union established in the fourth century) to a "post-Constantinian" model, in which Christianity came to exist as one option in a pluralistic religious market. Waldenström's success as a leader in this transitional period was due to his ability to mobilize thousands of people in layman-oriented activities, in which a democratic model for congregational life was explained as preferable. This mobilization was facilitated by his frequent use of print media outlets, both newspapers and books, to encourage readers to support voluntary common projects, like funding mission stations in Congo and China, as well as congregations and schools in Sweden and North America.

The important point made about Waldenström's use of print media was that it was not only used for communicating religious concepts, but also had both direct and indirect application to politics. While his devotional material remained focused on theology and explanations of scripture, by contrast, his newspaper articles and his travel accounts were heavily engaged in social-critical commentary. Some of the main primary sources used in this study were taken from a collection of letters and articles written in his later career, which were re-discovered in the 1980s, and as such represent some new material. In terms of religious pluralism, examination of these letters has demonstrated that Waldenström made arguments that religion should not be fully privatized, since cleansing the public sphere of religion would demonstrate a compromise of ideals of pluralism and free speech. This argument brought him into conflict with Viktor Lennstrand, but also into agreement on some points with another opponent, Hjalmar Branting, and even more so with Kata Dahlström, particularly on the nature of religious instruction in public schools. It is also here in the discussion of the appropriateness of religion in public that Waldenström first presented a defense of the rights of dissenters, a defense that he would later extend to the debates about the rights of strike-breakers during the labor movement (covered in Part III), as well as the rationale behind his moderate stance in the temperance movement (Part IV). The fact that he continued to voice his criticism of the state church, as a participant in the debates of the Church Assembly of the Church of Sweden in 1868, 1908, 1909, and 1910, demonstrate that the role Waldenström carved out for himself was ecumenical in nature, as well as that he remained invested in the success of the Church of Sweden long after his formal exit from the rolls of its clergy in 1882. This criticism was aimed at convincing the state church to democratize its structure, split from the state, and adapt to the pluralistic context it was entering as one free church among many, processes that have since occurred (albeit with glacial speed).

Part III focused on the role that Waldenström played in the politics of parliament and offers an explanation for his strong opposition to socialism in particular. His critique of socialism is examined through comparisons of his political views to those of Hjalmar Branting, as well as some of the recorded exchanges between these two opponents. These exchanges also demonstrate that each of these men heard and responded to the criticism of the other, indicating that the showdown between the Pietists and Socialists was not only a confrontation, but an important exchange. This exchange can explain in part how the overall course of Swedish politics developed in the direction of the hybrid form of ideologies known as Social Democracy, instead of a more purely Socialist form of government. It was also argued that Waldenström's independent politics and refusal to align too closely with any political party should be interpreted as a conscious choice in the defense of pluralism in the political arena. This is in contradistinction to past interpretations which have presented his behavior as erratic, meglomaniacal, or as doctrinaire conservatism. His own discourse was noticeably affected by this exchange, which is evident in how he picked up Socialist terminology and repurposed these words to claim (or reclaim) concepts that he thought belonged to Pietist Christianity, such as "open-mindedness," "freethinking," and "solidarity." The most significant discovery of that section, and perhaps of the entire study, is the role that Waldenström played in the elections of 1902 and 1905. In these campaigns, he advocated the introduction of proportional elections (instead of majoritarian elections), when many of his Social Democratic and Liberal opponents did not. As some of these opponents shortly thereafter came to reverse this stance, and since proportionalism has come to prevail in Swedish elections to the present, this is an important moment in which a religious leader can be seen directly advocating a policy that favored pluralism and which became the law of the land.

Part IV focused on the one specific issue that Waldenström invested the most time advocating in parliament, which was temperance. This section's main objective was to clarify the difference between two terms used in the period to designate different camps, the "absolutists" and the "moderates." It was explained here that Waldenström fits best in the moderate camp, as well as why that stance demonstrated an application of his philosophy of democratic pluralism. In order to locate him on the spectrum of moderates and absolutists, his discourse was compared to that of Johan Bergman, who represented the absolutists' viewpoint. As a moderate, Waldenström demonstrated a preference for education in addressing the social ills that stemmed from alcoholism, whereas the absolutists tended to prefer legislation as the means to accomplish these reforms. Further evidence of this is noted in the fact that Waldenström's discourse largely lacked the millenialist warnings that were so common in the speeches and writings of the absolutists. One of the main sources used in this section was his travel literature on North America, in which he gleaned wisdom from the varied experiences of temperance advocates in the areas he visited and reported these findings in an attempt to educate his Swedish and Swedish-American readers on the issue. A moment in which Waldenström directly impacted the temperance legislation in Sweden was during his service on *Maltdryckskommitén*. As a member on this committee, and in his role as the author of a subsequent report of the committee's findings, he advocated that a scientific basis should be used to determine which alcoholic beverages would be regulated and which could be sold with little or no regulation, recommending that this threshold be set at 2.5 percent. As a similar standard was later adopted in Sweden, which segregated such beverages based on percentage alcohol content, Waldenström's role here again appears to have been quite central. The so-called "local veto" was another complex aspect of the temperance movement, as well as an occasion in which he demonstrated a preference for decentralized regulation with provisions for dissenters (in this case for local magistrates to be able to opt out of the national alcohol laws—not popular referenda). In general, his politics in the temperance movement demonstrate a propensity to investigate and experiment with best practices, rather than to be rigidly wedded to specific legislation.

In drawing this exploration to a close, it is apparent that there are several aspects of the discussion of this topic that did not receive full treatment due to the constraints of the project. The organization of the study was designed to demonstrate the interconnectedness of three movements, and therefore focused only on the most central aspects of each. Each of these chapters could easily have been expanded into its own study, and future research into all of these topics would no doubt produce further insights into the folk movements. The political cartoons alone could be made into their own study, and one area that was not treated here was the differentiation between the satire of Waldenström and Pietism made by the Socialist newspapers and that made by the Liberals and the overall bourgeois press. There are also areas in which Waldenström's support of the Church of Sweden in his later career reflected similar sentiments as those expressed by Manfred Björkquist, one of the architects of the so-called "Folk Church" concept, which had advocated a continued national role for the state church that would extend into the pluralist period. Comparative study in this area would further illuminate the tension between civic religion and religious freedom. And lastly, while Waldenström's influence in North America is included in this study, particularly his commentary on American temperance politics, there remains a fruitful study that can be done on his impact on Swedish-American immigrants in the politics of their adopted homeland. His audience straddled the Atlantic Ocean, and the fact that he addressed politics on both sides simultaneously, demonstrates an exchange that went two ways, even though this study focused almost exclusively on the transfer of ideas that occurred from West to East.

These and other shortcomings aside, this study has the potential to augment the overall understanding of the role that religious movements like Pietism served in the secularization of European society. While Waldenström's case reflects the unique situation in Sweden, there are ways in which this case has parallels in other European countries of the same period. These similarities are striking. In a comparative study in 1999, Andrew Gould analyzed the relative success of liberal movements in Belgium, France, Germany, and Switzerland. As part of his conclusion, Gould identified the mechanism at work in the success of liberal democracy as being the relative distribution of power resources, noting that "... a wide distribution of power resources prevents any single group from exercising hegemony in a political system." This was presented as part of his effort to challenge the assumption that economic developments alone produced democracy. Gould held that the success of liberalism depended on the ability of liberals to orchestrate coalitions of different populations, in which religious populations played a decisive role. As it related to the countries of his study, Gould concluded that religious movements often cooperated with liberal movements. Dissenting religious groups often fractured the unity of religious life, which created cultural trends of non-conformity in protest of established religion and conservative dominance. When liberals were successful, it was often due to their ability to appeal to these diverse dissenting groups, all of whom had a vested interest in freedom from the establishment.[416] The coalitional character of liberalism was born out of a necessity to broker compromise between sometimes competing interests in order to challenge conservative regimes. Switzerland was deemed as the most successful place for liberals, as Gould saw them as having been successful in organizing coalitions that pitted Protestants against Catholics. In the case where liberalism was most defeated, Germany, Gould identified the reason for this as the result of the liberal groups' alienation and isolation of the Catholic population, which responded by allying itself with the conservative establishment.[417] In all of the cases presented by Gould, the level of participation of religious groups in liberal movements was indicative of the relative success of liberalism, and thus democracy. In another study on early nineteenth-century England, Hugh McLeod notes that although the upper class members of the religious revivals were associated with conservative ideas, the middle and lower classes often demonstrated political liberalism and radical sentiments.[418] This parallels the active interest of the lower classes in the Swedish revivals of the time, in which progressive political reform movements were often an outgrowth of participation in revivals.

These findings also underscore the necessity to treat religious ideologies within the framework of rational choice theory, instead of presenting religion as an irrational or emotional activity. For instance, as recently as the 1990s, religious movements were a marginal area of study within the field of sociology, as religious topics were not considered suitable for hard science. The reasons for this originated in the field's traditional orientation, which preferenced the study of human activity from a rational choice perspective (based on the assumption that humans act in their own best interest to optimize their ability to achieve various "goods"). Since religion often deals with intangible, and therefore scientifically unobservable, phenomena, it is no surprise that from a materialistic point of view, religion was discounted as a productive area of study. Lacking a framework for discussing religious decisions in terms of rational choice, religion was often neglected or explained as irrational behavior. However, as some sociologists and historians have pointed out in the past two decades, religions not only demonstrate measureable phenomena, but they also can be analyzed in terms of rational choice theories. Such was the contribution of Rodney Stark and Roger Finke in a landmark study on the rational aspects of religion (2000), in which the authors pointed out, among other claims, that the loyalty to religious paradigms that participants demonstrate is not merely sentimentality or fanaticism, but also can be explained by identifying the goods that these participants expect to receive by their actions. Loss of salvation or the betrayal of moral convictions can also be seen as goods that can be lost, and which can at times be valued more highly than material goods. The authors concluded that religiously motivated choices should therefore be considered as being as rational as any other aspect of human psychology, and furthermore that these ideals can be studied in terms of measurable data.[419] In the case of Waldenström, his preferences for liberal forms of government can be seen in terms of the advantages that these preferences would bring in this world, as well as in the next. Choices for political and social reforms were often quite practical, and not simply based in considerations about the afterlife.

A main area in which this study has the potential to contribute is to the field of Swedish political history itself, particularly in explaining the origins of the twentieth century political landscape. Political analyst Sheri Berman sees the success of the Social Democratic movement in Sweden as having been dependent on the unique assertion of what she calls the "primacy of politics." In contrast to the National Socialist models that succeeded in Germany in the 1930s, which abandoned democratic political practices, Social Democracy in Sweden prioritized democratic processes and saw pluralistic political structures as the means to achieve reform.[420] If this can indeed be said to typify the Swedish case, then this also suggests that Swedish democracy in its formative period was shaped more by ideological debate and exchange than by a single party's dominance, namely the Social Democratic party. This one political party governed the nation almost exclusively (interrupted only by brief intervals) for the better part of the twentieth century, from 1932–1976, which has been identified as the longest continuous rule of a single party of any democratic country in history.[421] This type of dominance of one party is surprising in a democratic context, and in the past has been interpreted as representing a homogeneity of ideology, rather than a "primacy" of democratic exchange in the political arena. However, the attempt has been made in this study to point out ways in which an outsider to the party like Waldenström could have influenced the development of the party's ideology.

The assumed destiny of Social Democratic party dominance and its basis in popular consensus, have been examined and challenged by one historian, Åsa Linderborg, who identified the dominant narrative of Swedish history as having been written with a distinct Social Democratic party perspective. The act of writing history is identified by Linderborg as having been used as a power resource in a rhetorical struggle between various political, ideological and socio-economic elements in society. Each of these groups, consciously and unconsciously, strove to use historical narratives as a means to gain power, as well as to establish legitimacy whenever that power was achieved. The dominant political party is thus seen as having been the most successful of the various societal elements in wielding this weapon. In contrast to the traditional grand narrative of the rise of a cohesive Social Democratic ideology, what Linderborg identified was a pitted battle between various groups who were vying for dominance at the turn of the century. Her study was an attempt to correct a deterministic view of the course of events.

> *There are no natural laws that dictate that society should look the way that it does, nor that the bourgeois class or the working class have not had several alternative courses of action. In regard to Swedish social democracy, it could have tried a more revolutionary path, or like Danish social democracy, a more liberal one. Reformism can manifest itself in many various forms and be more or less critical of the system, theory-driven, or pragmatic. Humankind always stands at various crossroads, there are no "historically-mandated decisions."*[422]

In her example here, the very identification of differences in the development of socialism in Denmark versus Sweden confirms the idea that even in two countries with very similar cultural and economic preconditions, the articulation of political values can be far from identical. The important contribution of her study is that it allows room for discussing how the various elements of Swedish society influenced each others' ideologies, and in particular how minority groups can affect the overall course of politics. It is not only those who are most closely aligned with the hegemonic ideology who are able to influence those in weaker positions. Rather it can reasonably be asserted that dissident political leaders and groups bring issues to the table that need to be addressed by the more dominant groups, thereby necessitating concessions on the part of the dominant groups. This impact of minorities is sometimes referred to as "third party" politics, in which minorities participate in the hope of achieving the inclusion of their causes and ideas in the national debates, even when these groups themselves have no chance of gaining dominance or winning parliamentary seats.[423]

In contrast with other Western democracies, such as in American politics, Swedish voters have not traditionally elected individuals to office, but instead have elected parties. As a result, those politicians who have been successful as "maverick" politicians have been very few, as explained by Stig Hadenius.

> . . . the typical Riksdag member is one of the group, one who does not stand out. Political groups and parties have been more prominent than individuals. Those who have had their own policies and thus influenced decisions in the Riksdag have been the exceptions.[424]

However, when considering the anomaly that is P. P. Waldenström, it becomes clear he demonstrates one of these exceptional "mavericks" in Swedish politics. He was a celebrity, and it was in large part due to his celebrity status, cultivated through print media outlets, that he was able to remain influential for twenty years in parliament. His success as a minority politician should be understood in terms of the ways in which his articulations impacted the overall discussion, rather than simply by counting the number of his motions which resulted in law. If historians follow the suggestion of Linderborg and Berman and view the political situation of the time as an unstable moment of contingency, rather than a steady march of an inherently democratic form of Social Democracy to national dominance, this can help explain why Sweden dodged the fate of two of its neighbors, the radical revolution of Russia and the National Socialist takeover in Germany. The fact that in both of these other cases, democratic pluralism was squarely defeated suggests strongly that the minority groups in Sweden who emphasized democratic pluralism in their political agendas may have played a greater role in the development of their country's politics than has yet been considered. Waldenström viewed the decades around the turn of the century as being a critical juncture in history. If Swedish voters and politicians did not sufficiently defend pluralism and make sure that it was written into the laws that were then being drafted regarding religious reforms, voting reforms, provisions for free speech, and temperance legislation, then crucial opportunities might have been missed.

Though this study has alluded to the concept of the "middle way," coined in the 1930s and popularized in the 1960s and 70s, this framework itself is worth problematizing, as it is based on assumptions of Swedish exceptionalism. The primary goal of this study was to trace the exchange of ideas between the various social movements, with Waldenström as the point of intersection, in order to see how democratic pluralism emerged in Sweden, and furthermore how it could be seen as an outgrowth of Lutheran Pietist ideals. As such, questioning whether or not Sweden was "exceptional" was not a primary focus. As much as possible, this study has attempted to underscore that this narrative of moderation was used by politicians in a variety of ways, which is why Linderborg's questioning of the Social Democratic Party's strategies of history writing was included. The study has highlighted how the construction of these narratives of moderation was a collaborative process, and that many participants in the public debates, including Waldenström, had a stake in this development.

It must be admitted that claims to Swedish exceptionalism should not be taken for granted. Historians in the last two decades have increasingly pointed out that the Swedish welfare state and democratic praxis resembles those of other western European nations in more ways than it diverges from them. Rolf Torstendahl has gone so far as to assert that, from the perspective of the early twenty-first century, Sweden's history can be framed as part of a "mainstream" Western European political culture, rather than following a rogue independent track. "Sweden [. . .] has been industrialized, bureaucratized and organized in stages according to a pattern which one finds in all West European states, at least north of the Po and the Pyrenees."[425] One can see that although development in Sweden took place with dramatically less domestic turbulence than Finland and Germany, and without the prior revolutions of France, similar trends can be seen in Norway, Denmark, Great Britain, and the Low Countries. Håkon Arvidsson frames the European perspective slightly differently, in that he identifies two main streams in European modernization—an "Anglo-Saxon" industrialization based on capitalist democracy on the one hand (demonstrated in Britain), and on the other hand, a form of modernization that became "traumatic," as in the case of the authoritarian, bureaucratic social capitalism of Germany, and Russia's forced industrialization without cultural modernization ("modernization run amok").[426] Political stability in Sweden was able to thrive, he says, because it was a peripheral nation, and escaped the more difficult contexts of other continental countries.[427] Also, among Arvidsson's list of factors that affected the tempo of modernization is the observation that development was hindered in those countries where religious institutions remained unaffected by concepts of modernism (Spain, Russia).[428] One can add that the strength of the revival movement in Sweden as a movement of reform, and particularly the democratic nature of the concepts its leaders espoused, can certainly be considered both influenced by modernism, as well as active in influencing modernism. Wilhelm Agrell, has theorized that Swedish politics was stable because of cultural limitations in the understanding of what pluralism meant. Pluralism in the Swedish political context came to emphasize consensus because it was based on cultural expectations of conformity, as well as a preference for effective reform through bureaucracy.[429] Waldenström demonstrates a variety of free-church politician who articulated a version of modern secularity that defined consensus as reserving places for dissenters, whether religious or not, and drew from traditions of classical liberalism as well as low-church Pietism in order to construct this definition.

In discussing Swedish policies (particularly its contested neutrality, which also can be seen as a sort of politics of moderation), Mikael af Malmborg also notes that local Swedish history fits into a broader Western framework. "The Western world comprises both a series of nation states and a transnational civilisation. [. . . This history] must be observed both as a general civilising process and as fluctuating geopolitical constellations which are specific to each state."[430] In other words, the local decisions of Swedish politicians and actors can diverge from the general directions for a time, but the differences between nations can reasonably be expected to level out in the long term. This does not necessarily mean a kind of determinism, but instead an acknowledgement that the local agency of the various national actors is connected to a broader exchange of ideas. It is to be expected that local innovations in terms of general Western concepts (democracy, liberalism, socialism, religiosity, secularity, and pluralism) might be exceptional for a time, but do not remain static. National actors, like Waldenström, should also be seen from an international perspective, as local agents in a much broader trend. Furthermore, it is not at all a stretch to see Waldenström in an international perspective, as he interacted with people and imported best practices from the United States, Canada, Norway, Denmark, Germany, and Great Britain.

It is also apparent that when it comes to evaluating the role of religious actors in politics, there remain challenges and opportunities for Scandinavian historiography. It has been alluded to here in this book that the religious awakenings of the nineteenth century have been marginalized and otherized. This is an understatement, and remains true. A recent example of this is the organization of topics in the 2012 volume of Norstedts *Sveriges Historia 1830-1920*. Early in this 657-page volume, attention is drawn to the role that the folk movements played in shaping the agenda of Swedish politics, without mentioning the religious awakening. It is not until several hundred pages later that a special section on the religious awakening is provided, which begins with the admission that "the awakenings were the oldest of the folk movements." One wonders then why they are the last mentioned. In this section, there is vague acknowledgement that the awakenings involved a social consciousness, but these religious ideas are not connected to long-term developments in Swedish politics and society. There is no mention of the scores of politicians in parliament during these decades who were considered "free-church" politicians. In contrast, five pages are devoted to ideas of the utopianist Nils Herman Quiding, who though fascinating, was not nearly as widely read as Rosenius or Waldenström. In the discussion of print media, their journal, *Pietisten*, is not mentioned once. As a remedy to this, chapter 4 of this book specifically outlined how extensive the readership of Rosenius and Waldenström's journal was, for the purposes of demonstrating that this journal rivaled and even surpassed many national secular papers.

Even more sympathetic historians have seemed to accept the idea of a disconnect between the awakening and political developments, assuming that secular politicians finished what religious "puritans" had only begun. Alf Johansson writes "The cosmos that had held together Swedish society had been a Lutheran-Puritan [he means "Pietist"] ethos in association with progressive thinking. Even after God had left the scene, the puritan ideals had lived on in secular form in the popular movements (*folkrörelser*) that had formed modern Sweden."[431] Johansson makes the rare observation among Swedish historians that there is an ideological connection between pietisms and progressivisms. This kind of observation is usually only made by church historians. However, one wonders exactly which year God "left the scene," or how this divine exit has been quantified. It is as though, in the style of Elvis, God needed someone to announce when he had left the *Riksdag* building. This is a poetic and amusing way of describing secularization, but these types of assumptions can reinforce the idea that politics became homogenously secular at some early moment, and potentially ignore the free-church politicians who remained present at the table after the 1910s. In fact, in 2004, a historical survey of the various Christian associations that had existed in the *Riksdag* over the previous century demonstrated that there were multiple waves of activity in these associations, and that there was even a marked *increase* in participation by parliamentarians in these groups following WWII extending through the 1970s. Worth noting is that these associations have regularly drawn members from all political parties, including even a few Communists. Hans Andreasson notes in this study that between 1964–1994, as many as one third of the entire *Riksdag* were members in these associations, and that even though Social Democrats were a minority, they nevertheless maintained a steady presence which averaged to be one out of every fifteen party members. Thus the participation of free-church and other Christian representatives is *disproportionately higher* than the national size of these religious groups.[432] The fact that these groups have had such a pluralist and ecumenical character is also striking, but perhaps not surprising in light of the pluralist themes that have been pronounced within the Rosenian and Waldenströmian circles. Religion has undoubtedly become a personal choice in Swedish society, and that is an important accomplishment and a cherished bedrock of modern pluralist democracy. But like many other personal matters, these religious worldviews remain informative in public, societal discussions.

This study can be an opportunity for renewed appraisal of religiosity in Swedish society, historically and currently. In the 1800s, Sweden experienced large-scale Christian revival movements which had ambitious goals and wide-reaching influence. In the early twenty-first century, there is the potential for similar patterns among Muslim populations and other religious minority movements that are entering the Swedish political landscape. Furthermore, despite narratives to the contrary, there remain Christians in Sweden. It would behoove Swedish politicians, historians and journalists to make every effort to avoid repeating this old assumption that religion is inherently a personal and irrational private concern or hobby. Theological ideas have mattered in recent history, too. The compartmentalization of religiosity to the realm of the private sphere is a bias that should be acknowledged as such and set aside. Without a doubt and despite its shortcomings, Swedish politics between the 1880s and the 1910s developed in the direction of more democracy, more parliamentary procedure, and an increasing climate of pluralism. Whether exceptional or not, this was not an automatic outcome of the age, but was dependent upon how human actors in Sweden interpreted their situation, and constructed narratives to optimize this situation in the creation of a new political order. These human actors generated narratives by making use of traditional concepts and vocabulary, repurposing them to address current concerns, and creating expectations among politicians and voters alike that politics in Sweden in the present and future would be based on ideals of democratic pluralism. And most impressive of all, this was a collaborative process.

Endnotes

Notes to Introduction

1. In a recent authoritative series on Swedish religious history (*Sveriges kyrkohistoria*), Waldenström was chosen as one of nine topics that received in-depth articles to represent major themes in the second half of the 1800s. Only one of these other topics was a person: the archbishop Anton Niklas Sundberg. See Dahlén, "Paul Petter Waldenström."

2. Lundkvist, "Popular Movements and Reforms," 193.

3. Unless otherwise specified, biographical facts from Waldenström's life are drawn from the following sources: *Svenskt biografiskt handlexikon* (1906); *Nordisk familjebok* (1893); *Nordisk familjebok* (1921); Tomson, *En Hövding*, Bredberg, *P. P. Waldenströms verksamhet*.

4. Lenhammar, *Budbäraren, Pietisten och Församlingsbladet*, 94; The estimated percentages of the population throughout this study are calculated using population statistics that are available by year on the Swedish Central Statistics Bureau, Statistiska centralbyrån, http://www.scb.se/; Per-Magnus Selinder has concluded that Pietisten often had a circulation greater than many secular publications during the period. See Selinder, "Mötesplatserna," 290.

5. Lenhammar, *Budbäraren*, 97.

6. Bredberg, *P. P. Waldenströms*, 20.

7. Kjellberg, *Folkväckelse i Sverige*, 283.

8. Waldenström later published a summary of this theory, *Om försoningens betydelse* (1873), a version of which was translated into English as *The*

Reconciliation. Who was to be Reconciled? God or Man? Or God and Man? Some Chapters on the Biblical View of the Atonement.

9. Numbers for the membership of the Swedish Mission Covenant are presented in the most recent history of that denomination. See Andreasson, *Liv och rörelse*, 141; Numbers on the adherants and extent of influence come from *Nordisk Familjebok* 1921; These numbers are based on the population information available by year on the Swedish Central Statistics Bureau, Statistiska centralbyrån, http://www.scb.se/.

10. "Four of Sweden's Greatest Men." *Chicago Sunday Times-Herald.* 5 Sept 1897. (WSA del I, vol 20); Much of the negative press came from newspapers of the Swedish Augustana Lutheran Synod. See Olsson, "Paul Peter Waldenström," 117.

11. The political parties were in their formative period during Waldenström's time in office. What was the Liberal party in the first decade of the 20th century later evolved into Folkpartiet, where a visible presence of Mission Covenanters continued through mid-century. See Andreasson, *Liv och rörelse*, 167.

12. "För den som menar, att kristendomen i och för sig är det radikalaste av allt och kommer med de längst gående anspråken, behöver det icke attributet radikal passar på den unge Waldenström. Däremot måste det te sig annorlunda för den som bedömer hans ställning ur modern socialdemokratisk synvinkel. En sådan måste finna stor likhet mellan honom och 'biskoparna.'" Bredberg. "Waldenströms 'radikalism.'" *Svenska Morgonbladet.* 14 Dec 1945. (Sigtuna Stiftelsens Pressklipparkiv).

13. Lindström, *I Livsfrågornas spänningsfält*, 10.

Notes to Part I

14. "... [P]å vänstra liksom på den högra sida af vägen finnes ett dike. Lika farligt som det är att köra ned i diket till vänster, lika farligt är det att köra ned i diket till höger, och lika visst som man måste reagera mot det ena, lika visst måste man reagera mot det andra. Det är en gammal berättelse, som de flesta nog känna till, om en godsägare, som skulle anställa en kusk. Det anmälde sig många till platsen. 'Huru nära kan du köra diket?' frågade han den förste af dem. Denne svarade: 'Så nära att det bara är en hårsmån, som skiljer hjulet från diket.' Den andre skröt lika mycket. Den tredje svarade: 'Jag kör aldrig nära diket, jag håller mig midt på vägen, ty det är tryggast.'

Det tyckte äfven godsägaren. Men inom våra politiska partier är det så, som borde den anses för den pålitligaste och bäste, som kan köra så nära diket, att åtminstone halfva hjulringen går utanför dikeskanten." (Waldenström, *Fosterländskt politiskt föredrag*, 8).

15. Schiller, "Years of Crisis," 197.

16. Weigel, *Against the Grain*, 171.

17. Lijphart, *Democracy in Plural Societies*, 17.

18. Ibid., 24.

19. See Stark and Finke, *Acts of Faith*, 39. Stark and Finke identify a bias within the study of religion in which religious phenomena have often been treated as irrationally motivated. In contrast, they assert that people are as rational about religion as they are about any other aspect of human life.

20. "Waldenströms försoningslära fick en avgörande betydelse för det demokratiska genombrottet i Sverige. Han slängde ut en svår dogmatisk lärofråga till folket och lät gemene man ta ställning själv om hur man skulle förstå försoningen. Nu gällde inte längre vad kyrkoherden och bekännelseskrifterna påstod. Läs själva i Bibeln, får ni se! [. . .] Kunde man nu själv bestämma om de himmelska tingen, var man givetvis kompetent att besluta i kommunala angelägenheter om skolor och kyrkbyggen och även om politiska riksfrågor!" (Quoted in Lindberg, "En strid i försoningens ljus," 45).

21. "[Institutionerna] var demokratiskt uppbygg[da], medlemmarna fick skolning i mötes-, organisations- och debatteknik. Nykterhetsrörelsen blev därför en utmärkt plantskola för den svenska demokratin. Både frikyrkorna och nykterhetsrörelsen ville i första hand förbättra de enskilda individerna och deras livsvillkor, men de började också att ställa krav på förändringar av samhället, politiska krav. Eftersom få av de manliga medlemmarna och ingen av de kvinnliga hade rösträtt, kom även dessa folkrörelser att engagera sig i rösträttsfrågan. De kämpade också för mötesfriheten och tryckfriheten." (Lindqvist, *Historien om Sverige*, 559–600).

22. "The Emergence of Swedish Democracy." Official site for Sveriges Riksdag. http://www.riksdagen.se/ 18/Feb/2010.

23. Bredberg, *Waldenströms verksamhet*, 40.

24. Ibid., 41–43.

25. Berggren, "Forward-Facing Angel," 73.

26. Stråth, "Neutrality as Self-Awareness," 150.

27. "Amerika synes mig likt en ung, rik, nervös fru med plymer, ringar, broscher, klädd i siden och sammet, turnyr samt skor med höga klackar, som göra henne längre, än hon verkligen är. Gamla Sverige liknar mer en blyg och anspråkslös mor med sjalett och bomullsförkläde. Det sitter mer guld utanpå hos den unga, men det bor mer guld i hjertat på den gamla." (Waldenström, *Genom Norra Amerikas*, 10).

28. Aksel Sandemose, *En flyktning krysser sitt spor*, 1933.

29. Henningsen, "Jante," 161–74.

30. Waldenström's mentor, C. O. Rosenius, made use of the term *lagom* in a way that fits this discussion of moderation as a guiding principle. Rosenius, "Citizenship in Heaven," in Safstrom, *Swedish Pietists*, 154.

31. Franzén, *Hjalmar Branting*, 215, 232; 1908 marked the year in which Social Democratic party leader Hjalmar Branting led the effort to exclude radicals like Hinke Bergegren from the party for the second time following a terrorist act that year. 1917 marked the year that the Social Democratic party split between moderates and its extremist left wing, which subsequently formed a communist party.

32. Childs, *Sweden*, 1936.

33. Berman, *Primacy of Politics*.

34. Linderborg, *Socialdemokraterna skriver historia*.

35. Hadenius, *Riksdag in Focus*, 197.

36. Bredberg, *P. P. Waldenströms*, 10, 13.

37. Lindström, *I Livsfrågornas spänningsfält*, 13.

38. Ibid., 10.; Lars Gustafsson recounts the same observation in *Litteraturhistorikern Schück*, 105; Numbers on the publication of *Squire Adamsson* are elusive, but the fact that the book has been published in eleven editions between 1863 and 2003 suggests an enormous contemporary readership, as well as an enduring posthumous legacy (the seventh edition was published in 1907, two years after the end of Waldenström's career in parliament). Lacking publication numbers on *Squire Adamsson*, one can compare with some of his other books and extrapolate. For instance, according to tallies of book sales recorded in the newspaper *Norrlands Posten*, from Dec. 1876 to July 1877 alone, thirty-one thousand copies of Waldenström's book *Herren*

är from ("The Lord is Good") were published, which would indicate that at least one out of 140 Swedes read the book that year. The book continued to be printed in newer editions after that as late as 1901, suggesting that the readership was far higher, particularly assuming some copies likely had more than one reader. Also in 1877, there were 230,000 copies published of a single sermon, "Du behöver frälsas" ("You need to be saved"). If all were sold, that would indicate a readership of 5 percent of the population, or one out of nineteen Swedes. Even if only half sold, the numbers are still staggering. See "Lysande bokspridning." *Norrlands Posten.* 23 July 1877. (Gävleborgs Arkiv, Gävle); Estimates are based on the population information available by year on the Swedish central statistics bureau, Statistiska centralbyrån, http://www.scb.se/.

39. "Kristen är en ångestfull flykting från jord och värld, brukspatron en i viss mån modern människa, splittrad, ständigt sökande efter en andlig identitet, delaktig i den nya tidens självanalys, reflexion och rastlöshet. Waldenströms allegori är i hög grad en svensk allegori, präglad av det svenska trossamhällets problematik." (Lindström, *I Livsfrågornas spänningsfält*, 15).

40. "Bokens framställning vittnar om ett genomreflekterat kulturmedvetande, ett försök att bestämma livsåskådningspluralismens alternativ och ta ställning till dem. Inte minst intressant är att författaren förser läsaren med så många invändningar mot kulturen i staden Evangelium och så många attraktiva argument för alternativa kulturer." (Lindström, *I Livsfrågornas spänningsfält*, 16).

41. Fish, "Rhetoric," 472–73.

42. Ibid., 476.

43. Ibid., 471.

44. Ibid., 473.

45. Augustine, *On Christian Doctrine*, 13–14.

46. D. W. Robertson explains Augustine's perspective on the Gospel's role in history. "Christianity was at once a logical outgrowth of late classical thought and, at the same time, an astonishingly brilliant fulfillment of the best traditions of ancient philosophy. . . . Paganism [according to Jerome Carcopino] 'groped and staggered in the pursuit of an ideal concerning which it could have only an obscure prescience. But when the message of the gospel reached its best thinkers, they believed that they have attained it in the flash of certainty which suddenly struck them.'" (Augustine, *On*

Christian Doctrine, ix-x); Augustine himself gives an example of the effectiveness of clear teaching in an example of his preaching in Caesarea in Mauretania, which he believed convinced the people to end their traditional practices of engaging in civil war (Ibid., 160-61).

47. Fish, *Doing What Comes Naturally*, 477.

48. Ibid., 493, 501.

49. Rorty, *Philosophy and Social Hope*, 36-38.

50. Ibid., 38-39.

51. Augustine's view of rhetoric is seen by Fish as negative because it appeals to the "cupidity" in human beings to deter them from their heavenly destination. "I call 'charity' the motion of the soul toward the enjoyment of God for His own sake, and the enjoyment of one's self and of one's neighbor for the sake of God; but 'cupidity' is a motion of the soul toward the enjoyment of one's self, one's neighbor, or any corporeal thing for the sake of something other than God. [...] The more the reign of cupidity is destroyed, the more charity is increased" (Augustine, *Christian Doctrine*, 88-89).

52. Bunyan's main character, Christian, does indeed explain his journey as one of linear forward progress. "If I go back to mine own country, that is prepared for fire and brimstone; and I shall certainly perish there. If I can get to the Celestial City, I am sure to be in safety there. I must venture: to go back is nothing but death, to go forward is fear of death, and life everlasting beyond it. I will yet go forward" (Bunyan, *Pilgrim's Progress*, 44).

53. Book of Rom 4:4-5 (composite translation from Waldenström's text).

54. Lindström explains the changes in Adamsson's names as a direct reference to Paul's discussion of justification by law versus justification by grace in Gal 4:30-31. (Lindström, *I Livsfrågornas spänningsfält*, 71).

55. Zinzendorf articulated this supremacy of experience in "Thoughts for the Learned and Yet Good-Willed Students of Truth," in which he states, among other things: "Religion must be a matter which is able to be grasped through experience alone, without any concepts." (*Pietists*, 291).

56. Waldenström, *Squire Adamsson*, 48.

57. Ibid., 61.

58. Ibid., 139-52.

59. Erickson, *David Nyvall*, 308.

60. Waldenström, *Squire Adamsson*, 83. The names are Förtröstansfull/Stark, Frimodig/Tvärsäker, and Upplyst/Självklok.

61. Ibid., 131.

62. For a relevant example of their similar views on the contentious issue of baptism, compare Rosenius's and Waldenström's discussion of this topic in *Swedish Pietists*, 120–39.

Notes to Part II

63. The motto, which is often attributed to Augustine, and appears here in Latin, German, Swedish, and English, can be found in a number of variations. Particularly notable is the difference between "doubtful things" versus "non-essential things." The motto was embraced by the Moravian community at Herrnhut, led by Count von Zinzendorf. Swedish Pietists were also known to reference it, including the Swedish Mission Covenant president Erik Jakob Ekman, who used it to frame the discussion about the doctrine of the atonement in the 1870s (*Den inre missionens historia*, Part 3, Vol. I, 1490); Waldenström was quite familiar with the theology of Moravian Pietism, as demonstrated in his commentary during his visits to missions conferences in Herrnhut in 1912 and 1913, as well as Halle and sites connected to the life of Martin Luther. Waldenström. Letters to the editors of Svenska Morgonbladet and Jönköpings Posten. 8 May 1912, 10 May 1912, 21 Apr 1913, 23 Apr 1913, 2 May 1913. (WSA del III, vol 3).

64. McLeod, *Secularisation in Western Europe*, 29, 51.

65. For examples, see Borg, *Old-Prussian Church*, xiii.; See also Gorski, *Disciplinary Revolution*, 85–90.

66. My understanding of classical Pietism and its influence in the Scandinavian Lutheran world has been profoundly shaped by its manifestations in North America, in particular through several generations of scholarship within the Evangelical Covenant Church. Modern attempts to interpret this legacy are exemplified by definitions given at two symposia held at North Park Theological Seminary in Chicago and later published in the Covenant Quarterly under the titles "The Pietist Heritage and the Contemporary Church" (1970) and "Contemporary Perspectives on Pietism: A Symposium" (1976).

67. Bexell, *Sveriges kyrkohistoria: Vol. 7*, 314; Johann Arndt's *True Christianity* (1605/1610) in particular had a long lifespan in Sweden, being published by the Evangeliska Fosterlands-Stiftelsen well through the 1800s.

68. Bexell, *Sveriges kyrkohistoria*, 101.

69. Ibid., 67. Rosenius and the EFS maintained a hesitancy to endorse the activity of participants whenever these activities resembled separatism, particularly when the practice of private communion services increased in the 1850s and 1860s.

70. Ibid., 111. The break between Waldenström and some of Rosenius's followers began in 1872 with the theological controversies ignited by Waldenström that year.

71. Amy Moberg defended the Rosenian line and attempted to dissuade Waldenström from publishing his atonement sermon in 1872. See Bredberg, *Waldenströms verksamhet*, 145.

72. Waldenström stubbornly held to this position even late in his career, encouraging both Swedish and North American Covenanters not to allow themselves to become denominations, but simply remain "missions societies." Waldenström. Letter to the editors of Missions-Wännen and Minneapolis Veckobladet. 13 July 1914. (WSA del III, vol 3).

73. See Safstrom, "Facing the Future Together."

74. Sattler, *God's Glory*, 76–77.

75. Although gendered differences existed between men and women in the revival, there were many instances of women assuming the role of teaching and interpreting scripture (though seldom as "preachers"). In Waldenström's own life, it is evident that several women held sway regarding theological interpretation, not least Amy Moberg, secretary for *Pietisten* during the Rosenius years. His aunt, Lina Benckert, was also central to his conversion. See Bredberg, *Waldenströms verksamhet*, 145; Bexell, 110; Waldenström, *Paul Peter Waldenströms minnesanteckningar*, 85.

76. Lenhammar, *Sveriges kyrkohistoria: Vol. 5*, 94, 98–100, 158–59.

77. Gonzalez, *Story of Christianity: Vol. 2*, 339.

78. Catholic historian George Weigel has recently critiqued these basic assumptions and the role assigned to religion in the Post-Constantinian era. Most relevant to this discussion is his assertion that religion cannot be

excluded from the public sphere if it is to truly be pluralistic. See *Against the Grain*.

79. Nordstrom, *Scandinavia Since 1500*, 44.

80. In the initial year of Pietisten's publication (1842), two articles appeared defining what the editors meant by invoking the Pietist identity and how they viewed ecumenism. See Safstrom, *Swedish Pietists*, 31–43.

81. Zinzendorf's concept that each individual church is a "trope" that completes the diverse whole that is the greater church is a paramount expression of this. Gritsch, *History of Lutheranism*, 155.

82. Scott and Rosenius, "Pietism," In *Swedish Pietists*, 34.

83. *Gud, den underbare*, 51.

84. Bexell, *Sveriges kyrkohistoria: Vol. 7*, 111.

85. For more on the activity of Waldenström in North America, see Safstrom, "Defining Lutheranism."

86. Waldenström's notes from a speech probably given around 1910 in the USA. "Landet." (WSA del I, vol 12).

87. Lenhammar, *Budbäraren*, 91.

88. Ibid., 92.

89. Ibid., 96.

90. Bexell, *Sveriges kyrkohistoria*, 108.

91. Hallingberg, "Tidningar, böcker," 309.

92. Stråth, *Sveriges Historia 1830–1920*, 134.

93. Lenhammar, *Budbäraren*, 92–94.

94. Waldenström. "Betalda bönehus." Letter to the editors of Svenska Morgonbladet and Jönköpings Posten. 8 Aug 1912. (WSA del III, vol 3).

95. Andreasson, *Liv och Rörelse*, 97–98.

96. Waldenström. Letter to Otto Högfeldt. 19 Mar 1915. (WSA del III, vol 3).

97. Noll, *Old Religion*, 67.

98. Brohed, *Sveriges Kyrkohistoria*, 17–18.

99. Johansson, P.P. *Waldenström i Kyrkomötet*, 204.

100. Bergsten, *Frikyrkor i samverkan*, 18–19. Bergsten presents the prevalent view that Waldenström's support for the Church of Sweden was inconsistent with his philosophy. I disagree, and suggest that Waldenström's defense of the Church of Sweden was a natural outgrowth of his philosophy concerning the public role of religion.

101. Johansson, P. P. *Waldenström i Kyrkomötet*, 201; Tomson, *Den radikale Waldenström*, 62–63; Tomson, *En politisk vilde*, 185. Tomson points out that Waldenström had referred to the persecution of Pietists and Salvation Army members in his defense of the free speech rights for Socialists in the "munkorgslag" debates in the Riksdag in 1889.

102. Nerman, *Hjalmar Branting: Fritänkaren*.

103. Johansson, P. P. *Waldenström i Kyrkomötet*, 26, 121, 197. This was followed up by a motion in 1908 that the half of the seats in the Kyrkomöte that were designated for laymen delegates should in fact be given to laymen, which was not yet the case (he pointed out that in 1868 he himself had been a layman delegate, although he was at that time a priest).

104. Ibid., 31; See also Waldenström, "Was the Apostle Peter Legally Married," in *Swedish Pietists*, 230–31.

105. Bexell, *Sveriges kyrkohistoria*, 132–35.

106. Johansson, P. P. *Waldenström i Kyrkomötet*, 132; See also Bexell, *Sveriges kyrkohistoria*, 253–55.

107. Brohed, *Sveriges kyrkohistoria*, 278. Civil bookkeeping was not transferred from the church to the state until 1991.

108. Bexell, *Sveriges kyrkohistoria*, 255.

109. Johansson, P. P. *Waldenström i Kyrkomötet*, 210.

110. Ibid., 204.

111. Ibid., 203.

112. Ibid., 306; See also Brohed, *Sveriges kyrkohistoria*, 24; Two major contradictions were apparent in Waldenström's argument for religious pluralism. One was that Waldenström made a precarious argument that atheists could not free their children from religious instruction as long as Sweden was constitutionally a Christian state (Johansson, 342). The other was that

he introduced a motion in 1910 that forbade foreign missionaries from spreading Mormon propaganda in Sweden, which passed. Native Swedes, he thought, should be free to discuss these teachings amongst themselves, but foreigners should not be allowed to disseminate material in person (Johansson, 360).

113. Waldenström, "Christian Congregation," in *Swedish Pietists*, 103–8.

114. See Johansson, *P. P. Waldenström i Kyrkomötet*, 223–24, 230, 342. Waldenström in his motion sought two things, ". . . dels att finna lämpliga former för upplösning av det nuvarande sambandet mellan kyrka och stat, dels att angiva den ordning, vari statens intresse för religionen må, efter en sådan upplösning, finna ett uttryck, som bäst motsvarar statens ändamål" (he articulated this better in his defense of his motion than he did in spelling it out in the actual motion).

115. Johansson, *P. P. Waldenström i Kyrkomötet*, 386.

116. Ivar, "Gudsförnekaren från Gävle."

117. *Berättelser om Gefle Arbetareförenings förvaltning år 1892.*

118. Ivar, "Gudsförnekaren från Gävle."

119. "Jag dör nöjd i tron på ett lyckligt framtidsfolk som lever utan illvilja, fördomar och vidskepelse, och ett samhälle där välvilja och godhet råda. Att arbeta för det släktet och det samhället är den högsta religionen, fast det nog dröjer århundraden, ja årtusenden, innan idealet varder förverkligat." (Quoted in Ivar, "Gudsförnekaren från Gävle.")

120. "Med Lennstrand går 'utilismen' som *antireligiösa sektrörelse* i graven. [. . .] Vi socialister föredraga vid särskilt den religiösa övertrons bekämpande en mindre bröstgänges metod; vi räkna på den naturvetenskapliga upplysningens stegrande spridning och framför allt, vi dela icke den ortodoxa utilismens ohistoriska, absoluta syn på tingen. Den är en senfödd plebejisk dotter till förra seklets aristokratiska rationalism. För vår del däremot se vi icke i de på varandra följande religionerna enbart eller främst en hop lögner, utan ställa frågan så: vilka historiska och sociala förutsättningar ha skapat de skiftande gudasagor, vari våra fäder nedlagt sina föreställningar om vad de icke veta? Med en sådan frågeställning förlorar kampen mot religionen sin udd, eller riktigare, den riktas icke mot följden: en viss religiös vidskepelse, utan mot orsaken: sociala missförhållanden, från vilka människorna tvingas att åtminstone i fantasin fly till en bättre, rättvisare värld än den som omgiver dem. I den mån denna nu ymnigt flödande källa till religiosit

tillstopas, blir religionen besegrad på ett radikalare sätt än med den ofta rätt ytliga utilistiska bibelkritiken: den dör bort som ett organ, vilket icke längre har någon användning, faller för indifferentismen, likgiltigheten, icke genom disputerande och diskuterande." (Branting, *Hjalmar Branting*, 33–34).

121. "Kristi lära har intet, absolut intet gemensamt med den dogmtro som av präster och stat utgives för 'kristendom'—och påtvingas ett värnlöst folks barn. Därför måste vi kräva att våra barn ej längre bli förgiftade av denna falska och bildningsfientliga dogmkristendom. Så upphöjd, vacker och människoälskande Jesu lära är, lika låg och usel och fientlig mot mänsklighetens broderskapslära är denna falska kristendom, som allt sedan stat och kyrka (den kristna) på Konstantin den stores tid kopplades samman, bjudits människorna. Staten har gjort kyrkan till sin medhjälpare när det gällt att hämma mänsklighetens utveckling. Man har försvårat vår kamp för att nå fram till ljus och klarhet. Därför måste vi bekämpa denna förfalskade kristendom, den av stat och präster mot vår vilja oss påtrugade kristendom, som nu likt en mara trycker folken ned till jorden. Men kristi lära, människokärlekens och broderskapets evangelium, låtom oss i alla goda Gudamakters namn ej bekämpa denna lära!" (Dahlström, *Bildning och Klasskamp*, 17–18).

122. Dahlström, *Leo Tolstoy*.

123. Dahlström, *Skolan och prästväldet*, 3–4.

124. Ibid., 15, 18.

125. Nerman, *Hjalmar Branting*, 174–75.

126. Ibid., 167.

127. Ibid., 9, 12.

128. "I betraktande därav, att religionen såsom samvetssak endast får bestämmas av den fria övertygelsen och att den världsliga makten följaktligen ej bör lägga hinder i vägen för den andliga friheten eller ingripa på det religiösa området, skall Föreningen söka att medelst möten, föredrag, petitioner och andra opinionsyttringar samt genom att verka på riksdagsmannavalen upphäva alla de lagar, förordningar och institutioner som tillsammans utgöra de statskyrkliga banden" (Nerman, *Hjalmar Branting*, 23–25).

129. "Hela denna utveckling bort från tvångsreligionen bottnar uppenbart i det mer eller mindre tydliga erkännandet att *religionen bör vara privatsak*. Konsekvent utförd är denna tanke oförenlig med statskyrkoprincipen. Men

vid en så ingripande reform som statskyrkans avskaffande är det uppenbart av stor vikt att gå i ordning med frågorna, så att den borgerliga staten icke bara handlöst släpper det band, varmed den håller kyrkan. Staten måste stå färdig att i allo taga konsekvenserna av tingens nya ordning och vara väl rustad mot de maktövergrepp, som alldeles säkert komma att försökas av vissa obskurant-samfund. De Waldenströmska, allt oftare återkommande lovsångerna över den katolska kyrkan, som aldrig böjt sig för statsmakten, men mäktigt härskar över miljoners själar, visa tydligt nog var våra svenska fripåvar se sina förebilder. Öppet har man ju redan på det hållet förordat kyrkans skiljande från staten i tid, d.v.s. medan den förra kan vid boskillnade ha utsikt att föra med sig maktmedel, som ett upplyst och klarsynt folk aldrig skulle lämna i sådana händer" (*Hjalmar Branting*, 90).

130. Waldenström. Letter to the editor of Svenska Morgonbladet and Jönköpings Posten. 20 Apr 1909. (WSA del III, vol 2). "Den katolska kyrkan är oböjlig, när det gäller att värna kyrkans frihet gentemot staten. De protestantiska däremot äro mjuka i ryggen som unga vidjor."

131. "I Elmhult blef en väldig diskusion. Där är ett af Waldenströms värsta nästen. Trots det ohyggligaste väder var lokalen proppad, och de hade rest dit både från Onsby o Hästveda. Där var nästan uteslutande religiösa och ytterst märkliga yttranden gjordes af dessa—mot skenkristendom och dogmtro" (Dahlström, *Brev till Hjalmar Branting*, 414).

132. Nerman, *Hjalmar Branting*, 169.

133. Ibid., 167.

134. Waldenström. Letter to the editors of Svenska Morgonbladet and Jönköpings Posten. 11 May 1912. (WSA del III, vol 3).

135. "Skola ej lärjungarne derigenom lära att tänka, att bibelordet är jämförelsewis mindre wigtigt än det dogmatiska lärosystemet? [. . .] I stället för att läroboken skulle wara en nyckel till Bibelns rätta förstånd och såsom sådan åtfölja bibelläsningen, så får nu Bibeln wara nöjd med den äran att åtfölja läroboken, så neml. att ur Bibeln i läroboken infogas härifrån och derifrån sammanförda s. k. dicta probantia (bewisställen)" (Waldenström, *Bibelläsning i skolan*, 5–6).

136. "Men den bibliska historien kan lika litet ersätta Bibeln, som planscher öfwer wexter kunna ersätta de lefwande wexterna sjelfwa. De äro goda jemte hwarandra, såwidt neml. den bibliska historien anwändes blott såsom en handledning till den kortfattade öfwersigten, men hon kan lika litet blifwa

Bibeln, som planchewerket kan blifwa naturen" (Waldenström, *Bibelläsning i skolan*, 11).

137. Waldenström, *Bibelläsning i skolan*, 27.

138. Ibid., 17.

139. Ibid., 19.

140. Ibid., 10.

141. Ibid., 27.

142. Ibid., 10.

143. "Wår öfwersättning är skrifwen på ett språk, som fått namn af kyrkospråket, hwilket tillbedes med en pietet, som om Guds Ande hängde på gamla kasusändelser och tyska ordställningar. [...] Hade apostlarna tänkt, att kyrkospråket skulle wara ett språk, som ingen talade eller skref och få förstådo, aldrig hade de skrifwit på den hellenistiska dialekten" (Waldenström, *Bibelläsning i skolan*, 56–57).

144. Ibid., 54.

145. Ibid., 59.

146. Waldenström, *Reform av kristendomsundervisningen*, 6.

147. Ibid., 8.

148. Ibid., 14.

149. Ibid., 24.

150. Ibid., 25.

151. Ibid., 28.

152. "Så som samfärdselmedlen utveckla sig och därmed äfven förbindelserna mellan de olika världsdelarne och folken, synes det mig böra höra till religionsundervisningen på det högsta stadiet att meddela lärjungarne en kort öfversikt af de förnämsta hedniska religionsformerna, såsom Bramaism, Buddaism, Konfucianism, Sintoism, religionsformer som visat sig mäktiga att skapa en jämförelsevis hög kultur. Så mycket påkallad torde en sådan undervisning vara, som den kristna missionen bland de hedniska folken med hvarje år växer i omfång och kraft. Den skulle också för vidgandet af lärjungarnes andliga vyer vara af mycket större betydelse än åtskilligt, som de nu få inhämta, och som därför gärna kunde lämna rum

för att bereda plats åt det nämnda" (Waldenström, *Reform av kristendomsundervisningen*, 29).

153. Waldenström. Letter to the editor of Stockholms Dagblad. 3 Jan 1912. "Svar till lektor Åhfeldt angående kristendomsundervisningen vid våra läroverk." (WSA del III, vol 3).

154. "[...] Jag skall aldrig upphöra att kämpa för föräldrars grundlagsenliga rätt att af skolan fordra bibliskt kristen religionsundervisning för sina barn. Men denna rätt innebär ock frihet att taga barnen undan en undervisning, som går i motsatt riktning. Däraf följer ingalunda såsom någon konsekvens rättighet för rationalister, materialister o.s.v. att fritaga sina barn från en bibeltroende undervisning, så länge svenska folket legaliter bekänner sig till den luterska reformationen, hvars utgångspunkt och grundprincip är den heliga Skrifts auktoritet såsom ofelbar norm för kristen tro, lif och gudstjänst. Helt annat blir förhållandet, om den dag kommer, då svenska staten utstryker den kristna religionen från sitt program. Då säger det sig själft att kristendomsundervisning alldeles aflägsnas ur statens skolor och på sin höjd ersättes med allmän 'objektiv' religionshistoria, där buddismen får precis samma rätt som kristendomen och madame Blavatsky sättes med Kristus på den ena sidan och Muhammed eller Konfucias—för att icke säga Josef Smith—på den andra. [...] Ha t. ex. metodister och andra dissenters rättighet att befria sina barn från skolans religionsundervisning, därför att den icke är metodistisk etc., så vore det väl märkvärdigt, om svenska kyrkans medlemmar skulle i längden förvägras samma rätt gentemot en undervisning, som undergräfver denna kyrkans egna grundpriciper." (Ibid.).

155. "Lektor Å talar ett skarpt omdöme öfver den stora katekesen. Därvid talar han om dogmatik och religion såsom i viss mån motsatser. Det borde han icke göra, huru modärnt sådant tal än är. Ty det vet lektor Å lika väl som någon annan, att ingen religion gifves utan dogmatik. Så snart jag säger barnet, att det finnes en Gud, så talar jag dogmatik. Så snart jag säger, att denne Gud älskar världen, att han skapat världen, att han sändt Jesus för att frälsa världen o.s.v.—då undervisar jag i dogmatik. Om det än är sannt, att religionens väsen är tro på Gud, så är det lika sannt att all tro på Gud framställer tro om Gud." (Ibid.).

156. Waldenström. Letter to the editors of Missions-Wännen and Minneapolis Veckobladet. 29 Jan 1912. (WSA del III, vol 3). "Det låter så vackert, när man säger: 'Vi ha biblen, den är nog, därför behöfva vi ingen dogmatik.' Det är alldeles så taladt, som om någon sade: 'Vi ha naturen, och då behöfva vi ingen naturlära.' Endast grof okunnighet kan tala så. [...] Det gäller då att

fortfarande studera bibeln för att justera, rätta, fullständiga sin dogmatik, så som det gäller för naturforskaren att alltjämt studera naturen för att komma till en alltjämt fullständigare och riktigare uppfattning af henne."

157. William Bredberg's *Waldenströms verksamhet till 1878* is the most extensive in this area. For an account in English, see Karl A. Olsson, *By One Spirit*.

158. Waldenström, "Was the Apostle Peter Legally Married," in *Swedish Pietists*, 230–31.

159. Nerman, *Hjalmar Branting: Fritänkaren*, 14.

160. Tomson, *En politisk vilde*, 25.

161. Waldenström. Letter to the editors of Svenska Morgonbladet and Jönköpings Posten. 12 Feb 1912. "Den Gullberg–Hamrinska motionen om dop och jordfästning som förrättas af frikyrkliga predikanter." (WSA del III, vol 3). "Kunna vi komma därhän—och dit skola vi komma, därom är ej tu tal—då ha vi vunnit allt, hvad vi behöfva, så länge en persons borgerliga ställning i något afseende kan bero därpå, att det kan styrkas, att han är döpt."

162. ". . . göra frikyrkopredikanterna till ett nytt statskyrkligt prästerskap, om än af lägre ordning (men så att säga halfofficiellt). Det må Gud bevara oss ifrån" (Ibid).

163. Waldenström. Letter to the editors of Svenska Morgonbladet and Jönköpings Posten. 15 Feb 1912. "Ytterligare några ord om den Gullberg–Hamrinska motionen." (WSA del III, vol 3); "Det tillhör inte riksdagen att gifva någon person rättighet att döpa. Därför skall församlingen icke af honom begära någon sådan. Hvad riksdagen må vara med om att besluta, det är, huru statskyrkoprästen skall anteckna ett dop i statskyrkans ministerialböcker. Därmed punkt."

164. Rosenius, "Spiritual Priesthood," in *Swedish Pietists*, 109–12.

165. Kierkegaard discusses the elusive nature of establishing authority in the modern era in "Two Ages" (1846) and "Two Ethical Religious Essays" (1849), among other places.

166. Eldebo, "Är Guds kärlek så gripande att ingen enda orkar bestå?"

167. Sundström, *Arvet från Waldenström*, 116.

168. "Waldenström var mycket luthersk på socialetikens område. Likväl såg han gränser för underdånigheten. När överheten direkt upphäver sig över Guds lagar och kränker trosfrihet och samvete har den kristne rätt till lydnadsvägran. Vidare gäller det att de kristna medborgarna har rätt att med lagliga medel ersätta en dålig överhet med en bättre. En kristen är över huvud taget medansvarig för sitt samhälles utveckling. Det är kristen medborgarplikt att i politisk verksamhet föra in kristna värderingar i lagstiftning och reformarbete" (Sundström, *Arvet från Waldenström*, 116).

169. Waldenström. "Den nya politiska situationen I." Letter to the editors of Svenska Morgonbladet and Jönköpings Posten. Not dated. (likely Feb 1914). (WSA del III, vol 3).

Notes to Part III

170. Rosenius, "Diversity of God's Children," in *Swedish Pietists*, 116.

171. Schiller, "Years of Crisis," 199.

172. Ibid., 227.

173. Stråth, *Sveriges Historia*, 427.

174. Anna Lindhagen. "Värkar religionen hindrande på arbetarrörelsen?" 3 Oct 1902. *Arbetarbladet*. (Kungliga biblioteket). To this question Lindhagen answers "yes," pointing to their antagonism toward all reforms. As this was a Gävle paper, she is most certainly including Waldenström in this evaluation, as she refers to "narrow pietism" (trång pietism). Furthermore she calls for religion to be a private matter for this reason.

175. Linderborg, *Socialdemokraterna skriver historia*, 131–32. Linderborg, like many historians, has identified Bergegren's removal as part of the party's housecleaning efforts in response to outside criticism of anarchist agitators.

176. Waldenström, *Fosterländskt politiskt föredrag*.

177. The summary of the social conditions in Sweden in the period are drawn from the following sources: Hadenius, *Riksdag in Focus*; Nordstrom, *Scandinavia Since 1500*; Stråth, *Sveriges Historia 1830–1920*.

178. Franzén, *Hjalmar Branting*, 142; Schiller, "Years of Crisis," 195 (notes by S. Koblik).

179. Hadenius, *Riksdag in Focus*, 166.

180. Ibid., 155–56.

181. See Andreasson, *Liv och rörelse*, 167.

182. Even the moderate Branting had drawn inspiration from the events in Paris as a young man. See Franzén, *Hjalmar Branting*, 42.

183. Waldenström, *Fosterländskt politiskt föredrag*, 8.

184. Tomson, *En politisk vilde*, 35.

185. Berman, *Primacy of Politics*.

186. In her book, Linderborg makes the case that the socialist party emphasized its radical nature, thereby recasting central figures like Branting as being more revolutionary than they actually were. Her thesis is therefore complementary to Sheri Berman's observations in that it explains how historians were inclined to neglect the classical liberal heritage altogether.

187. Furthermore, the understanding of pluralism that is being advanced here is one that understands pluralism to be a positive and even deliberately-orchestrated situation, not merely the presence of multiple viewpoints. This would be opposed to some understandings in which pluralism is seen as a *modus vivendi*, or undesirable situation. In this positively defined pluralism, participants seek to maintain a delicate balancing act between arguing their own case and leaving room for constructive dissent.

188. Stråth, *Sveriges Historia*, 185.

189. Ibid., 186.

190. "Det sanna frisinnet söker att sätta sig in i olika tänkandes åskådning. Det gifver skäl och tar skäl. Finner det bättre skäl hos motståndaren, än det själft har att bjuda på, så blygs det icke att ändra sin ståndpunkt och mening. Att däremot under sådana förhållanden, envist hålla fast vid en ståndpunkt som man en gång fattat, det är egensinne, det är envishet i ful bemärkelse. En sådan person är en tjurskalla, och det är ingen vacker titel. Må vi därför vara i sanning frisinnade. Må vi försöka att sätta oss in i deras åskådning, som tänka annorlunda än vi, i de skäl, som de ha för sin mening, samt i öfverenstämmelse därmed bedöma dem." (Waldenström, *Fosterländskt politiskt föredrag*, 4).

191. "Till Gefle frisinnade och arbetarvalmän!" *Arbetarbladet*. 19 Sept 1902; "Valet i Gefle: Skall ärligheten segra?" *Arbetarbladet*. 4 Sept 1905. (Kungliga biblioteket).

ENDNOTES

192. Tomson, *Den radikale Waldenström*, 62–63.

193. The main newspapers consulted were *Arbetarbladet*, *Gefle Dagblad*, *Söndags Nisse*, and *Svenska Morgonbladet* during the election years of 1902 and 1905, housed in microfilm at Kungliga biblioteket.

194. Franzén, *Hjalmar Branting*, 215, 232. Hjalmar Branting had led the effort to exclude radicals like Hinke Bergegren from the party in November of 1906, as well as again in June of 1908. When the bomb exploded in Malmö, it was seen as confirmation of the dangers of anarchism; the three men involved were self-proclaimed "unghinkar" or "Young Hinkes."

195. Stråth, *Sveriges Historia*, 188.

196. Quoted in Tomson, *En politisk vilde*, 42.

197. Nils Olof Franzén makes this claim as to Branting's political strategy in his biography. "Det är reformismens väg han [Branting] pekar ut; den är förvisso fylld av kamp och strid, men striden utkämpas på den demokratiska utvecklingens villkor. Det hände att Branting även i fortsättningen talade om framtiden i den marxistiska 'vetenskapens' ordalag. Men det var offer på den försvagade trons altare. Det var ord som i grunden stred mot den gärning han ägnade sin helhjärtade kraft. Den gärning för vilken han fick utkämpa sina bittraste strider—striderna mot dem till höger som fruktade eller hatade den parlamentariska demokratin och mot dem till vänster som föraktade den och ville ersätta den med något slags proletariats diktatur." (Franzén, *Hjalmar Branting*, 167–168).

198. An example of this can be seen in Herman Lindqvist's popular history, *Historien om Sverige*, 559–600.

199. Franzén, *Hjalmar Branting*, 47–48.

200. Branting. *Hjalmar Branting tal och skrifter*: Vol. *10*, 27. Lennstrand "hade i uppväxtåren den då ännu icke som hycklare avslöjade Waldenström till lärare."

201. Ibid., 33–34.

202. Branting, *Hjalmar Branting tal och skrifter*: Vol. *11*, 87.

203. Lagerlöf, *Jerusalem*, 106.

204. Branting, *Hjalmar Branting tal och skrifter*: Vol. *11*, 10.

205. Branting, *Hjalmar Branting tal och skrifter*: Vol. *10*, 288.

206. "Vår svenska socialistiska arbetarrörelse har ett program, som är lyckligt fritt från teoretisk doctrinarism och därför också stått ej blott orubbat utan också okritiserat inom partiet självt i nu över 11 år. Vi ha också visat oss i vår praktiska politik lyckligt fria från den intransigenta doktrinarism, som i sin rätlinjighet offra möjligheten att uträtta *något*, därför att det icke står till att få *allt* eller ens det *mesta* genast efter vårt huvud. Med stigande makt följer nu förpliktelsen att gå vidare på denna samma väg. Vi ha lovat vid valen Sveriges arbetande folk att göra vad vi kunna för att främja dess rätt och bästa. Då är det också vår plikt att som parti göra redligt *vår* anpart för att söka bringa till stånd en sådan vänstersamling, att vägen jämnas denna gång för ett *verkligt* demokratiskt genombrott. Personliga stämningar eller antipatier måste i det arbetet vika för de stora sakliga synpunkterna." (Branting, *Hjalmar Branting tal och skrifter: Vol. 4, 7*).

207. Branting, *Hjalmar Branting tal och skrifter: Vol. 4, 5*.

208. "Flertalet ledamöter i Social-Demokratens kontrahentförsamling var nog den sortens socialdemokrater. De var reformister, utan revolutionärt sinne, ännu kvar i liberala och frisinnade tankegångar ärvda från hemmen, förvärvade i hantverksbetonade fackföreningar, i frikyrkorörelsen eller godtemplarrörelsen. Ideologiskt kanske mera hemmahörande där än hos Marx. Det var den typen av arbetare i kontrahentförsamlingen som lyfte Branting till chefsposten i SD och ville ha honom som ledare i striden för ett bättre samhälle." (Sundvik, *Branting eller Palm?*, 161).

209. Falk, *Socialistprästen*, 115.

210. *Berättelser om Gefle Arbetareförenings förvaltning år 1886*, 7; *Berättelser om Gefle Arbetareförenings förvaltning år 1891*, 7; *Berättelser om Gefle Arbetareförenings förvaltning år 1892*, 8; *Berättelser öfver Gefle Arbetareförenings verksamhet under år 1901*, 9. (Arkiv Gävleborg).

211. From Branting's foreword to Spak's *Gammal och ny moral*. "Som kristen präst ser författaren alldeles naturligt, världsutvecklingen främst med moralistens ögon. Marxismens särmärke är däremot att för densamma den *ekonomiska* utvecklingen är historiens drivkraft, genom att denna skjuter fram eller undergräver olika klassers maktställning, medan moralen helt enkelt uttrycker på sitt område olika tiders och klassers *behov* samt vexlar med dessa. Av dessa klasser se vi, frånsett nutiden, här föga, men läsa mycket om enskilda morallärares förkunnelse och deras idéers fullkomning fram mot det absoluta. Moralen lösgöres alltså från den miljö, vars produkt den enligt Marxismen är, och svävar som andlig makt över den mänskliga utvecklingen, ledande denna mot det absoluta ideal, som redan finnes oss givet av

Kristus. Det behöver knappt tilläggas att författaren gör som varenda teolog före honom, de s.k. frisinnade liksom de ortodoxa; en var omdiktar ganska fritt sin Kristusbild efter sin egen föreställning om moralisk fullkomlighet."

212. Waldenström. Letter to the editor (unspecified—perhaps Minneapolis Veckobladet). 9 Sept 2010. (WSA del III, vol 2).

213. "De moderna 'troende,' som så högröstat just nu bekänna sin bokstavstro på allt 'som står skrivet,' skulle alldeles säkert gripas av helig fasa och raseri, om de någonsin i misshugg råkade slå upp sitt Gamla testamente och där fingo se huru våldsamt profeterna tygade till sin tids överklass." (Spak, *Gammal och ny moral*, 36).

214. Waldenström. Letter to the editor (unspecified). 30 Oct 1908. (WSA del III, vol 2). "Och hvad är socialismen från kristlig synpunkt sedt? Jag skall till svar anföra några ord af en af de socialistiske riksdagsmännen. Han säger: 'För en stor del blir kyrkan och bönehuset en tillflyktsort för lifvet. Dessa människor äro lika oemottagliga för sundt förnuft, sanning och rättvisa som förnäcklade lik. Det är lika omöjligt att bibringa en dylik individ upplysning och vetande som att förmå en höna att lära sig multiplikationstabeller. Då sålunda religionen är ett hinder för arbetarerörelsens frammarsch, så börjar partiet rikta sin agitation ej endast mot statskyrkoreligionen eller kristendom, utan mot allt, hvad som med rätta bör betraktas såsom religion.' Ja, så låter det, där man talar rent språk. Men ändå finnes det många fromma kristna, som icke kunna se någon egentlig fara uti socialismen, ja som ondgöras öfver fälttropet: 'Front mot socialismen!'"

215. Lundkvist, "Popular Movements and Reforms," 193.

216. Ibid., 182.

217. Kjellberg, *Folkväckelse i Sverige*, 297.

218. Andreasson, *Liv och rörelse*, 167.

219. Tomson, *En politisk vilde*, 35.

220. Schiller, "Years of Crisis," 207, 218, 225–26.

221. Waldenström. Letter to editor of Missions-Wännen and Minneapolis Veckobladet. 28 Sept 1908. (WSA del III, vol 2). "Ett förfärligt väsen hafva vi haft af riksdagsmannavalen, som försig gått under september månad. Det har varit grufliga slitningar. Den öppet och energiskt kristusfientliga socialismen har tagit en mängd platser, därvid understödd af de s.k. liberalerna. Dessa å sin sida har till tack därför erhållit socialisternas stöd för somliga

sina kandidater. Men de veta mycket väl, att så snart de hjälpt socialisterna fram så långt, att de kunna reda sig själfva, så sparka de ut sina hjälpare. Så ha de gjort på flere ställen vid årets riksdagsmannaval särskildt i Stockholm, där de sparkat ut flera liberaler. Liberala tidningar, som inse socialismens fara och bekämpa densamma, hafva klagat på 'högern' därför, att den icke velat hjälpa dem mot socialisterna. Men på samma gång ha de varit fullkomligt främmande för den tanken, att segern mot socialisterna hade på flere ställen kunnat vinnas, om liberalerna understödt högerns kandidater. Men nej. Hellre ha de då röstat med socialisterna, utan att besinna, hvarthän sådant leder."

222. Waldenström. "Staaf i kajutan Branting vid rodret." 29 Sept 1911. (WSA del III, vol 2). "De liberala talarne ha väl försökt lugna allmänheten. Men Branting har talat rent språk. Han har låtit liberalerna veta, att de icke komma någon väg utan socialisternas hjälp. Utan dessa stå de totalt maktlösa. Men han har också låtit dem veta, att de icke kunna påräkna socialisternas hjälp utan grundliga vederlag. Han har låtit dem veta, att deras egentliga uppgift är att bana väg för socialismen, som är den slutliga arftagaren. [. . .] Huru länge en vänsterregering skall kunna hålla stånd emot socialismen, det kommer att bero på högern. Detta har hvarje något så när bildad person länge kunnat inse. Det är också från de moderatas sida upprepade gånger sagdt. Äfven så pass liberala tidningar som Aftonbladet och Svenska Dagbladet ha insett det och betänksamt skakat på hufvudet. Men hvarken Brantings eller Lindmans ord ha kunnat öppna ögonen på de liberala väljarena. [. . .] För 15 å 20 år tillbaka höjdes röster, som påpekade faran af socialismens framträngande. Då svarades—och jag fick själf mottaga det svaret—'Hvad har man att frukta af en handfull socialister?' Det betraktades som skuggrädsla. Och nu? Nu är socialisternas parti det dominerande i riksdagen. Det är det parti, som alltid kommer att fälla utslaget i hvarje fråga, där liberala och moderata komma att stå emot hvarandra. [. . .] Och så visas det klarare än dagen för hvar och en, som icke förblindar sig själf, att talet om en underhusparlamentarism är en stor humbug. Ty den förutsätter med nödvändighet ett majoritetsparti i Andra Kammaren och icke bara en koalition af två hvarandra ganska skarpt motsatta partier, hvilkas enda egentliga gemensamma intresse är att störta den bestående regeringen. Så snart det kommer till ett positivt politiskt arbete, så må herr Staaff tala, huru mycket han vill, om en 'fruktbärande samverkan'—Herr Branting har på ett ganska beskt sätt låtit honom veta, att någon annan samverkan icke kommer i fråga än en sådan som befordrar socialismens intresse. Branting kan därför, hvad ögonblick han finner lämpligt, störta en liberal regering, ifall högern icke räddar henne. Så står saken i verkligheten."

223. Palme, *Karl Staaff*, 177.

224. Nyman, *Kommittépolitik och parlamentarism*, 94.

225. Ibid., 108.

226. Register till Riksdagens protokoll med bihang 1867–1899, 1900–1910. (Riksarkivet.)

227. Nyman, *Kommittépolitik och parlamentarism*, 99.

228. Lövgren, *Oscar Ahnfelt*, 50–51.

229. Linderborg, "Historical Romanticism," 87.

230. Waldenström. "Den nya politiska situationen—I." Feb 1914. (WSA del III, vol 3). "Vill man ha bort konungamakten, så gör då om vår konstitution, säg adjö åt konungen och sätt dit en president i stället. Det blir reellt, det blir sanning."

231. Waldenström. Letter to the editors of Svenska Morgonbladet and Jönköpings Posten. "Den nya politiska situationen—II." 20 Feb 1914. (WSA del III, vol 3). "Wi ha en grundlag. Enligt denna är konungen den, som regerar riket—konungen, den personliga, icke ett kungligt neutram eller fantom. Att grundlagen stadgar så, det måste alla erkänna, äfven de som ifrigt önska, att det icke vore så. Men bredvid grundlagen har man framarbetat något däremot ehördande, som man nu kallas 'konstitutionell praxis,' hvilken så småningom blifvit en partisignal och 'kommit till genombrott' (!) genom valen 1911. Nu har konflikt uppstått. Konungen håller fast vid grundlagens uttryckliga, af ingen bestridda, än mindre af några vederlagda ord. Det liberala partiet sätter den nämnda praxis öfver grundlagen, 'Denna praxis,' sade socialisten herr Staffen i första kammaren 'är det verkliga konstitutionella lifvet, medan grundlagen endast är ett temporärt uttryck för uppfattning vid ett visst tillfälle. Då denna praxis nått en viss utveckling, är tiden inne att äfven ändra grundlagens bokstäfver.' Däri träffade han säkert alldelles riktigt vensterns verkliga mening. Här erkännas alltså med klara och sanna ord, att den nuvarande konflikten beror på motsatsen mellan grundlagens ord å ena sidan och en 'omkring grundlagen uppvuxen konstitutionell praxis,' och så inträffar det märkliga, att konungen som i enlighet med sin villkorliga pligt och kungaed, håller fast vid grundlagen, anklagas för att handla okonstitutionellt, ju 'sätta vår konstitution i fara,' medan det för tillfället maktägande partiet och dess regering, som besvurit samma grundlag som konungen, trotsar på att handla konstitutionellt och värna vår konstitution, när det medvetet handlar i strid mot dess otvetydliga ord.

Och sådant gå äfven kristna riksdagsmän med på! Att det finnes personer, som önska en fullt genomförd parlamentarism efter engelskt mönster, där ministären är regent och konungen ett slags sekraterare, som kontrasignera ministärens beslut, det kan man förstå. Att de arbeta för detta mål, det är deras rätt, och ingen skall klandra dem för det. Men det skall ske genom att ändra grundlagen."

232. Waldenström. Letter to the editors of Svenska Morgonbladet and Jönköpings Posten. "Den nya politiska situationen—III." 26 Feb 1914. (WSA del III, vol 3).

233. Waldenström. "När vi se Sveriges kung inför oss..." Not dated. (WSA del I, vol 7).

234. "Gefle—23 Maj—Gif akt!" 23 May 1902. *Arbetarbladet*. (Kungliga biblioteket). Waldenström is sarcastically referred to here as "hr utskottsledamoten."

235. Stråth, *Sveriges Historia*, 175.

236. "Lektor Waldenström i Rösträttsfrågan." 22 May 1902. *Gefle Dagblad*.; "Lektor Waldenström i Rösträttsfrågan." 23 May 1902. *Gefle Dagblad*. (Kungliga biblioteket).

237. "Gefle—19 Sept—Geflevalet i dag." 19 Sept 1902. *Arbetarbladet*. (Kungliga biblioteket). Here the following terms were connected to Waldenström: "waldenströmska Jesuitism," "största vinglare," "svartaste kulturfiende," "intolerantaste frikyrkoapostel," "vidriga waldenströmska läsarokets tryck."

238. "Geflevalet 1899." 8 Aug 1902. *Arbetarbladet*. (Kungliga biblioteket).

239. "Den 18 Sept—Inför afgörandet." 18 Sept 1902. *Gefle Dagblad*. (Kungliga biblioteket).

240. "Hr Waldenström." 29 Aug 1902. *Arbetarbladet*. (Kungliga biblioteket).

241. "Fria ord—Riksdagsmannavalet." 17 Sept 1902. *Gefle Dagblad*. (Kungliga biblioteket).

242. "Frisinnade valmän. 'Fria ord—Riksdagsmannavalet.'" 16 Sept 1902. *Gefle Dagblad*. (Kungliga biblioteket).

243. D. "Fria ord—Riksdagsmannavalet." 16 Sept 1902. *Gefle Dagblad*. (Kungliga biblioteket).

244. J. N. "Fria ord—Riksdagsmannavalet." 19 Sept 1902. *Gefle Dagblad.* (Kungliga biblioteket).

245. Karl H Lindh. "Fria ord—Riksdagsmannavalet." 19 Sept 1902. *Gefle Dagblad.* (Kungliga biblioteket).

246. "Fria ord—Till Gefle frisinnade och arbetarvalmän." 19 Sept. 1902. *Gefle Dagblad.* (Kungliga biblioteket).

247. "Många moderata valmän. 'Fria ord—Till Gefle moderata valmän.'" 19 Sept 1902. *Gefle Dagblad.* (Kungliga biblioteket).

248. "Den 20 Sept—Valresultat—Brodin-Waldenström återvalda." 20 Sept 1902. *Gefle Dagblad.* (Kungliga biblioteket).

249. "Fria Ord—Upprop till valmännen i Gefle." 8 Sept 1905. *Gefle Dagblad.* (Kungliga biblioteket). This article was signed by Gefle Frisinnade valmansförening, Gefle Arbetareförening, Gefle Godtemplare, Gefle Templare, Gefle arbetarekommun, and Strömsbro gårdsägareförening.

250. Untitled article. *Norrlands Posten.* 27 Aug 1884; Untitled article. *Norrlands Posten.* 6 Sept 1884. (WSA del I, vol 9).

251. *Berättelser öfver Gefle Arbetareförenings verksamhet under år 1901,* 9.

252. "Valmän!" Advertisement. 19 Sept 1902. *Gefle Dagblad.* (Kungliga biblioteket). This was signed by Gefle Moderata Valmansförening, Gefle Handtverksförening, Gefle Nykterhetsförening, Gefle Minuthandelsförening, and Gefle Fastighetsegareförening.

253. Valman. "Fria Ord: Gefle-valet." 7 Sept 1905. *Gefle Dagblad.* (Kungliga biblioteket). "Då så stora och dyrbara inträssen stå på spel måste väl hvarje samvetsöm valman låta alla personliga sympatier för den eller den kandidaten vika och lämna sin röst endast åt den, som bestämdt förklarat sig icke under några förhållanden vilja medverka till rösträttsreformens förfuskande genom införandet af proportionella val."

254. "D:r David Bergströms föredrag." 7 Sept 1905. *Gefle Dagblad.* (Kungliga biblioteket).

255. "Den 7 Sept—Geflevalet." 7 Sept 1905. *Gefle Dagblad.* (Kungliga biblioteket).

256. "Fria ord—Upprop till valmännen i Gefle." 8 Sept 1905. *Gefle Dagblad.* (Kungliga biblioteket). " ... kom ihåg att det icke gäller personer, utan

sak. I lektor Waldenström har proportionalismen och Första kammaren sin säkraste anhängare."

257. "Storartad vänsterseger. Starbäck-Lindh valda." 9 Sept 1905. *Gefle Dagblad*. (Kungliga biblioteket).

258. Tomson, *En politisk vilde*, 205.

259. Ibid., 200-9.

260. Waldenström. "Stockholm den 13 Aug—Lektor Waldenström och rösträttsfrågan." 13 Aug 1902. *Svenska Morgonbladet*. (Kungliga biblioteket).

261. "Det s.k. kommunalstreket har jag alltid bekämpat såsom en alltför lös och vacklande grund för den politiska rösträtten. [. . .] Kommunalstrecket är, efter en mycket kort lifstid, begrafvet äfven af dem, som födt det fram till världen. Utan tvifvel har man ock allmänt insett, att det är onaturligt och farligt, att grunden för medborgarnes politiska rösträtt skulle stå icke i grundlagen utan i kommunallagen. Och så är denna den enda tvistepunkten mellan mig och Liberala samlingspartiet för alltid förfallen. Detta har nu inom riksdagen varit min ställning och min verksamhet i rösträttsfrågan, och utom riksdagen har jag upprepade gånger—särskildt i mitt fosterländska tal vid landtbruksmötet i Gäfle—uttalat mig för politisk rösträtt åt varje hederlig medborgare. Vid sist nämda tillfälle uttalade jag ock min tro, att den tiden icke vore långt aflägsen, då vi skulle komma därtill. Hädanefter lär det väl icke heller inom riksdagen kunna bli tal om någon rösträttsreform annat än på den allmänna, af hvarje bevillningsstreck oberoende rösträttens grund. Och det må förlåtas mig, om jag smickrar mig med den tron, att just min kamp mot Liberala samlingspartiets kommunalstreck rätt väsentligt bidragit att bringa situationen fram till denna punkt, som nu synes bli en verklig samlingspunkt." (Ibid.).

262. "Man kan tycka, att en smula rättskänsla, om än aldrig så liten, skulle för en tidning, som kallar sig frisinnad, omöjliggöra en så grof förvrängning af allmänt kända fakta. Men sådant är partityranniet" (Ibid.).

263. "Stockholm den 9 Aug—Samling seger—splittring nederlag." 9 Aug 1902. *Svenska Morgonbladet*; "Stockholm den 14 Aug—Den Waldenströmska kandidaturen." 14 Aug 1902. *Svenska Morgonbladet*; "Valrörelsen." 10 Aug 1905. *Svenska Morgonbladet*. (Kungliga biblioteket); "Situationen är nu tämligen klar. Högern, de moderate, handtverkarne och de frikyrklige—dit hör ock Gäfle nykterhetsförening—ena sig kring lektor Waldenström. Hvilken deras andre kandidat blir, beror alldeles på hur skeppsbyggmästare Brodin kommer att ställa sig till proportionalismen."

264. "Stockholm den 14 Aug—Den Waldenströmska kandidaturen." 14 Aug 1902. *Svenska Morgonbladet*. (Kungliga biblioteket).

265. "Hvarför proportionella val?" 21 Aug 1905. *Svenska Morgonbladet*. (Kungliga biblioteket). "Vid proportionella val få alla partier sitt, - alla grupper af någon betydelse erhålla riksdagsmän till ett antal, som svarar mot gruppernas storlek. Majoriteten får flere och därmed sin naturliga belöning, minoriteten blir icke lottlös. Känslan häraf minskar stridens hetsighet, dämpar lidelserna, främjar lugn och besinning. Hvarje parti väljer fritt sina män, som det har fullt förtroende till, och dessa kandidater i sin ordning bäras fram af sina meningsfränder; det är på deras förtroende de hvila, de behöfva icke söka gunst åt alla håll, icke fria med löften åt alla partier. De proportionella valen skipa rätt mellan partierna, främja karaktär och själfständighetskänsla hos både partier och kandidater."

266. "Hvart majoritetsvalen leda, fick man det klaraste bevis på vid de senaste allmänna valen i Sachsen. Socialisterna utgjorde 58 proc. af valmanskåren och eröfrade 22 platser af 23; alla de borgerliga elementen tillsamman—42 proc. af valmanskåren!—fingo gemensamt 1 plats!" (Ibid.).

267. "Stockholm den 9 Aug—Samling seger—splittring nederlag." 9 Aug 1902. *Svenska Morgonbladet*. (Kungliga biblioteket).

268. Waldenström. Letter to the editor (unspecified). 1 June 1907. (WSA del III, vol 1). "Både i Aden och Suez fick jag tidningen från Sverige och gladde högligen öfver att se, att rösträttsfrågan ändtligen blifvit löst och det på proportionalistisk grund. Må Gud leda allt till godo för vårt land och folk. En bedröflig syn i vårt fosterland företar det socialistiska tyranniet, som blir alltmer brutalt och våldsamt. De liberala tidningarna anklaga den socialistiska tidningspressen såsom orsaken till den gräsliga förvildning som man nu får skåda. Men den tänker föga på, att det är deras egen under lång tid fortsatta kurtis för socialismen som ej blott beredt den socialistiska pressen tillfälle att i lugn och ro så sin draksådd utan äfven vattnat utsädet, så att det kunnat växa med sådan fart, som det gjort." [. . .] Elsewhere he described his eagerness to receive word on developments at home: "Huru det bränner i mig att få veta rösträttsfrågans utgång i mitt kära fädernesland, kan hvar och en lätt förstå. Det är emellertid en underbara begåfvning svenska folket har att lösa viktiga frågor. Riksdagen och regeringen pusta och arbeta år efter år, innan de kommer till något, kanske i mångt och mycket ganska otillfredsställande, resultat. Men när 'folket' kommer tillsammans i en skog eller på folkets hus, då är saken snart klar. Det går som psalmen i kyrkan: klockaren tar upp och angifver tonen, och sedan går det af sig själf.

Få se, om jag i Aden får några underrättelse om, huru riksdagen afgjort den viktiga rösträttsfrågan. Må Gud leda allt så, att det må hända vårt land till välfärd."

269. Waldenström. Letter to the editor of Missions-Wännen. 8 Jan 1908. (WSA del III, vol 1). "På det politiska området är det jämföreslsevis lugnt, sedan de uppslitande, mångåriga rösträttstriden mynnat ut i det rösträttsbeslut, som antogs af förra riksdagen, och som nog kommer att äga bestånd. Detta beslut innehöll, att valen skola ske proportionellt, d.v.s. så att hvarje mer betydendepolitiskt parti kan i riksdagen få in så många representanter, som motsvara partiets styrka i valmanskåren. Det blir således icke möjligt för majoriteten att helt och hållet stänga ut minoriteten. Och det är rättvist. Det s.k. liberala partiet bekämpade med en [??] energi de proportionella valen. Men nu ha händelser inträffat, som gjort, att 'liberalerna' sannolikt äro mycket belåtna öfver, att det blir proportionella val. Man har nämligen på senare tiden haft några s.k. fyllnadsval, där liberalerna med det närvarande valsättet förlorat platser dels åt den s.k. högern dels åt socialisterna. Och det varslar om, hvad de möjligen hade att att [sic] vänta, om ej proportionella val infördes, på samma som rösträtten blefve allmän. Nu säga liberalerna, förstås, icke: 'Det är bra för oss, att vi få proportionella val.' Nej, däri skulle ligga ett erkännande större, än man kan vänta af dem. Men de säga så nedlåtande, att de vid nästa val icke skola göra något för att få det nyss fattade beslutet kullkastadt. Och det är vackert af dem, att de vänligen afstå från att krassa räddningsbåten, medan skutan håller på att kantra."

270. "Prässen om Geflevalet." 12 Sept 1905. *Arbetarbladet*. (Kungliga biblioteket).

271. Valand. "Gefle—När maran släpper." 12 Sept 1905. *Arbetarbladet*. (Kungliga biblioteket). "Som bekant har W. på senaste tiden uppträtt som den mäst fanatiske motståndare till arbetarerörelsen, röstat för åkarpslagar, svikit i rösträttsfrågor m. m., m. m."

272. "Gefle—Riksdagsmannavalet—Det frisinnade valmötet." 22 Aug 1905. *Arbetarbladet*. (Kungliga biblioteket).

273. "Mot proportionssystemet." 4 Sept 1905. *Arbetarbladet*; "Gefle—Valet i Gefle." 2 Sept 1905. *Arbetarbladet*. (Kungliga biblioteket).

274. "För Dagen 9 Sept—Gestrikland har valt." 9 Sept 1905. *Arbetarbladet*. (Kungliga biblioteket).

275. M. "Gefle—'Jättehumbugen från Gefle.'—Waldenström vill bli omvald." 3 Aug 1905. *Arbetarbladet*; "Norrlandsfrågan och de proportionella valen." 2 Sept 1905. *Arbetarbladet*. (Kungliga biblioteket).

276. Valand. "Gefle—När maran släpper." 12 Sept 1905. *Arbetarbladet*. (Kungliga biblioteket).

277. E. R. "För Dagen 9 Sept—Gestrikland har valt." 9 Sept 1905. *Arbetarbladet*. (Kungliga biblioteket). "Hr. Waldenström har äntligen fallit på sina gärningar och i hans fall förkroppligas det arbetande och skattdragande folkets ljungande protest mot förstakammarplanerna i rösträttsfrågan, mot krigspolitiken, mot klasslagstiftningen, kort sagt mot hela den störtflod af reaktion som var nära att dränka nationen men som nu allt folket, med ens vaknat till lif och medvetande om sin stykra, skakar af sig som en pinsam dröm."

278. M. "Gefle—'Jättehumbugen från Gefle.'—Waldenström vill bli omvald." 3 Aug 1905. *Arbetarbladet*. (Kungliga biblioteket). "De skydda nämligen *minoriteten*. Men att skydda den rösträttslösa, till stor del i rättsligt hänseende utan tak öfver hufvudet stående *majoriteten* för den af 5,000-gradiga rösträttsorättvisor omgärdade minoritetens öfvervåld, undantagslagar, hungertullar och militärbördor har aldrig fallit P.W. in. Det är endast minoriteten som behöfver mera skydd, 'så den kan få ett ord med i laget,' fastän den redan förut är enväldshärskare i kommunalstämmor, stadsfullmäktige, landsting och första kammare. Sådant är P.W:s program! Klasslagstiftningsfrågorna *tiger* han med. Hans ställning där är också tillräckligt känd."

279. Christian II was a perennial symbol of tyranny for the Swedes; "Lektor Waldenström i Rösträttsfrågan." 22 May 1902. *Gefle Dagblad*; "Lektor Waldenström i Rösträttsfrågan." 23 May 1902. *Gefle Dagblad*. (Kungliga biblioteket).

280. "Den 9 Sept—Gefle-valet. Doktor Larsons programtal." 9 Sept 1902. *Gefle Dagblad*. (Kungliga biblioteket).

281. "De organiserade arbetarne och Gefle-valet." 12 Sept 1902. *Gefle Dagblad*. (Kungliga biblioteket).

282. "Hvad är en sträjkbrytare?" 29 Aug 1905. *Arbetarbladet*. (reprinted from "Newyorker Volkszeitung") (Kungliga biblioteket). "En sträjkbrytare är för sitt yrke, hvad en landsförrädare är för sitt land, och äfven om han i krigstid är till stor nytta för den ena parten, så blir han efter fredsslutet föraktad af båda parterna. Är hjälp af nöden, så är han den siste som bispringer, men kan han bli delaktig af något gott, som han icke själf varit

med om att åstadkomma, då är han den förste som griper till. Hvad hans egna angelägenheter beträffar, är han den störste egoist och kan för ett par 'silfverpänningar' förråda familj, vänner och fosterland. Han är en landsförrädare i smått, som först säljer sina arbetskamrater, för att sedan själf, när freden blifvit sluten, bli såld af sina arbetsgifvare. Han föraktas af båda parterna och af hela mänskligheten. Han är en fiende till sig själf, till nutides och framtiden!"

283. Olson, *Logic of Collective Action*.

284. The summary of the situation in Sweden around the time of the 1909 strike is drawn in part from Axel Strand's introduction to Haste's *Dokument från storstrejken*, and Schiller's *Storstrejken 1909*.

285. "Det är tydligt, att de nordiska länderna hade två vägar att välja på, antingen att organisera arbetsmarknaden med sikte på förhandling och avtal, vilket inte uteslöt öppen strid vid tillfälle, eller med sikte enbart på strid. Vilken väg skulle de välja?" (Schiller, *Storstrejken 1909*, 10).

286. Schiller, *Storstrejken*, 63.

287. Ibid., 57.

288. Waldenström. Letter to the editor (unspecified). Undated (between July and Sept 1909). (WSA del III, vol 2). "Huru öfver alla gränser brutal strejkledningen är, därpå må ett par exempel anföras. Nådigt har, den medgifvit, att läkare få åka till de sjuka, att sjuka få skjutas till sjukhus, att mjölk får köras till sjukhusen, att lik få utföras till begrafningsplatserna. Men detta allt endast på det villkor, att hvarje därvid tjänstgörande kusk begär och erhåller särskildt tillståndsbevis från den s.k. landsorganisationen, d.v.s. strejkledningen."

289. "Värst af allt har dock det nedriga aftalsbrott varit, som bestått däri att typograferna allmänt nedlagt arbetet så godt som öfver hela landet. Typografförbundet är just det, som först och mest verkat för att åstadkomma kollektiva aftal mellan arbetare och arbetsgifvare. Ett sådant aftal består också och förbjuder uttryckligen strejk eller lockout under aftals tiden. Men heder och tro betydde nu ingenting. Tidningarna miste sin tryckeripersonal. Endast en tidning fick komma ut nämligen Socialdemokraten, som dock för tillfället bytte om namn och kallade sig Svaret. Den öppet förklarade afsigten var att sätta tumskruf på den del af pressen, som var motståndare till storstrejken" (Ibid.).

290. Waldenström. Letter to the editor (unspecified, presumably Vecko-bladet). 9 Sept 1909. (WSA del III, vol 2). "Man må ha huru stort intresse som hälst för arbetarnes väl—brott måste man dock låta vara brott, äfven då det begås af arbetare, ju t.o.m. när det sker mot arbetsgifvare. Våra arbetare äro djupt att beklaga för deras brist på omdöme och deras lätthet att förtro sig åt bedragare. Synnerligen svår har de troende arbetarnes ställning blifvit. Skaror af dem hafva, förlamade af en oförklarlig feghetens ande, låtit sig släpas med under de gudlösa tyrannernas krutpiska. Må Gud frälsa dem! Må Gud bryta sönder deras bördas ok och deras skuldras ris och deras plågares staf (Es. 9). Men 'ingenting ont, som ej har något godt med sig.' Nu hafva ögonen öppnats äfven på de blinda till att se, hvad socialdemokratin bär i sitt sköte, och hvilken förbannelse den är just för arbetarne, trots dess lögnaktiga skräfvel om sitt stora intresse för dem. Nu skola väl ock alla sansade arbetare, och i all synnerhet de troende, få kraft att slita sig lös från all 'solidaritet' med dem, som hata och håna deras Gud och frälsare. Det är för resten oförklarligt, huru det någonsin kunnat bli tal om några sådan solidaritet—solidaritet mellan Kristus och Belial. Nu skola vi väl också få lagar, som effektivt skydda arbetsvilliga mot strejkares förföljelser samt göra det klart för alla, att i Sverige skall råda frihet att arbeta och försörja sig och att hvar och en, som förgriper sig på den friheten, förgriper sig på staten själf."

291. Waldenström. Letter to the editors of Missions-Wännen and Minneapolis Veckobladet. 12 Oct 1909. (WSA del III, vol 2). "Här äro fackföreningarne tvångsanslutna till socialismen, och Svenska arbetareförbundet, som försökt bilda fackföreningar, som varit oberoende af socialismen, har måst utstå otroligt hätska förföljelser."

292. Schiller, *Storstrejken*, 29.

293. Waldenström. Letter to the editors of Svenska Morgonbladet and Jönköpings Posten. 11 May 1912. (WSA del III, vol 3). "Här i Tyskland har stark rörelse i dagarne uppstått genom tvenne socialdemokratiska händelser, som äro rätt betecknande. En socialdemokratisk skriftställare i Solingen har blifvit utesluten ur partiet därför, att han i ett utgifvet arbete kritiserat några af socialdemokratiens programspunkter. Tidningar anmärka helt spetsigt, att man sålunda börjat med kätteriprocesser inom socialdemokratien, 'alldeles som inom kyrkan.' Jo, ja men. Man börjar med att bryta alla 'borgerliga' band och slutar med att pålägga band, som äro sjufaldt värre."

294. "Folkfesten i Bomhus." 1 Aug 1902. *Arbetarbladet*. (Kungliga biblioteket).

295. Tomson, *En politisk*, 185.

296. "Det är herrarna inte obekant, att vi äro ett gott stycke inne på en statssocialism, i vilken staten tager hand om vissa samhällsklasser, tillförsäkrar dem vissa fördelar, hjälper till att hålla priset uppe på deras varor osv., och det är ett bland socialdemokratiens förnämsta yrkanden, att staten på samma sätt skall taga hand om den arbetande befolkningen, tillförsäkra den en viss maximiarbetstid, en viss minimilön osv., något som en stor del av Sveriges innebyggare genom statens mellankomst redan äga" (Quoted in Tomson, *Den radikale Waldenström*, 60).

297. Schiller, *Storstrejken*, 38.

298. "Den 10 Sept—Skola vi vara med?" 10 Sept 1902. *Gefle Dagblad*. (Kungliga biblioteket).

299. "Politik och religion." 12 Sept 1902. *Gefle Dagblad*. (Kungliga biblioteket).

300. "Kristendom." 4 July 1902. *Arbetarbladet*. (Kungliga biblioteket). "Kristus var fattig, en tiggare, som icke visste hvart han skulle luta sitt trötta hufvud. Han predikade fattigdomens rätt till öfverflödet. Han förklarade, att förr kunde en kamel gå genom ett nålsöga, än en rik man komma in i himmelriket. Men hans efterföljare, prästerna, hur göra de? De ha väldiga inkomster [*in footnote*: P.P.W. dock bara 22,000 utom extra aktieinkomster], de lefva i lyx och öfverflod och den öfverste själaherden, Kristi ståthållare på jorden, som äfven kallas påfve, har 500 millioner placerade i goda säkerheter i Englands bank. En sann Kristi efterföljare! [. . .] Jo, det skall bli på ett annat sätt! Ty vi vilja blifva kristna—inga profitkristna, inga bastardkristna, utan socialister, d.v.s. sanna kristna. Vi vilja predika kärlek, jämlikhet och rättvisa för de undertrykta och förslafvade."

301. Workman. "Den röda tråden." 27 Mar 1902. *Arbetarbladet*. (Kungliga biblioteket).

302. Spak, *Gammal och ny moral*, 45.

303. Waldenström. "Landet." Not dated (probably given around 1910 in the USA). (WSA del I, vol 12).

304. Waldenström. Untitled note for speech on patriotism. Undated. (WSA del I, vol 12).

305. Waldenström, "Landet."

306. Waldenström. "Solidaritet." *Pietisten*. 22 Dec 1909. 366. "Solidaritet är ett ord, som nu för tiden mycket ofta användes. Det är ett vackert ord,

namnet på en mycket skön *dygd*, nämligen sammanhållning och samhörighetskänsla inom en viss krets och för ett bestämt ändamål. [...] När medborgare i ett land äro genomträngda av känslan att de utgöra *ett* folk, så att säga *en* kropp i många lemmar, samt var och en i sin mån med glädje göra, vad de förmå, för att stödja fosterlandet och befordra dess väl, då är det solidaritet, en högst berömvärd dygd. En sådan solidaritet kan även finnas inom olika föreningar, olika folkklasser, olika yrkesklasser o.s.v. Den tjänar då i högsta grad till att stödja, stärka, uppfostra de enskilda medlemmarne samt befordra deras bästa. Det finnes dock en gräns, utöver vilken solidariteten icke får gå. Solidaritet i sådant, som är orätt, är ett lika avskyvärt brott, som solidaritet i det goda är en berömvärd och välsignelsebringande dygd."

307. "Men det gives ett annat område, där solidariteten borde spela en mycket större rol, än den i allmänhet gör, och det är i församlingen. Där om någonstädes böra de särkilda medlemmarne känna sig riktigt solidariska, riktigt samhöriga, riktigt ansvariga för varandra, enligt apostelns ord: när en lem lider, så lida alla lemmarne med, när en lem förhärligas, så förhärligas de alla. Att hålla ihop såsom ett i församlingen, stödjande, tjänande, bärande varandras bördor o.s.v., det är en av de härligaste dygder, som kunna tänkas eller nämnas." (Waldenström. "Solidaritet").

308. Waldenström. Letter to the editors of Svenska Morgonbladet and Jönköpings Posten. Apr 1911. (WSA del III, vol 2).

309. Waldenström. Letter to an unspecified editor (likely Veckobladet). 9 Sept 1909. (WSA del III, vol 2). "Nu skola väl ock alla sansade arbetare, och i all synnerhet de troende, få kraft att slita sig lös från all 'solidaritet' med dem, som hata och håna deras Gud och frälsare."

310. Waldenström. "Hvad fosterlandet behöfver" (speech notes). Undated. (WSA del I, vol 12).

311. In their introduction to a collection of Branting's speeches, the editors, Alvar Alsterdal and Ove Sandell, note: "Med den demokratiska inställningen följde respekten för oliktänkande och beredskap till samverkan. Lika oförsonlig som Branting var i kritiken av orättvisor och missförhållanden, lika villig var han till samarbete med andra framstegsvänliga krafter. Allt eftersom arbetarrörelsen växte i makt och mognad blev Branting alltmer inställd på kompromisser och samlade lösningar—en hållning som stundom ådrog honom kritik från de mer otåliga inom partiet. Med sin utomordentliga politiska känslighet sökte Branting alltid utvinna det bästa möjliga ur en situation. Tillkomsten av den liberal-socialistiska regeringen 1917 och den stora författningsuppgörelsen året därpå kan sägas utgöra krönet på

denna strävan. Branting visste att de djupare liggande konflikterna i samhället hade klasskaraktär. Men han förkunnade ingen oförsonlig klasskamp. Hela samhället skulle lyftas materiellt och kulturellt. Arbetarrörelsen skulle ytterst vara en kulturrörelse." (*Socialism och demokrati: Ett urval av Alvar Alsterdal och Ove Sandell,* 9).

312. Waldenström. Letter to the editors of Missions-Wännen and Veckobladet. 5 Sept 1911. (WSA del III, vol 2). "En annan nyhet i den pågående valagitationen har varit, att de olika partierna utsändt automobiler öfver hela landet med restalare, som på vägar och torg och andra platser hållit agitationstal. Dessa automobiler ha haft olika färger. De moderatas ha varit blå, socialdemokraternas röda, de liberalas hvita. Själf har jag icke sett mer än en af dem. Det var i Luleå. Den var röd och kom såsom ett urväder en kväll. Den trumpetade, där den for fram. Så samlades folk, och tal höllos halfva natten ute under bar himmel."

313. Waldenström. "Från de stora sommarmötena I." 18 June 1911. (WSA del III, vol 2).

314. Stein, *Philipp Jakob Spener*, 118.

315. Gritsch, *History of Lutheranism*, 150.

316. Waldenström. Letter to the editors of Svenska Morgonbladet and Jönköpings Posten. 2 May 1912. (WSA del III, vol 3).

317. Kjellberg, *Folkväckelse i Sverige,* 290. The first two deaconesses were actually commissioned in Bethlehem Church in Stockholm in 1855.

318. Waldenström, *Genom Norra Amerikas Förenta Stater,* 320–25, 435; Waldenström, *Nya Färder i Amerikas Förenta Stater,* 6, 29, 32, 85, 134, 155, 157, 334, 351, 458, 524, 535.

319. Waldenström. Letter to the editors of Svenska Morgonbladet and Jönköpings Posten. 11 May 1912. (WSA del III, vol 3).

320. Stråth, *Sveriges Historia,* 285–88.

321. Waldenström. Letter to the editors of Missions-Wännen and Veckobladet. 15 Jan 1910. (WSA del III, vol 2). "En annan bestående rest af den där verksamheten äro de då upprättade s.k. arbetsstugorna i Norrbotten. I stället för att af de insamlade nödhjälpmedlen kasta almosor hit och dit i de fattiga hemmen att af deras innevånare strax uppätas, tog man hand om barnen i arbetsstugor, där de ej blott fingo husrum, mat och kläder, utan— hvad vida mer var—fingo uppfostran, fingo lära sig arbeta och därigenom

utbildades till att i framtiden kunna redbart förtjäna sitt uppehälle. Af de nödhjälpsmedel, som jag erhöll från Amerika, använde jag en del till hjälp för dessa arbetsstugor, men sedan jag mottagit det ofvan nämnda klandret af förbundet, så måste jag sluta. 'Folket skulle ha pengarna såsom gåfva och icke såsom betalning för arbete,' hette det utan prut. Och så blev det."

322. Waldenström. Letter to the editors of Missions-Wännen and Veckobladet. 3 May 1913. (WSA del III, vol 3).

323. Waldenström. Letter to the editors of Svenska Morgonbladet, Jönköpings Posten, and Ansgari Posten. Jan 1915. (WSA del III, vol 3).

324. Stråth, *Sveriges Historia*, 425.

325. Waldenström. Letter to unspecified editor. 13 July 1903. (WSA del I, vol 7). "Men sorgligt är att den själfegande bondeklassen på detta sätt alltmer förvandlas till en klass af bolagsarrendatorer. Huru man skall råda bot på detta, är ett stort socialt problem hvars lösning ännu icke är funnen. För resten är det en rörelse, som går genom hela världen, att de stora sluka upp de små. Stora riken sluka de små, stora affärer sluka de små o.s.v. Kapitalets makt växer med en förfärande styrka."

326. Tomson, *Den Radikale Waldenström*, 47.

327. Arvidsson, "Reflections," 49.

328. Tomson, *Den radikale Waldenström*, 44–45.

329. See Larsson, *Väckelsen och Sundsvallsstrejken 1879* and Svärd, *Väckelserörelsernas folk i andra kammaren 1867–1911*.

Notes to Part IV

330. Waldenström. "Vid årskiftet." Letter to the editors of Svenska Morgonbladet and Jönköpings Posten. Not dated (likely Dec 1915 or Jan 1916). (WSA del III, vol 3).

331. Tomson, *En politisk vilde*, 22–23.

332. "Här i Sverige blef tillverkning och försäljning af fosfortändstickor för kort tid sedan förbjuden, och det dels på den grund, att en eller annan därmed sysselsatt arbetare, som var oförsiktig, ådrog sig sjukdom, dels därför, att det hände, att kvinnor använde giftet från dessa stickor till fosterfördrifning. Allt det där är idel småsaker i jämförelse men den förödelse, som alkoholen vållar. Det veta alla. Men ändå skall alkoholen vara lös, och

finnes det någon plats, som vill skydda sig emot honom, så skall det kosta en oerhörd kamp och agitation å nykterhetsvännernas sida." (Waldenström, *Nya Färder*, 189).

333. "Superiet är icke minst bland de upplysta och bildade klasserna. Äfven kyrkliga fester hos oss anser man icke kunna firas utan 'vin och starka drycker.' När makar vigas, skall det supas; när barn döpas, skall det supas; när en familjemedlem begrafves, skall det supas; när en kyrka inviges, och en kyrkoherde installeras, skall det supas. Det äldsta minne jag från pojkåren har af en begrafning var, att värden klingade med prästen och sade: 'Det är sista gången vi supa upp den gamla Stina.' Alla beklaga det, men ingen har mod att bryta seden" (Waldenström, *Nya Färder*, 403).

334. Bergman, *Modärn kultur*, 8. Bergman notes the influence of the abolitionist movement on the temperance movement in Sweden.

335. See *Absolutism och personlig frihet*. Much of this debate focused on the tension between moderates and absolutists ("*moderatister*" and "*absolutister*"); among the people who spoke in defense of the absolutists' position was another leader in the movement, E. W. Wretlind.

336. Johansson, *Systemet lagom*, 40, 10–11.

337. Burchell, *Evolution of Green Politics*. In his comparison of the development of green parties in several Western European countries, Burchell includes the Swedish *Miljöpartiet de gröna*. In this comparison, the green parties have distinguished themselves as so-called "new social movements" in that they resist complete institutionalization into the dominant political system and maintain external criticism. However, he concedes that since the 1960s, some accommodation to the dominant political process has actually taken place, bringing forth a more moderate form of the movement. The overall trend that I see in Burchell's analysis is that in the Swedish experience, environmentalism has accomplished a consensus with other political parties, in which environmental priorities are embraced to varying degrees by all parties. I suspect that this is the result of the development of the moderate element.

338. "America is addicted to foreign oil. It's an addiction that threatens our economy, our environment and our national security. It touches every part of our daily lives and ties our hands as a nation and a people. The addiction has worsened for decades and now it's reached a point of crisis." http://www.pickensplan.com/theplan/ 7/Apr/09.

339. Daniels, *Doomsday Reader*.

340. Skarstedt, *Nykterhetsrörelsens Banérförare*.

341. These include Johan Bergman (seventeen pages), Edvard Wavrinsky (twelve pages), Per Wieselgren (ten pages), Sigfried Wieselgren (ten pages), and August Berglund (nine pages). Waldenström tied with two people, Ernst Beckman and Carl Oskar Berg.

342. "De högermän som var anslutna till riksdagens nykterhetsgrupp, 1908 var det 31 av 109 riksdagsledamöter, tillhörde vanligtvis kretsen kring de mer moderata nykterhetivrarna med P. P. Waldenström i spetsen." [Johansson is citing Lydia Svärd, 337] (Johansson, *Systemet lagom*, 71–72).

343. Tomson, *En politisk vilde*, 150–79; Tomson, *Den Radikale Waldenström*, 165–73.

344. Waldenström, *Kampen för nykterhet*. The speech was apparently stenographed at its original delivery at the Nordiska Nykterhetsmötet in Stockholm in July of 1902.

345. Ibid., 22.

346. "Sedligheten är ett system av dygder, och osedligheten är på sätt och vis ett system av laster. Därför ser icke heller den Heliga Skrift räddningen däri, att en människa lägger bort utövningen av den eller den synden, utan hon ser räddningen i *människans fullständiga moraliska upprättelse*" (Ibid., 18).

347. Lagerlöf, *Körkarlen*, 406.

348. Waldenström, *Låt glaset stå! Nykterhetsföredrag*, 5.

349. Waldenström, *Nya Färder*, 401.

350. Ibid., 403.

351. "Denna högst märkliga rörelse stannade emellertid snart af, och inom kort talade just ingen mer om fru Nation. Herren var icke i stormvädret. De sönderslagna glasen ersattes med nya, speglar och andra af hennes yxa förstörda föremål reparerades, och rusdrycksfloden strömmade åter i sin gamla fåra, bortryckande, dränkande och begrafvande unga och gamla, rika och fattiga, män, kvinnor och barn, huslig lycka, ungdoms hälsa, ålderdoms tröst." (Waldenström, *Nya Färder*, 405).

352. Waldenström. Letter to the editors of Svenska Morgonbladet and Jönköpings Posten. July 1910. (WSA del III, vol 2). Waldenström attended "Svenskarnes dag" on July 22, and mentioned that Carrie Nation had spoken during the week and that he had even received a commemorative pin

in the shape of an axe, a symbol of her order of the "Knights of the Axe." Waldenström joked that it was the only "order" that he had ever belonged to.

353. ". . . nykterhetsåsikterna icke äro hos majoriteten så mogna, som fordras för att i längden härda ut mot likörligans oerhörda uthållighet och makt. Det är ingen konst att arbeta upp en tillfällig entusiasm för en viss sak. Men det är betydligt svårare att underhålla denna entusiasm i fortsättningen." (Waldenström, Nya Färder, 282).

354. Bergman, Nykterhetsrörelsens världshistoria, 161. Bergman identifies Waldenström as the leading temperance man in the Riksdag during the 1890s, followed by Ernst Beckman and Carl Ekman; See also Tomson, Den radikale Waldenström, 165.

355. "Jag hatar all obskurantism, all trångsynthet och all fanatism med ett hat som är så intensivt, att språkets starkaste ord äro för svaga för att ge ens approximtivt riktigt uttryck åt dess glöd. Men lika intensivt hatar jag dryckenssederna." (Bergman, Modärn kultur, 3).

356. Bergman, Modärn kultur, 9.

357. Ibid., 14.

358. Bergman, Per Wieselgren, 86–90.

359. Bergman, Ett ord till den bildade, 20. Bergman claimed that scientists as a whole had moved away from moderation, and toward a full endorsement of absolutism.

360. Bergman, Modärn kultur, 15–16.

361. Ibid., 10.

362. Bergman, Några ord om nykterhetssakens historiska, 11; Bergman, Vägen till folknykterhet, 12.

363. Waldenström, Maltdryckskomiténs förslag, 29.

364. Tomson, En politisk vilde, 22.

365. Waldenström, Nya Färder, 402.

366. Waldenström, Genom Norra Amerika, 411.

367. Kjellberg, Folkväckelse i Sverige, 276–77.

368. "Ett malplaserat likhetstecken." 3 Oct 1902. Arbetarbladet. (Kungliga biblioteket).

369. Waldenström, Untitled speech notes, on temperance. Not dated (filed with other material from 1912). (WSA del I, vol 12).

370. Waldenström, "Det kan vara lärorikt." Not dated (filed with other material from 1912). (WSA del I, vol 12).

371. Waldenström, *Genom Norra Amerika*, 41.

372. Waldenström, *Nya Färder*, 189.

373. Tomson, *Den Radikale Waldenström*, 169.

374. Bexell, *Sveriges kyrkohistoria*, 105; Waldenström. "Man skall åtminstone icke försvara det." Not dated (likely Mar or Apr 1912). (WSA del III, vol 3).

375. Waldenström, *Genom Norra Amerika*, 408.

376. Waldenström, "Kampen mot rusdryckerna." Letter to the editors of Svenska Morgonbladet and Jönköpings Posten. 20 Nov, 1914. (WSA del III, vol 3).

377. Waldenström, *Vad Gud kan vilja säga Sverige genom det i Europa pågående kriget*.

378. Waldenström, *Maltdryckskommiténs förslag*, 5.

379. Ibid., 43, 62–63.

380. Ibid., 30.

381. Ibid., 31–32, 34.

382. "De som öfvervaka lagen, blunda också för öfverträdelserna i den tron, att när lagen är galen, så har länsman rättighet att vara klok och handla efter den gamla domareregeln: 'Det rätt och skäl icke är, det kan icke heller vara lag.'" (Waldenström, *Maltdryckskommiténs förslag*, 36).

383. Ibid., 37, 39, 49.

384. Ibid., 51.

385. Ibid., 53.

386. Ibid., 62–63; The "Appendix" of my original dissertation manuscript includes a list of surviving letters. These letters were sent to Waldenström on behalf of individuals and temperance organizations around the country, and reflect some of the 500 responses that Waldenström elicited with his

newspaper article, in which he asked for reports to be sent in about their experiences with alcohol and proposals for improving the laws. The majority of these responses placed importance on restricting the ability for train conductors to consume alcohol. They also congratulated Waldenström on his pronouncements on the matter in the Riksdag. The letters are preserved at Riksarkivet: Waldenströmska släktarkivet, P.P. Waldenströms Arkiv vol B:4 Brev 1883-1917; See also, WSA del I, vol 13.

387. "Det nykterhetsarbete, som nykterhetssällskapen i vårt land bedrifva och som af Eders Kongl. Maj:ts Befallningshafvande i deras femårsberättelser upprepade gånger blifvit så väl vitsordadt, har naturligtvis i främsta rummet till uppgift att på öfvertygelsens väg motarbeta drykenskapen. Det inse och praktisera de äfven. När man stundom beskyllt dem för att hafva öfvergifvit denna väg och vilja sätta lagstiftningsåtgärder i det moraliska nykterhetsarbetets ställe, så är det en orättvis beskyllning. Men då lagstiftningen—allt eftersom den är god eller otillfredsställande—kan väsentligen stödja eller motverka det moraliska nykterhetsarbetet, så måste verksamheten *äfven* rikta sig på åstadkommande af en lagstifning, som, så vidt möjligt är, undanrödjer eller minskar de hinder, som hon har att kämpa med. Detta är icke något nytt. Nykterhetsverksamheten har från första början gestaltat sig så. Hennes första seger i lagstifningsväg var också den största, hon någonsin vunnit, då husbehovsbränningen upphäfdes." (Waldenström, *Maltdryckskommiténs förslag*, 29).

388. Waldenström, *Genom Norra Amerika*, 428.

389. Ibid., 616.

390. Ibid., 492–93.

391. Waldenström, *Nya Färder*, 39.

392. Waldenström, *Genom Canada*, 24.

393. "... innan anordingarna voro färdiga, beslöto stadsfullmäktige, att en krog skulle läggas där, och parken sålunda göras till en fallgrop för folket. Det är så svenskt, så svenskt. Hvilken skam för vårt härliga land!" (Waldenström, *Nya Färder*, 38).

394. Waldenström, *Nya Färder*, 101–2, 115, 183–87.

395. Ibid., 49.

396. Ibid., 188.

397. Carlson, *History of North Park College*, 296–97. Carlson recounts the active student interest in engaging in the temperance movement as an extra curricular activity.

398. "Att hänskjuta frågors avgörande till mängdens omröstning måste i regel bliva detsamma som att undandraga dem den lugna, insiktsfulla prövningen och giva dem till pris åt lidelsernas virvelvindar. Och det är jag rädd för, även om det någon gång kan gå bra. Jag tror alls icke, att allmän folkomröstning i alkoholfrågan skulle väsentligen förändra förhållandena i vårt land i det stora hela. På de flesta ställen skulle det förbli, som det är, på somliga ställen skulle ändring ske till det bättre, på somliga ställen till det sämre." (Tomson, *Den Radikale Waldenström*, 170).

399. Waldenström. "Man skall åtminstone icke försvara det." Not dated (likely Mar or Apr 1912). (WSA del III, vol 3).

400. Waldenström. "Lokalt veto." 4 Sept 1911. (WSA del III, vol 2). "Men nu har man i ordet 'lokalt veto' skjutit in en annan betydelse—en betydelse, som det icke har—nämligen rättighet för alla en kommunens myndiga medlemmar att per capita rösta om, huruvida rusdrycksförsäljning skall tillåtas eller ej. För närvarande är det de kommunala myndigheterna, som afgöra den saken. Och de hafva skött sig så bra i den punkten, att de allra flesta kommuner i landet redan ha och länge haft rusdrycksförbud. Hädanefter lär det väl också komma att gå vidare i den riktningen, sedan den kommunala röstskalan blifvit så väsentligt ändrad i demokratisk riktning."

401. Waldenström. "Alkoholfrågan och partierna." Not dated (likely Sept 1911). (WSA del III, vol 2). "För nuvarande har den allra största antalet kommuner lokalt veto, d.v.s. rusdrycksförbud. Om nu Konungens Bfhds rättighet att bevilja utskänkning upphäfves, så ökar detta antal ännu mer, allrahälst med den nya kommunala röstskalan. Låt oss skatta oss lyckliga, om vi i ett slag vinna så mycket som detta. Det är bättre att försöka taga ett steg i sänder och lyckas än att spilla tid och kraft på att taga två steg i stöten och misslyckas."

402. Waldenström. Letter to the editor of Missions-Wännen and Veckobladet. 28 Mar 1912. (WSA del III, vol 3).

403. Waldenström, *Genom Norra Amerika*, 314. "Ja, ja, hvem vet! Jag har ofta tyckt, att Missionsvännen begått ett stort misstag, då den sålunda gjort "allt eller intet" till sitt mål."

404. Johansson, *Systemet lagom*, 71-72 (Johansson is citing Lydia Svärd, 337).

405. "I allmänna valmansförbundets valprogram 1908 upptogs symptomatiskt nog nykterhetfrågan till behandling under rubriken 'Uppfostran och folkhälsa,' inte 'Social lagstiftning'. Denna markering indikerar att man från valmansförbundets sida valde att betrakta nykterhetsfrågan som en folkhälsofråga med betoning på uppfostran och sedlighet, snarare än en fråga som kunde lösas inom ramen för en mer aktiv sociallagstiftning." (Johansson, *Systemet lagom*, 71–72).

406. Waldenström, *Nya Färder*, 523.

407. Ibid., 282.

408. Waldenström, *Genom Norra Amerika*, 245.

409. Ibid., 87.

410. Waldenström. "Från de stora sommarmötena II." 26 June 1911. (WSA del III, vol 2).

411. Waldenström. "Vid årskiftet." Letter to the editors of Svenska Morgonbladet and Jönköpings Posten. Not dated (likely Dec 1915 or Jan 1916). (WSA del III, vol 3). "Nykterhetslagstiftningen har under lång tid—trots tillfälliga mistag—varit stodd i framåtskridande till det bättre. Åskådningarna likaså. Men allt, som ska äga bestånd, måste växa fram inifrån utåt, och det går sakta. Det skulle bli inspektion av en landtbruksskola en vår. Föreståndaren lät eleverna hugga en mängd björkar och sätta upp dem till en allé. Det såg mycket bra ut, och han fick beröm av inspektören, som ej visste annat, än att björkarna voro växte på platsen. Men inom kort vissnade de. De hade ingen rot. Historien är en verkligheten och må tjäna såsom en lämplig bild af en lagstifting, som går för fort, som löper förbi det allmänna rättsmedvetandet, äfven om den löper i rätt riktning. Man må beklaga tillkomsten av det s.k. frihetsförbundet huru mycket som hälst. Men enligt min tro är det uttryck av en reaktion, som kan bli farlig nog för det politiska nykterhetsarbetet. Denna reaktion har nämligen gjort synnerligen aktuell den ytterst viktiga frågan om gränserna för samhällets rätt att ingripa på det privata livets område. Ty lika visst som en sådan rätt finnes, lika visst måste de finnes gränser för densamma—för så vidt makt icke är samma som rätt. Äfven jag beklagar tillkomsten av frihetsförbundet. Men jag finner den i alla fall lätt förklarlig, och jag har väntat något sådant där, allt sedan nykterhetsvännerna i Andra Kammaren af sin orubbliga tro på det lokala vetots välsignelse läto förleda sig till det enligt min tro okloka steget att förkasta, hvad som då stod att vinna. Det gäller nu att upptaga det politiska nykterhetsarbetet i öfverenstämmelse med den situation, som är, samt tacka Gud för, hvad som vinnes, så länge något ännu kan vinnes. Hvad vi äfven i

denna punkt behöfva, är ett verkligt frisinne, som icke blott vill utan äfven tror på möjligheten af ett samförstånd samt arbetar därför [...]."

412. There appear to have been more than one organization that had "*frihetsförbundet*" in its name at this time (which may or may not have been directly associated with each other) and sorting out which organization Waldenström is referring to here has been non-conclusive. As Waldenström's article suggests, *frihetsförbundet* was asserting the rights of the individual in the temperance movement. For instance, one of the organizations called *ekonomiska frihetsförbundet*, was radical on the question of taxes, and had been inspired by American currents of thought. They called for one tax, therefore undoing existing taxes on alcohol. Another organization called *frihetsförbund* appears to have also had Swedish-American inspiration, and even published works by Thomas Paine into Swedish. See Paine, *Förnuftets tidehvarfv*.

413. Waldenström. Letter to the editors of Missions-Wännen and Veckobladet. 27 Jan 1916. (WSA del III, vol 3).

414. Waldenström. Letter to the editors of Missions-Wännen and Veckobladet. 31 Oct 1910. (WSA del III, vol 2); Waldenström. Letter to the editor of Gäfleposten. Not dated (likely 1908). (WSA del III, vol 2); Waldenström had been alarmed to find that many friends of temperance within his church had voted for Starbäck, his former opponent, with the simple explanation being that he was a liberal and that he had promised to vote for local veto. Waldenström interpreted this as misrepresentation of his actual motives, particularly since he characterized Starbäck as an alcoholic.

415. Origins for Waldenström's contextualized understanding of the truth can be traced to his interpretation of scripture. Regarding the appropriateness of remarriage, for instance, Waldenström gave a contextual answer: "Men liksom alla bud, som icke röra rent moraliska ting, så har icke heller detta allmängiltig betydelse. Under vissa förhållanden kan det vara rätt och godt och apostoliskt att göra, hvad som under andra förhållanden vore motsatsen." (Waldenström, *Nya Färder*, 283–84).

Notes to Conclusion

416. Gould, *Origins of Liberal Dominance*, 122.

417. Ibid., 116–18.

418. McLeod, *Secularisation in Western Europe*, 23.

419. Stark and Finke, *Acts of Faith*.

420. Berman, *Primacy of Politics*.

421. Hadenius, *Riksdag in Focus*, 197.

422. "Det finns inga naturgivna lagar som säger att samhället behöver se ut som det gör, och att varken borgarklassen eller arbetarklassen haft några alternativa handlingsvägar. Vad gäller den svenska socialdemokratin, har den kunnat prova en mer revolutionär väg, eller liksom den danska socialdemokratin, en mer liberal. Reformismen kan uppträda i många olika former och vara mer eller mindre systemkritisk, teoribehäftad eller pragmatisk. Människan står alltid inför olika vägval, det finns inget som heter 'historiskt nödvändiga beslut.'" (Linderborg, *Socialdemokraterna skriver historia*, 25).

423. Sifry, *Spoiling for a Fight*.

424. Hadenius, *Riksdag in Focus*, 156.

425. Torstendahl, "Sweden in a European Perspective," 42.

426. Arvidsson, "Reflections," 52–53.

427. Ibid., 59–60.

428. Ibid., 59.

429. Agrell, "In the Innermost Sanctum."

430. af Malmborg, "Europe's Wars," 134.

431. Johansson, "If you seek his monument," 183.

432. Andreasson, *Kristet föreningsliv i riksdagen*.

Bibliography

Manuscript Collections

Riksarkivet, Stockholm (The Swedish National Archives). Waldenströmska Släktarkivet (The Waldenström Family Collections). Abbreviated in notes as WSA.

Published Sources

Absolutism och personlig frihet; Föredrag af Joseph Hermelin jämte efterföljande diskussion å Norrlands nation i Upsala den 27 mars 1900 i anledning af rektor J. H. Bergendals uttalande i nykterhetsfrågan. Stockholm: Svenska Nykterhetsförlaget, 1900.

Agrell, Wilhelm. "In the Innermost Sanctum: Reflections on the Mythology of Sweden's Neutrality Policy and the History of Questioning." In *The Swedish Success Story?*, edited by Kurt Almkvist and Kay Glans, 187–97. Stockholm: Ax:son Johnson Foundation, 2004.

Anderson, Philip J. "Paul Peter Waldenström and America: Influence and Presence in Historical Perspective." *The Covenant Quarterly* 52.4 (1994) 2–21.

Andreasson, Hans. *Kristet föreningsliv i riksdagen: En studie av riksdagens kristna grupp och dess föregångare.* Stockholm: Sveriges Riksdag, 2004.

———. *Liv och rörelse: Svenska Missionskyrkans historia och identitet.* Stockholm: Verbum, 2007.

Arvidsson, Håkon. "Reflections on the Dilemma of Modernization." In *The Swedish Success Story?*, edited by Kurt Almkvist and Kay Glans, 47–60. Stockholm: Ax:son Johnson Foundation, 2004.

Augustine. *On Christian Doctrine.* Translated by D. W. Robertson, Jr. Upper Saddle River, NJ: Prentice Hall, 1958.

Berättelser om Gefle Arbetareförenings förvaltning år 1886. Gävle: Gefle-Postens Tryckeri, 1887.

Berättelser om Gefle Arbetareförenings förvaltning år 1891. Gävle: Ahlström & Cederbergs Boktryckeri, 1892.

Berättelser om Gefle Arbetareförenings förvaltning år 1892. Gävle: Otto Serranders Tryckeri, 1893.

BIBLIOGRAPHY

Berättelser öfver Gefle Arbetareförenings verksamhet under år 1901. Gävle: Gefle-Postens Tryckeri, 1902.

Berggren, Henrik. "The Forward-Facing Angel: Nationalism and Modernity in Sweden in the Twentieth Century." In *The Swedish Success Story?*, edited by Kurt Almkvist and Kay Glans, 67–79. Stockholm: Ax:son Johnson Foundation, 2004.

Bergman, Johan. *Ett ord till den bildade och bildningssökande ungdomen*. Stockholm: Svenska Nykterhetsförlaget, 1908.

———. *Modärn kultur och modern nykterhetsrörelse; Föreläsning hållen å akademiska föreningens salong i Lund den 4 oktober 1899 af D:r Johan Bergman*. Stockholm: Svenska Nykterhetsförlaget, 1900.

———. *Några ord om nykterhetssakens historiska utveckling och nuvarande läge. Föredrag hållet vid opinionsmötet i Stockholm den 27 oktober 1934 av professor J. Bergman*. Stockholm: Häroldens tryckeri, 1934.

———. *Nykterhetsrörelsens världshistoria: En framställning av nykterhetssträvandenas utveckling genom tiderna*. Stockholm: Oskar Eklunds Bokförlag, 1928.

———. *Per Wieselgren; Minnesteckning af D:r Johan Bergman*. Stockholm: Svenska Nykterhetsförlaget, 1900.

———. *Vägen till folknykterhet;Debatten Bratt—Bergman å Södra latinläroverkets aula i Stockholm den 2 mars 1913*. Stockholm: Oktoberkommitten för förbudspropaganda, 1914.

Bergsten, Torsten. *Frikyrkor i samverkan: Den svenska frikyrkoekumenikens historia 1905–1993*. Borås: Libris Verbum, 1995.

Berman, Sheri. *The Primacy of Politics: Social Democracy and the Making of Europe's Twentieth Century*. New York: Cambridge University Press, 2006.

Bexell, Oloph. *Sveriges kyrkohistoria: Vol. 7: Folkväckelsens och kyrkoförnyelsens tid*. Stockholm, Sweden: Verbum, 2003.

Borg, Daniel R. *The Old-Prussian Church and the Weimar Republic: A Study in Political Adjustment, 1917–1927*. Hanover, NH: University Press of New England, 1984.

Branting, Hjalmar. *Hjalmar Branting tal och skrifter: Vol. 4: Kampen för demokratin II*. Stockholm: Tidens Förlag, 1927.

———. *Hjalmar Branting tal och skrifter: Vol. 10: Stridskamrater och Vänner*. Stockholm: Tidens Förlag, 1929.

———. *Hjalmar Branting tal och skrifter: Vol. 11; Litteraturkritik och varia*. Stockholm: Tidens Förlag, 1930.

———. *Socialism och demokrati: Ett urval av Alvar Alsterdal och Ove Sandell*. Stockholm: Norstedts, 1998.

Bredberg, William. *P. P. Waldenströms verksamhet till 1878; Till frågan om Svenska Missionsförbundets uppkomst*. Stockholm: Missionsförbundets Förlag, 1948.

Brohed, Ingmar. *Sveriges Kyrkohistoria: Vol. 8: Religionsfrihetens och ekumenikens tid*. Stockholm: Verbum, 2005.

Bunyan, John. *The Pilgrim's Progress*. Cornwall, NY: Dodd, Mead, 1968.

Burchell, Jon. *The Evolution of Green Politics: Development and Change within European Green Parties*. London: Earthscan, 2002.

Carlson, Leland H. *A History of North Park College*. Chicago: North Park College and Theological Seminary, 1941.

Childs, Marquis W. *Sweden, The Middle Way*. New Haven, CT: Yale University Press, 1947.

Clifton-Soderstrom, Michelle A. "'Happily Ever After?' Paul Peter Waldenström: Be ye reconciled to God." *Ex Auditu* 26 (2010) 91–106.

"Contemporary Perspectives on Pietism: A Symposium." *The Covenant Quarterly* 34 (1976) 1–2.

Dahlén, Rune. "Paul Petter Waldenström—bibelteolog och väckelseledare." In *Sveriges kyrkohistoria: Vol. 7: Folkväckelsens och kyrkoförnyelsens tid*, edited by Oloph Bexell, 299–305. Stockholm: Verbum, 2003.

———. "Waldenströms View of the Bible." *The Covenant Quarterly* 52.4 (1994) 37–52.

Dahlström, Kata. *Bildning och Klasskamp*. Lysekil: E. F. Larssons Boktryckeri, 1909.

———. *Brev till Hjalmar Branting och Fredrik Ström*. Edited by Rut Berggren. Lund: Arkiv förlag, 1987.

———. *Leo Tolstoy som kristen samhällsreformator*. Karlstad: Eget förlag, 1908.

———. *Skolan och prästväldet: Föredrag av fru Kata Dahlström*. Karlstad: Värmlands folkblads tryckeri, 1907.

Daniels, Ted, ed. *A Doomsday Reader: Prophets, Predictors, and Hucksters of Salvation*. New York: New York University Press, 1999.

Ekman, E. J. *Den Inre Missionens Historia: Från Början af 18:de Århundrade till Närvarande Tid*. Stockholm: E. J. Ekmans Förlagsexpedition, 1902.

Eldebo, Runar. "Är Guds kärlek så gripande att ingen enda orkar bestå? En analys av E. J. Ekmans apokatastasitanke." In *En historia berättas—om missionsförbundare*. Edited by Rune Dahlén & Valborg Lindgärde, 65–78. Falköping: Kimpese, 2004.

Erickson, Scott E. *David Nyvall and the Shape of an Immigrant Church: Ethnic, Denominational, and Educational Priorities Among Swedes in America*. Uppsala: University of Uppsala Press, 1996.

Falk, Hans. *Socialistprästen; H. F. Spak 1878-1926*. Stockholm: Carlsson, 1998.

Fish, Stanley E. "Rhetoric." In *Doing What Comes Naturally; Change, Rhetoric, and the Practice of Theory in Literary and Legal Studies*, 471–502. Durham, NC: Duke University Press, 1989.

Franzén, Nils Olof. *Hjalmar Branting och hans tid: en biografi*. Stockholm: Bonniers, 1985.

Frisk, Donald C. *Covenant Affirmations: This We Believe*. Chicago: Covenant, 1981.

Fritzson, Arne. "En Gud som är god och rättfärdig." In *Liv och rörelse: Svenska missionskyrkans historia och identitet*, edited by Hans Andreasson, et al., 361–72. Stockholm: Verbum, 2007.

Gonzalez, Justo L. *The Story of Christianity: Volume 2: The Reformation to the Present Day*. San Francisco: Harper Collins, 1985.

Gorski, Philip S. *The Disciplinary Revolution: Calvinism and the Rise of the State in Early Modern Europe*. Chicago: University of Chicago Press, 2003.

Gould, Andrew. *Origins of Liberal Dominance: State, Church, and Party in Nineteenth Century Europe*. Ann Arbor, MI: University of Michigan Press, 1999.

Gritsch, Eric W. *A History of Lutheranism*. Minneapolis: Fortress, 2002.

Grundström, Jakob. *Waldenström och Samhällsfrågorna*. Gefle: Richards Förlag, 1938.

Gud, den underbare. Stockholm: BV-Förlag, 2008.

Gustafsson, Lars. *Litteraturhistorikern Schück; Vetenskapssyn och historieuppfattning i Henrik Schücks tidigare produktion*. Stockholm: Almqvist & Wicksell, 1983.

Hadenius, Stig. *The Riksdag in Focus: Swedish History in a Parliamentary Perspective*. Arlöv: Berlings, 1997.

Hallingberg, Gunnar. *Läsarna: 1800-talets folkväckelse och det moderna genombrottet.* Stockholm: Atlantis, 2010.

———. "Tidningar, böcker, förlag och moderna medier." In *Liv och rörelse: Svenska missionskyrkans historia och identitet,* edited by Hans Andreasson, et al., 305–21. Stockholm: Verbum, 2007.

Haste, Hans. *Dokument från storstrejken 1909.* Introduction by Axel Strand. Stockholm: Pogo, 1979.

Henningsen, Bernd. "Jante, or the Scandinavian Law of Mediocrity. On One Factor in the Identity of the Welfare State." In *The Swedish Success Story?* Edited by Kurt Almkvist and Kay Glans, 161–74. Stockholm: Ax:son Johnson Foundation, 2004.

Hirschman, Albert O. *Exit, Voice, and Loyalty: Responses to Decline in Firms, Organizations, and States.* Cambridge, MA: Harvard University Press, 1970.

Hjelm, Norman A. "Augustana and the Church of Sweden: Ties of History and Faith." In *The Heritage of Augustana: Essays on the Life and Legacy of the Augustana Lutheran Church,* edited by Harland H. Gifford and Arland J. Hultgren, 19–36. Minneapolis: Kirk, 2004.

Hofberg, Herman, et al., eds. *Svenskt biografiskt handlexikon.* Stockholm: Albert Bonniers, 1906.

Ivar, Ulf. "Gudsförnekaren från Gävle." *Arbetarbladet.* January, 18 2009. Online: www.arbetarbladet.se/merlasning/ulfivarshistoria.

Jarlert, Anders. *Sveriges kyrkohistoria: Vol. 6: Romantiken och liberalismens tid.* Stockholm: Verbum, 2001.

Johansson, Alf W. "If you seek his monument, look around! Reflections on national identity and collective memory in Sweden after the Second World War." In *The Swedish Success Story?,* edited by Kurt Almkvist and Kay Glans, 175–186. Stockholm: Ax:son Johnson Foundation, 2004.

Johansson, Lennart. *Systemet lagom: Rusdrycker, intresseorganisationer och politisk kultur under förbudsdebattens tidevarv 1900–1922.* Lund: Lund University Press, 1995.

Johansson, O. P. *P. Waldenström i Kyrkomötet; Hans motioner och anföranden i kyrkliga och teologiska frågor vid fyra kyrkomöten.* Stockholm: Svenska Missionsförbundets Förlag, 1931.

Kihlberg, Leif. *Karl Staaff Regeringschef, Oppositionsledare 1905–1915.* Stockholm: Albert Bonniers, 1963.

Kjellberg, Knut. *Folkväckelse i Sverige under 1800-talet; uppkomst och genombrott.* Stockholm: Carlssons, 1994.

Lagerlöf, Selma. *Herr Arnes penningar, Liljecronas hem, Körkarlen.* Viborg: Albert Bonniers, 2005.

———. *Jerusalem.* Pössneck: Albert Bonniers, 2007.

Larsson, Tage. *Väckelsen och Sundsvallsstrejken 1879.* Stockholm: Gummesson, 1972.

Lenhammar, Harry. *Budbäraren, Pietisten och Församlingsbladet: Studier i svenska religionsperiodika.* Uppsala: Litteraturvetenskapliga Institutionen Uppsala Universitet, 1981.

———. *Sveriges kyrkohistoria: Vol. 5: Individualismens och upplysningens tid.* Stockholm: Verbum, 2000.

Lijphart, Arend. *Democracy in Plural Societies: A Comparative Exploration.* New Haven, CT: Yale University Press, 1977.

Lindberg, Lars. "En strid i försoningens ljus: Waldenström omläst och omvärderad." In *En historia berättas—om missionsförbundare*, edited by Rune Dahlén & Valborg Lindgärde, 43-63. Falköping: Kimpese, 2004.

Linderborg, Åsa. "Historical Romanticism and Development Optimism: On the Historical Perception of Social Democracy." In *The Swedish Success Story?*, edited by Kurt Almkvist and Kay Glans, 81-95. Stockholm: Ax:son Johnson Foundation, 2004.

———. *Socialdemokraterna skriver historia: Historieskrivning som ideologisk maktresurs 1892-2000*. Stockholm: Atlas, 2001.

Lindqvist, Herman. *Historien om Sverige: Från istid till framtid*. Stockholm: Norstedts, 2002.

Lindström, Harry. *I Livsfrågornas spänningsfält; Om P. Waldenströms Brukspatron Adamsson—populär folkbok och allegorisk roman*. Stockholm: Verbum, 1997.

Lövgren, Oscar. *Oscar Ahnfelt; Sångare och folkväckare i brytningstid*. Stockholm: Gummessons, 1966.

Lundkvist, Sven. "Popular Movements and Reforms." In *Sweden's Development from Poverty to Affluence, 1750-1970*, edited by Steven Koblik, 180-93. Minneapolis: University of Minnesota Press, 1975.

Malmborg, Mikael af. "Europe's Wars and the Swedicisation of Peace." In *The Swedish Success Story?*, edited by Kurt Almkvist and Kay Glans, 133-46. Stockholm: Ax:son Johnson Foundation, 2004.

McLeod, Hugh. *Secularisation in Western Europe 1848-1914*. New York: St. Martin's, 2000.

Missionsförbundets Minneskrift, 1885-1910: Publicerad med anledning af Svenska Evangeliska Missionsförbundets i Amerika Tjugufemårsjubileum i Chicago, 21-26 Juni, 1910. Minneapolis: Augsburg, 1910.

Nerman, Ture. *Hjalmar Branting: Fritänkaren*. Stockholm: Tidens Förlag, 1960.

Noll, Mark. *The Old Religion in a New World: The History of North American Christianity*. Grand Rapids: Eerdmans 2002.

Nordisk familjebok. Stockholm: Nordisk Familjeboks Expedition, 1893.

Nordisk familjebok. Stockholm: Nordisk Familjeboks Expedition, 1921.

Nordstrom, Byron J. *Scandinavia Since 1500*. Minneapolis: University of Minnesota Press, 2000.

Nyman, Torkel. *Kommittépolitik och parlamentarism: Statsminister Boström och rikspolitiken 1891-1905. En studie av den svenska parlamentarismens framväxt*. Uppsala: University of Uppsala Press, 1999.

Ollén, N. P. *Paul Peter Waldenström: En Levnadsteckning*. Stockholm: Svenska Missionsförbundets Förlag, 1917.

Olson, Mancur. *The Logic of Collective Action*. Cambridge, MA: Harvard University Press, 1965.

Olsson, Karl A. *By One Spirit*. Chicago: Covenant, 1962.

———. "Paul Peter Waldenström and Augustana." In *The Swedish Immigrant Community in Transition; Essays in Honor of Dr. Conrad Bergendoff*, edited by J. Iverne Dowie and Ernest M. Espelie, 107-20. Rock Island, IL: Augustana Historical Society, 1963.

Paine, Thomas. *Förnuftets tidehvarfv: En undersökning angående sann teologi och fable-teologi*. Translated by K. J. Ellington. Stockholm: Frihetsförbundets förlag, 1906.

Palme, Sven Ulric. *Karl Staaff och storstrejken 1909*. Stockholm: Bonniers, 1959.

Phelan, John E., Jr. "Reading Like a Pietist." *The Swedish-American Historical Quarterly* 63.2–3 (2012) 202–24.
Rorty, Richard. *Philosophy and Social Hope*. New York: Penguin Putnam, 1999.
Safstrom, Mark. "Defining Lutheranism from the Margins: Paul Peter Waldenström on Being a 'Good Lutheran' in America." *The Augustana Synod and the Covenant Church: Contact, Conflict, and Confluence 1860–2010*. Swedish-American Historical Quarterly 63.2-3 (2012) 101–34.
———. "Facing the Future Together: A Look at the Reasons for and the Implications of the Merger of the Covenant, Methodist, and Baptist Churches in Sweden." In *The Covenant Companion* (October 2011) 24–27.
———. "Making Room for the Lost: Congregational Inclusivity in Waldenström's *Squire Adamsson*." *The Covenant Quarterly* 71.3–4 (2013) 52–72.
———. *The Swedish Pietists: A Reader: Excerpts from the Writings of Carl Olof Rosenius and Paul Peter Waldenström*. Edited and translated by Mark Safstrom. Eugene, OR: Pickwick, 2015.
Sattler, Gary R. *God's Glory, Neighbor's Good: A Brief Introduction to the Life and Writings of August Hermann Francke*. Chicago: Covenant, 1982.
Schiller, Berndt. *Storstrejken 1909: Förhistoria och orsaker*. Gothenburg: Akademiförlaget, 1967.
———. "Years of Crisis, 1906-1914." In *Sweden's Development from Poverty to Affluence 1750–1970*, edited by Steven Koblik, 197–228. Minneapolis: University of Minnesota Press, 1975.
Selinder, Per-Magnus. "Mötesplatserna—samling, söndring och sändning." In *Liv och rörelse: Svenska missionskyrkans historia och identitet*, edited by Hans Andreasson, et al., 289–304. Stockholm: Verbum, 2007.
Sifry, Micah. *Spoiling for a Fight: Third-Party Politics in America*. New York: Routledge, 2002.
Skarstedt, Waldemar. *Nykterhetsrörelsens Banérförare: Biographier af nutida svenska nykterhetskämpar*. Stockholm: N. J. Schedins Bokförlag, 1903.
Spak, H. F. *Gammal och ny moral; Betraktelser med anknutning till storstrejkens erfarenheter*. Stockholm: Socialdemokratiska arbetarepartiets förlag, 1911.
Stark, Rodney, and Roger Finke. *Acts of Faith: Explaining the Human Side of Religion*. Berkeley: University of California Press, 2000.
Stein, K. James. *Philipp Jakob Spener: Pietist Patriarch*. Chicago: Covenant, 1986.
Stråth, Bo. "Neutrality as Self-Awareness." In *The Swedish Success Story?*, edited by Kurt Almkvist and Kay Glans, 147–60. Stockholm: Ax:son Johnson Foundation, 2004.
———. *Sveriges Historia 1830–1920*. Stockholm: Norstedts, 2012.
Sundström, Erland. *Arvet från Waldenström; Läsestycken från Waldenströms skrifter med inledning och sammanfattningar av Erland Sundström*. Falköping: Gummessons, 1978.
Sundvik, Ivar. *Branting eller Palm? Ledarstreden 1885-1887*. Stockholm: Tidens förlag, 1981.
Svärd, Lydia. *Väckelserörelsernas folk i andra kammaren 1867–1911—Frikyrkliga och lågkyrkliga insatser i svensk politik*. Diss. Lund University, 1954.
"The Emergence of Swedish Democracy." Official site for Sveriges Riksdag. Online: http://www.riksdagen.se/2/18/2010.
"The Pietist Heritage and the Contemporary Church." *The Covenant Quarterly* 28 (1970) 1–4.

Tomson, Ragnar. *Den radikale Waldenström; Bidrag till undersökning av P. Waldenströms radikala år intill tiden omkring år 1890*. Stockholm: Missionsförbundets Förlag, 1945.

———. *En Hövding; Minnesteckning över P. Waldenström till 100-årsdagen av hans födelse*. Stockholm: Svenska Missionsförbundets Förlag, 1937.

———. *En politisk vilde i 25 riksdagar; P. P. Waldenström i Sveriges Riksdag 1885–1905*. Stockholm, Sweden: Svenska Missionsförbundets Förlag, 1942.

Torstendahl, Rolf. "Sweden in a European Perspective—Special Path or Mainstream?" In *The Swedish Success Story?*, edited by Kurt Almkvist and Kay Glans, 33–46. Stockholm: Ax:son Johnson Foundation, 2004.

Wadström, Berhard. *Ur Minnet och Dagboken: Anteckningar från Åren 1848–1897*. Stockholm: Fosterlands-Stiftelsens Förlags-Expedition, 1900.

Waldenström, Paul Peter. *Bibelläsning i skolan: Ett ord i en wigtig fråga*. Stockholm: A. L. Norman, 1867.

———. *Brukspatron Adamsson: Eller hvar bor du?* 5th edition. Stockholm: Pietistens Expedition, 1891.

———. *Dop och barndop; Samtal mellan Natanael och Timoteus*. Stockholm: Svenska Missionsförbundets Förlag, 1923.

———. *Fosterländskt politiskt föredrag 1908*. Karlstad: Nya Wermlands Tidningen, 1908.

———. *Genom Canada; Reseskildringar från 1904*. Stockholm: Normans Förlag, 1905.

———. *Genom Norra Amerikas Förenta Stater; Reseskildringar*. Stockholm: Pietistens Expedition, 1890.

———. *Kampen för nykterhet*. Stockholm: Svenska Missionsförbundets Förlag, 1916.

———. *Låt glaset stå! Nykterhetsföredrag*. Uppsala, Sweden: SSUH Förlag, 1897.

———. *Maltdryckskommiténs förslag med inledning och reservationer*. Stockholm: Normans, 1900.

———. *Nya Färder i Amerikas Förenta Stater; Reseskildringar*. Stockholm: Normans, 1902.

———. *Om försoningens betydelse*. Stockholm: Pietisten och A. L. Normans, 1873.

———. *Paul Peter Waldenströms Minnesanteckningar 1838–1875*. Ed. Bernhard Nyrén. Stockholm: Svenska Missionsförbundets Förlag, 1928.

———. *The Reconciliation. Who was to be Reconciled? God or Man? Or God and Man? Some Chapters on the Biblical View of the Atonement by P. Waldenström, PhD*. Translated by J. G. Princell. Chicago: John Martenson, 1888.

———. *Reform av kristendomsundervisningen vid det högre allmänna läroverket: Betänkande ingifvet till Statsrådet och chefen för Kongl. Ecklesiastikdepartmentet*. Stockholm: Normans, 1900.

———. "Sermon for the Twentieth Sunday after Trinity, 1872." In *Covenant Roots; Sources & Affirmations*. Edited by Glenn P. Anderson, Translated by Herbert E. Palmquist, 113–31. Chicago: Covenant, 1980.

———. "Sjuttio år." *Pietisten*, 22 Dec 1911.

———. *Squire Adamsson: Or, Where Do You Live? An Allegorical Tale from the Swedish Awakening*. Translation with Introduction and Notes by Mark Safstrom. Seattle: Pietisten, 2013.

———. *Vad Gud kan vilja säga Sverige genom det i Europa pågående kriget*. Stockholm: Svenska Missionsförbundets förlag, 1914.

———. "Var Aposteln Petrus Lagligt Gift?" In *Jungfrutalare i riksdagen: Berömda riksdagstal från Engelbrekt till Per Albin*, edited by August Borgström, 221–23. Stockholm: Natur och Kultur, 1947.

Weigel, George. *Against the Grain: Christianity and Democracy, War and Peace*. New York: Crossroad, 2008.

Westin, Gunnar. *George Scott och hans verksamhet i Sverige*. Stockholm: Svenska kyrkans diakonisyrelsens bokförlag, 1929.

von Zinzendorf, Nicolas Ludwig. "Thoughts for the Learned and Yet Good-Willed Students of Truth." In *Pietists: Selected Writings*, edited by Peter C. Erb, 291–95. New York: Paulist, 1983.

About the author

Mark Daniel Safstrom, PhD, is Lecturer of Swedish and Scandinavian Studies at the University of Illinois at Urbana-Champaign, where he teaches courses in Scandinavian literature and history. His research focuses on various aspects of the history of social movements and revivalism in Scandinavia, and he has previously published *The Swedish Pietists: A Reader*, and a translation of Paul Peter Waldenström's allegorical novel, *Squire Adamsson: Or, Where Do You Live?* He completed a doctoral degree in Scandinavian Languages and Literatures at the University of Washington in 2010. This book is based on his dissertation of the same title.

www.ingramcontent.com/pod-product-compliance
Lightning Source LLC
Chambersburg PA
CBHW071237230426
43668CB00011B/1473